FULL EMPLOYMENT WITHOUT INFLATION

By the Same Author

Full Employment (1941)
Full Employment and Free Enterprise (1947)
Insuring Full Employment: A United States Policy for Domestic Prosperity and World Development (1964)
Essays on Full Employment, 1942-1972 (1972)

FULL EMPLOYMENT WITHOUT INFLATION

Papers on the
Economic Performance Insurance
(EPI) Proposal

JOHN H. G. PIERSON

ALLANHELD, OSMUN   Montclair

ALLANHELD, OSMUN & CO. PUBLISHERS, INC.

Published in the United States of America in 1980
by Allanheld, Osmun & Co. Publishers, Inc.
19 Brunswick Road, Montclair, New Jersey 07042

Library of Congress Cataloging in Publication Data

Pierson, John Herman Groesbeck, 1906–
   Full employment without inflation.

   Consists chiefly of selections from the author's Essays
on full employment, 1942-1972.
      Includes index.
      1.   United States—Full employment policies—Addresses,
essays, lectures.   I.   Pierson, John Herman Groesbeck,
1906-   Essays on full employment, 1942-1972.
III.   Title.
HC106.5.P5385   339.5   79-5446
ISBN 0-916672-39-5

Printed in the United States of America

To William R. Leonard

Contents

Preface

The purpose of this book is to describe and advocate an approach to economic stabilization that would assure continual full employment in the United States and at the same time greatly facilitate the control of inflation. The novel element in that approach is something I call Economic Performance Insurance, or EPI.

My use of this term goes back (as will appear from these papers) only as far as 1970. The same concept, however, has been the heart of my proposal from the outset. "National income insurance" I called it in 1942—reluctantly, I remember, since that phrase can be misunderstood as referring to *values*, whereas *flows* of money and activity are what is meant.

EPI can be summarized in a single sentence. The President would each year recommend and Congress decide on lower and upper limits to employment and consumer spending and on contingent measures to be activated by the President without further Congressional debate whenever either of those totals threatened to go below or above its pre-set limits. But words can convey just so much. The grooves in which conventional thinking runs do not easily accommodate an essentially simple but unfamiliar proposition of this kind. A new idea in political economy is hard to communicate, even spelled out at length.

Economists who talk about full employment are nowadays often regarded as old-fashioned and out of touch with current reality. The thought seems to be that the significance of this issue is dictated by fashion, like the width of a necktie!

Such an absurdity must surely be due to statistical disagreements and inflation. When the composition of the labor force is changing rapidly, and the key statistical series are admittedly imperfect, and economic theory fails to supply an applicable definition, who is to say exactly what (small) reported percentage of residual unemployment is the *correct* measure of "full" employment? For practical purposes, however, this entire difficulty vanishes under the EPI method whereby the President and Congress, with all of the doubts and conflicting opinions in plain view, would name the *official* measure, hold performance to *that* throughout the year, and adjust the target numbers in the light of experience one year later.

The weightier reason for caution on full employment is, of course, inflation. Those who believe that reducing unemployment must increase inflation may even conclude that full employment would be a mistake. Or, if uncomfortable with that conclusion or with the underlying trade-off premise or both, they may decide that the two evils have to be attacked simultaneously but by wholly separate means. In point of fact the remedies *are* separate for price rises caused by the oil shortage or by depletion of any other natural resource, but otherwise they are largely the same for inflation as for unemployment. At least, the EPI guarantees would greatly ease the cost-push pressures *other* than those from oil etc. and would come close to ending the demand-pull pressures altogether.

Would this require regimentation and arbitrary controls? No, these proposals take the merits of individual initiative seriously (although there are limits to those merits in view of the gap between the free-enterprise theory and the reality) and what they do is point the road to follow if we Americans want to control our destiny *without* giving up our freedom.

Perhaps the most striking other feature of EPI is the way it would help to liberalize foreign trade by ending the historic fear of a shortage of markets, which is the main thing enabling protectionist interests to gain governmental support for trade restrictions. Thus we could, for example, become the good neighbor of Third World countries all around the globe that both they and we would prefer to have us be.

*   *   *

To my fellow economists with a working interest in the same objectives I suggest that any real differences of opinion between us will probably be limited to three issues. First of all I affirm, while some others will no doubt deny, that my full-employment proposals and theirs differ more in kind than degree. Perhaps it is foolish even to discuss a question like that, but I must say again here that to give a binding *promise* is something quite other than to set a *goal* and then (in the face of wrong forecasts, unexpected events, and divided counsels) merely do "the best that we can" toward achieving it!

The second issue arises whenever someone thinks that my proposal is against, or perhaps disregards the importance of, his or her proposal. That is a misconception in principle. EPI is an umbrella policy, potentially consistent with any and all other measures, be they "liberal" or "conservative," for promoting prosperity and stability at the full-employment level. (My private views on the kinds of other measures our country needs have been indicated repeatedly, of course. Two examples may be cited here. Certainly, special job programs should be expanded to reduce the "structural" joblessness of disadvantaged groups in decayed inner cities. Indeed, this is especially urgent. Certainly also, monopolistic interferences with free markets have to be held in check. Even Galbraithian selective price and wage controls should be used if shown to be really necessary, although in a program equipped with EPI I doubt that they would be.)

The third issue obviously is over whether the operations called for under EPI could be carried out. Would the plan work in practice? This final question, to be sure, is not resolvable in advance of an actual trial; probability is the most that can be claimed. Given the various kinds of "leeway" the plan envisages, I do think that that probability will be found to exist.

To go back for a moment—the umbrella function of EPI has a further aspect that might escape notice at first, namely its bearing on the role of economic theory. Economic theory is of absorbing interest to many scholars, and one can only honor those of them who have done their job well. But there are certain critical problems that need to be solved in the real world while the opportunity is still there. One is the problem treated in this book, and here the availability of an insurance-type solution makes it evident that, as I wrote in another book, "lack of dedication to a theory could become a comparatively harmless affliction."

* * *

The papers in this collection are presented in reverse chronological order. A short chapter from the book mentioned just above—*Insuring Full Employment*, published by Viking Press in 1964—appears here as Chapter 19. All the others from before 1973 have been taken from my Scarecrow Press book, *Essays on Full Employment, 1942–1972* (which is, however, reproduced only in part; Chapters 3, 5, 8, 10, 12, 14, 19, 21 and 22 are omitted). Acknowledgments for reprinting them are repeated at the appropriate points in the present volume. I also want to thank *The New York Times* for permission to reprint two 1976 letters to the editor, and the *Journal of Post Keynesian Economics* for permission to present the full text of an article that appeared in their Summer 1979 issue in abridged form.

J. H. G. P.
January 1980

FULL EMPLOYMENT WITHOUT INFLATION

1

The Importance and Practicality of Guaranteed Full Employment

This article is written in the hope of drawing fresh attention to the neglected subject of *guaranteed* full employment. My aim is to show (1) that guaranteed (assured, permanent) full employment is part of the critically needed new order of priorities for the United States, and (2) that an approach centering around "economic performance insurance" can achieve it in a practical way, helping both to control inflation and strengthen private enterprise.

The fact that no theoretically satisfying definition of "full" employment can be formulated for today's imperfectly competitive labor market is immaterial. Once we agree to maintain full employment without fail, the rigor of the definition becomes operational, not abstract. First, the lobbying by interest groups as Presidential recommendations and Congressional decisions are going forward will (given such agreement) lead to the designation of some particular rate of unemployment or level of employment as being the officially certified equivalent of full employment for the year ahead. Then *that* official standard, whatever it happens to be, must be scrupulously adhered to. This will bear repeating. The rigor of the definition cannot lie in choosing some theoretically satisfying standard (there isn't any), but rather it must lie in absolutely upholding whatever numerical standard has in fact been chosen.

If critics—from labor or business, for instance—then feel that the chosen standard is too loose or too tight to reflect the underlying concept, they can agitate for adjustment of the numbers when the new standard is being set the following year. Thus nobody under these procedures is expected to do the impossible, but the government *is* periodically required to seek a good working answer to the question, declare what it is, commit itself to that answer, and honor that commitment.

This article appeared in abridged form, with the title "EPI: Economic Performance Insurance," in the Summer 1979 issue of the *Journal of Post Keynesian Economics*. The proposal has been developed in a series of my books and articles, from 1941.

The underlying concept of course is that there should be no *involuntary* unemployment, over and above the "necessary frictional" amount. (*Some* small percentage—for people just entering the labor market, or laid off temporarily, or moving from one job to another—is inevitable under present methods of counting.) In other words, the objective is to have a situation in which there will always be job opportunities, at fair levels of pay and under decent working conditions, for all men and women who are able to work and who give suitable positive evidence that they want to. For persons who wish to work but are not able to work effectively, the better solution appears to be not to "bend" the concept but rather to provide training and other relevant forms of assistance on a generous scale, to help them become able.

THE STRATEGIC IMPORTANCE OF THE ISSUE

Much of the worst damage that involuntary unemployment does is hidden from direct view, and this, I believe, largely explains why the need to have full employment on a permanent basis is not more widely recognized than it is. That need, in my opinion, is critical; the neglect of it, highly dangerous; and the study of how to meet it, an obligation upon economists in the first instance. But the subject is shrouded in taboos, and plagued besides by a general sense that a cure for the problem cannot be found, and so the neglect continues.

A familiar point is that our unemployment spells enormous waste.[1] Consumers and business both lose in obvious ways, and government, with reduced tax revenues and expanded public assistance, runs "passive" budget deficits. People abroad are disappointed in their hopes for American assistance. Our society finds that it is not able to afford even high-priority domestic investments in city rehabilitation, mass transport, conservation, energy research, low-cost housing, education, health.

Akin to this is the personal poverty question. Abolishing individual and family poverty in the United States would be enormously simplified under continuing full employment because of the great increase in the amount of paid labor—and, incidentally, the lessened chances for certain employers to pay substandard wages. While special income-support programs would still be needed, since many people cannot and should not work, our present antipoverty effort could be drastically curtailed.

But dollar considerations are still not the heart of the matter. Closer to that is the relation between inadequate job opportunity and discrimination on the basis of race, sex, age, and other factors. The drive for equal employment opportunity—not to speak of affirmative action on jobs—simply cannot hope for real success without continuing full employment. The efforts must surely be persevered in anyway, but they will truly succeed only when the supply of job opportunity is large enough to match the *total* demand.

Even worse, involuntary unemployment in a free society destroys personality. Income maintenance programs can't prevent this, since the urge to take part in society's active business (not the "work ethic" but something more universal) remains defeated at every turn. From a humane point of view this is as fundamental a criticism of our economic system as could be imagined. Besides, our whole society will tend to grow weak if this process continues. Many hard-core jobless will turn to crime; others will become demoralized to the point where they expect, or perhaps even want, nothing better than to live a life on the dole.

In two other ways also our business cycles and unemployment are causing divisions that could prove fatal to the nation in the end. Recessions, actualized or even merely anticipated, often impel powerful organizations in business, labor, and agriculture to push their financial claims too vigorously and get into serious conflict with the general interest—usually by causing more price inflation. Editors and highly placed government officials will then ask those organizations to show responsibility. But it is safe (although unpopular) to say that the concept of responsibility will never take very firm root with the parties concerned until the government itself assumes its own responsibility for holding the economy at a satisfactory level.

At the same time, our unemployment problem builds up the pressure to adopt restrictive foreign-trade measures, and so our international relations are strained too. Protectionist measures may sometimes (while raising domestic prices) produce a net gain in domestic jobs—often they do not—but certainly they undermine the larger national interest by sacrificing vital opportunities for international cooperation. For instance, we easily tire of giving the Third World countries economic aid, and we freely advise them to "move from aid to trade" (as indeed they want to, without our admonition), but then we find ourselves unwilling to provide them with the export markets they obviously must have in order to make that move. This is surely an embarrassing position for a great power vis-a-vis those much weaker members of the family of nations.

In sum, the inadequacy of our basic economic policies keeps us collectively poorer than we need to be, exaggerates the welfare burden, reinforces discrimination against women and minorities, destroys the self-reliant character of millions of Americans by showing them that their contributions are unwanted, pits interest groups too hard against society as a whole, and undermines our foreign relations, especially with the Third World. This is a course that needs to be reversed before it brings us to disaster.

The indictment would certainly have to be softened if guaranteed full employment were in fact impossible in a free society. Or even if, although possible, it would still entail serious offsetting disadvantages. But neither of those objections can be sustained. Not only is guaranteed full employment perfectly possible but it would greatly *help* us to find the answers to the other questions we face in our relations within our society, with other nations, and with the environment.

For the environment, the practical issue today is not whether the long-term investments that are so critically needed to create a more habitable world would provide the vast numbers of new jobs that environmentalists themselves foresee; of course they would! Rather, it is whether enough of them can be carried out. For the likelihood is that many of them will *not* be carried out soon in the absence of an *independently* legislated policy of guaranteed full employment with inflation control. Only a policy like that would assure the existence, elsewhere in the economy, of the jobs needed to offset those that are lost when environmentally dangerous or wasteful industries have to be shut down; and would see to it that certain prices were lowered, elsewhere, to offset the increases in costs and prices that the introduction of antipollution equipment often makes necessary.[2]

It is true—looking now at feasibility—that technology is likely to put economic policy to the test; computers and automation are raising more severe employment difficulties than many economists had anticipated.[3] But those difficulties are not insurmountable. To conclude that they are—to think that soon there will just not be enough work to go around—is to ignore both the immense amount of work still needed in today's world and the possibility and desirability of instituting work-sharing arrangements when or if we really do start to run out of useful things to do.

THE INADEQUACY OF CURRENT CONCEPTS

We are in a long pause between the historic discovery that depressions aren't acts of God and the awareness that cycles and unemployment can be abolished altogether.[4] In my opinion, this pause is needlessly prolonged by three factors: (1) As just said, the worst dangers from unemployment have been largely ignored. (2) So long as the *modus operandi* has not yet been understood, some persons suppose that guaranteed full employment would be too rigid or too disruptive—that it would stifle free enterprise, give the Administration too difficult a task, rob Congressional committees of their prerogatives, and so on. In fact, no such results need follow, as I will show. (3) Finally, many economists have seriously underestimated the difference between combatting unemployment and really ending it.

All sorts of policies, taken in isolation, would stimulate the economy and combat unemployment, and not a few have been overplayed as answers—not necessarily by exaggeration of their positive effects but by disregard of all the elements of uncertainty as to events and other legislation and even their own more indirect repercussions. For example, liberals (with whom I usually agree, on most issues) often talk as though full employment could be had as a side-effect of the extra mass purchasing power or government spending to be gained by winning the *other* victories they hope to achieve.

Here we have the by-product theory of full employment. As Sir William Beveridge put it, "If we attack with determination, unity and clear aim the four giant evils of Want, Disease, Ignorance and Squalor, we shall destroy in the process their confederate—the fifth giant of Idleness enforced by mass unemployment."[5] But Sir William saw clearly that he had to invoke "unity" to envisage an end even to "mass" unemployment, and no unity in support of the liberal—or any other!—program is in sight in America today.

Actually, current theories and proposals simply will not *unaided* give us guaranteed full employment. The better ones would, if enacted, help to reduce unemployment, but they uniformly fail to provide a final "insurance" device, something to make *sure*.[6] For guaranteed full employment *two* things are needed: not only policies to give us a reasonably good first approximation, but also a clearly formulated last-resort "insurance" plan in the form of *contingent or standby devices that are certain to be called into action to the extent that the first approximation fails to satisfy the guarantee.*

Even if some Presidential economic adviser should calculate "perfectly," Congress would find reasons to change the program, which consequently, barring coincidence, would end up either smaller or larger than it started out to be. Nor would Congress often correct perfectly an *im*perfect Presidential program. All approaches that depend on having exactly the right full-employment program formulated ahead of time are, therefore, inherently fallible. This much could no doubt be shown mathematically.

Of course our government really proceeds on a different premise altogether, the premise that economic fluctuations, when not held sufficiently in check by the built-in stabilizers like unemployment compensation, can be corrected by introducing contra-cyclical measures on an *ad hoc* basis. Thus, when the President or Congress thinks that a recession threatens, a bill will be introduced to lower certain taxes or perhaps pay out tax refunds. But this approach must fail too, if only because of the excruciatingly long time that tax changes always take to become law, given the conflicts of opinion. The flavor of it comes out in Senator Russell Long's remark (spring of 1978) that most of the tax changes proposed by President Carter "simply cannot pass and would do more harm than good if they did."[7]

Congressional tax debates are essential, naturally. The reform portions of tax bills involve basic policy issues that Congress *has* to consider fully, and so do *certain parts* of stabilization—questions like: what stabilization results does Congress want to achieve? what continuing methods are best for bringing those results near? and what "last resort" methods should be used if, as and when any final adjustment actually proves to be needed? Much of the rest of stabilization is technical, however, or else it merely involves the *execution* of policy, and so it should not be taking up Congressional time.

ECONOMIC PERFORMANCE INSURANCE

The way out of these perplexities does not lie in having the right thinkers on social and economic policy overpower the wrong thinkers (overpowering is a bad idea anyway) but rather in agreeing on a specific change in stabilization procedure. Our federal government needs to end the present guesswork, confusion, and delay by substituting responsible advance policy decisions (1) on certain precisely formulated goals and (2) on standby measures to assure achievement of those goals.

My proposal on this is called, for want of a better term, economic performance insurance, or EPI for short. EPI would be an added element in fiscal policy, used to gain control over the *level* of operation of the economy as a whole but not (lest that point be misunderstood) over the individual producer. It would function with the least effort if policies to spread purchasing power, develop new energy sources, encourage initiative and investment, prevent monopolistic extortion, break down structural rigidities, improve existing monetary institutions, and so on were highly developed, since that would leave EPI itself with relatively little work to do. But there is no need to assume miraculous progress in those other directions.

What EPI would do is amend present general policy legislation governing the annual procedure aimed at full employment, so that thereafter: (1) the President would each year recommend specific levels of employment and consumer spending to be guaranteed, and methods to be used as necessary for honoring those guarantees; (2) Congress would then accept or modify those Presidential recommendations; and (3) the Executive Branch, without further Congressional intervention, would execute the given mandate by activating the approved standby measures to the extent found necessary.

Guaranteed Employment Level

There would be a firm commitment to continuous full employment as defined in quantitative terms in advance. Either (a) a certain national rate of *un*employment, considered not higher than "necessary frictional" unemployment, would be specified; or (b)—as will be assumed here—the commitment would be to the national level of *em*ployment that in turn was expected to hold unemployment at the rate envisaged in (a).

The seasonally adjusted figure for civilian employment in the BLS-published monthly series (the household survey)[8] would, therefore, be examined each month to see whether it corresponded to the civilian labor force figure implied by the department's annual labor force projection, minus "necessary frictional" unemployment. If the employment guarantee were stated as a single average figure for the year as a whole, that could then serve as the guaranteed mid-year level, from which the other monthly targets would have to differ somewhat, being diminishingly lower at first and then increasingly higher.

Not only should unemployment not rise above the intended rate but it should not fall far below that rate either, lest a too tight, "overemployment" situation be thereby created. Total *em*ployment should therefore be kept from falling below a certain specified level and also from rising very much above that level. In other words, the commitment would be to hold employment within a defined range or band, above a certain minimum or floor but below a certain maximum or ceiling (and not, of course, at a precise point, which would clearly be impractical). How wide this band should be is a question that needs to be studied. Provisionally—but only as a starting point for discussion—I suggest that a 1 percent variation might create a situation that was neither too loose nor too tight; if at some point the floor were 100 million persons, the ceiling would then be 101 million.

Guaranteed Level of Consumer Spending

It is self-evident that production for market, unlike planned production, expands or contracts mainly in response to the indicated size of the market as a whole. Under EPI there would be a second firm commitment, to a pre-set level of *consumer* spending, with performance monitored by reference to the seasonally adjusted current rate of personal consumption expenditures published quarterly by the Commerce Department. Again it would be a question of holding the figure within a specified range or band rather than on a precise line, and here the band might be, I think, somewhat wider than for employment—say a 2 percent difference between bottom and top, although that again is only a preliminary suggestion, subject to modification in the light of study.

The Full Employment and Balanced Growth Act of 1978, amending the Employment Act of 1946, requires the President to propose, and Congress to review, annual numerical short-term and medium-term goals for employment and unemployment and also for production, real income, productivity, and prices. This is intended to help achieve, as rapidly as feasible, full employment and production, increased real income, balanced growth, price stability, a balanced federal budget, an improved trade balance, and several other major goals. There can be no question that our society has a number of important economic goals that need to be worked for simultaneously and achieved as nearly as possible. The contrasting point to be made about firm commitments or *guarantees*, however, is that these can hardly exceed two in number. (Take, say, the older "employment, production, and purchasing power" maintainance formula. If total purchasing power is to be fixed in advance, production—the GNP—must be free to vary somewhat, by expansion or contraction of last-resort projects, to assure maintenance of a pre-set level of employment.)

There are several reasons why consumer spending should be the second guarantee. First and foremost, this would permit full employment to be guaranteed without any implication that a bigger government sector would be the means of fulfillment. This additional guarantee, in other words, is what would make the guaranteeing of employment itself realistically possible in the United States. Second, the pre-set ceiling on consumer spending—aided by the ceiling on employment—would be a powerful weapon against demand-pull inflation, as discussed later. Third, as explained immediately below, this control, applied to the largest component part of the market, would in fact assure producers of an adequate *total* market at all times, regardless even of the state of our foreign-trade balance. (The other components of demand, moreover—private domestic investment, government purchases of goods and services, and net exports—do not lend themselves to precise advance determination in an unplanned economy.)

Consider how the *right* level of consumer spending for guarantee purposes would be established. The first step would be to estimate a "full-employment GNP," i.e. to guess as shrewdly as possible the aggregate amount of expenditures for goods and services needed to keep the economy operating at the full-employment level in the year ahead, given the expected rate of price increase (for which, naturally, as low a goal would be set as practicable). Next, estimates would be developed for gross private domestic investment; government spending on goods and services at federal, state, and local levels; and—obviously a minus quantity today—net exports. Finally, the necessary (operationally speaking) level of personal consumption expenditures would be derived by subtracting the algebraic sum of those estimated other GNP components from the estimated full-employment GNP. Being the residual number, the consumer spending commitment would accomodate itself to the desired size of the federal government's program; the less government spending intended, the more consumer spending needed, and conversely. And it would accommodate itself too to the state of the trade balance that seemed most likely to develop in the light of circumstances and the foreign policy that our country wanted to follow.

Hence an American EPI system could be highly acceptable both at home and abroad. First, establishing these procedures involving the whole GNP would tell producers of goods and services that, between them, they would always find a big enough total market. Furthermore, the method of determining the consumer spending guarantee— by having all items wanted by the President and Congress for their own sake, but not any others, included in the subtotal *subtracted* from the estimated necessary GNP to arrive at that—would be altogether favorable to private producers. For it would certify that all parts of the full employment not public by deliberate choice would be reserved to the private domain. We would therefore always have the GNP level we needed without having a public sector level that we as a nation didn't want. The Gordian knot that has seemed to tie promises of full employment to threats of bigger and bigger government would be effectively cut.

Finally, as regards foreign trade, the present situation in which the United States (like most other nations) intensifies its pursuit of export markets and its resistance to imports whenever its domestic market shrinks would become obsolete. For after that we could consciously adjust the size of our domestic market, via the consumer spending guarantee, to whatever export or import surplus seemed indicated on broadest policy grounds. In a word, our trade policies would no longer need to be governed by the historic fear of a shortage of markets, and we could wear our good-neighbor face more often. One noteworthy corollary effect would be that sales of arms abroad could no longer be defended as necessary for bolstering our domestic economy.

Final Adjustment of Employment

To honor its promise, the federal government would have to stand ready to raise or lower the job total quickly when that need arose. The frequency and extent of that need would be reduced by the *other* promise, the assured maintenance of consumer demand at the presumptively adequate level, and by the probability that the inevitable estimating errors would partially offset each other. Still, it remains incontrovertible that under guaranteed full employment the government would have to be prepared to come in as employer of last resort. There would thus have to be (1) a permanent "reserve shelf" or "reservoir" of public service and public works jobs, and (2) unprecedented arrangements to assure its prompt use, whether for expansion or for contraction, whenever upward or downward adjustment was called for to honor the guarantee.

The reserve shelf should certainly include only works and services of instrinsic value, including activities already being carried out on some level as well as new projects. To enable work to be started and tapered off quickly, undue dependence on equipment with inflexible delivery or operating schedules should be avoided. A wide spectrum of "industry" fields and occupational skills should be represented. The shelf should include local, state, and federal projects, many to be operated on a contract basis by profit-making construction firms or nonprofit agencies. Since it must obviously have nationwide coverage, the geographical apportionment formula for expansions and contractions would raise important questions for the President and Congress to decide. One of the main factors in setting up special work programs today, however, namely differences in the severity of unemployment from area to area, would become far less important for the *reserve* shelf (as distinct from the ongoing "first resort" work against "structural" unemployment in blighted areas etc.) once national full employment was guaranteed.

Although building and maintaining this reserve shelf would be the most laborious undertaking necessitated by EPI, the psychological resistance that similar undertakings have met in the past should largely disappear. Any fear of a creeping governmental encroachment at the expense of private enterprise would be clearly unwarranted under the EPI system, since marginal contractions of publicly sponsored jobs would be as likely to be called for as marginal expansions (i.e., if the consumer spending calculations aimed at the midpoint in the guaranteed employment range). And it would be absurd to suggest that adjustments utilizing the reserve shelf could not be very greatly speeded up, once given the will in Washington to keep that device always ready for immediate use.

Final Adjustment of Consumer Spending

Holding to the guaranteed job level would keep income flowing at a rate tending to yield approximately the correct return flow of consumer spending. Still, a guarantee of consumer spending would presuppose the federal government's readiness to raise or lower the current rate *directly* when that proved necessary. Doing that has been simplified by progress in computer technology and the rapid expansion of all sorts of transfer payments. Since there are many alternative solutions, a certain amount of continuing debate over the best solution might well occur among the President's economic advisers and in Congress.

It may of course be asked whether the government *can* control the consumer spending level, which depends in the end on *individuals'* decisions on the use of their purchasing power—whether to spend or to save their income. Those who have closely observed how the rate of consumer saving has varied at different stages in recent business cycles may especially be expected to feel some concern on this particular point. Practically speaking, however, in a situation in which business cycles were no longer occurring, I think it must be allowed that the chances are really nonexistent that the government could be defeated in its efforts to raise or lower consumer spending by operating upon the level of disposable income. How, in those circumstances, could the national propensity to consume suddenly become so capricious?

Only two of the possible final-adjustment methods will be mentioned here. One would entail raising or lowering slightly the withholding rate on the personal income tax, after preferably first adding a negative income tax feature so as to avoid having to use separate, special devices for reaching low-income households. Enough has been written about the negative income tax to show that its introduction would be feasible.[9] A guaranteed household income plan, effectuated through such a negative tax, furthermore deserves consideration as an antipoverty measure—*provided* always that full employment be guaranteed too, lest the income-guarantee plan perpetuate the division between those who can get jobs and those who can't. Under EPI the allowances (negative income taxes) would then be raised, and the positive income taxes lowered, whenever it was necessary to increase consumer spending so as to meet the guarantee, while the positive income taxes would be raised, and the allowances lowered—although never below their base level—in the opposite case.

Another alternative, first suggested years ago,[10] would be to institute a standby two-way federal tax-or-bonus scheme at consumer sales points. Under this plan, when consumer spending was running too low, all buyers of goods and services at retail would receive from the sellers special coupons or stamps. Unlike food stamps, these income-booster coupons would be convertible into cash at a bank or post office if promptly presented. On the other hand, when consumer spending was running too high, the device would become a sales tax, automatically reducing the amount of consumer spending received by business, net of this tax, as much as necessary for purposes of guarantee fulfillment.

Legislation and Operations

Two kinds of legislative action are required, the first being new permanent legislation to amend the present law. Permanent legislation could obviously not bind future Congresses on questions of specific substance, but it would, as does the Congressional Budget Act of 1974, call on future Congresses to follow certain specific procedures.

Incidentally, it would need to amend Section 301 of that Budget Act, which might otherwise be held to prevent authorization of *contingent* modifications of budget outlay and revenue totals as required for maintaining guaranteed levels of employment and consumer spending. The Budget Act pointedly avoids requiring budget *balance* in any given year, and should equally clearly not push the idea of advance budget *rigidity* to the point where that would prevent the maintenance of full employment. A drafting amendment is, therefore, required, to indicate that modifications in the pre-set annual outlay and revenue totals called for under the budget law would be permissible, if specifically occasioned by last-resort actions needed to honor the commitments under the employment law.[11] With that change made, neither act would contravene the other.

Once adopted, the new employment law would have the President each year recommend in his Economic Report (1) lower and upper limits to employment and consumer-spending guarantees for the year ahead,[12] and (2) contingent or standby measures for the adjustment of both magnitudes, as already explained. Congress would then each year have its Joint Economic Committee analyze those recommendations, and would after that follow a procedure leading to a concurrent resolution setting forth its own decisions on those same points.

To illustrate, suppose that these procedures had been in effect for the year 1977, when unemployment averaged 7 percent, civilian employment averaged 90.55 million persons, the GNP was $1887 billion, and consumer spending came to $1207 billion. *If* the President had been in a position to propose a 3.5 percent limit to unemployment instead, he would have recommended holding employment, say, between 94 and 95 million and—I am simplifying the calculation[13]—holding consumer spending between $1320 and $1345 billion (based on an estimated full-employment GNP of $2062 billion). And *if* Congress had then decided on a tighter definition of full employment, say 3 percent unemployment, but a smaller government program and hence an offsetting, larger amount of consumer spending, the guarantee figures as modified by Congress could have been: employment, 94.5–95.5 million and consumer spending, e.g., $1360–$1385 billion.

Note again that, under the EPI proposal, the decisions finally reached on numerical limits and on methods of enforcement would be binding decisions. Congress would not be giving the President *discretionary* authority for dealing with economic fluctuations. On the contrary, while final-balancing operations, when required, would be conducted by the Executive Branch without further Congressional intervention, resort to those operations would be *mandatory* to honor the specific promises given by Congress and would be precluded in other circumstances.

Objection might be raised to having Congress exercise this authority, binding upon the President. If so, then a procedure involving the opportunity for Presidential vetoes and Congressional overrides could be used instead, although a testing of the

Constitutional question raised by such an objection might be welcomed first. What is essential, however, is simply that, under EPI, the annual process of setting the stage for the next economic year would have to end with definite, unambiguous decisions on the lower and upper limits to the guarantees, and on the standby methods for use in enforcing those limits.

The regular committee system of Congress would meanwhile deal with authorizations and appropriations as it does now. For example, tax reforms shaped by the Senate Finance Committee or by Ways and Means would not clash with the standby tax adjustment mechanism, but would only affect (by altering after-tax income and its distribution) the likelihood that those mechanisms would have to be called into play.

Let me turn now to the operating side of EPI. A special unit, most likely in the Labor Department, would be charged with initiating action to raise or lower employment, and one in the Treasury Department (or possibly a joint task force of IRS, HEW and CEA?) with triggering additions to or subtractions from consumer spending. These experts would need good judgment for solving problems of timing. One group would be working with preliminary tabulations of employment data due to be published about three weeks after the period to which they applied; the other, with data on consumption expenditures for which the Commerce Department publishes preliminary figures some three weeks after the end of each quarter. Both would obviously have to keep close watch also on a wide array of forecasts for individual industries and on other relevant economic data.

Although statistical leads and lags would be much less troublesome in the absence of business cycles than they are today, very real technical difficulties would remain, both in knowing the facts and in getting operational decisions carried out. Since the mandate would be to stay within designated bands or ranges, corrections would commonly have to be introduced on an anticipatory basis. Postponing action until either indicator was already too low or too high would breach the continuity of the pattern before correction could take hold. Again, once correction did take hold, how soon should action be terminated?

Yet there seems no reason to doubt that these problems could be solved. Firstly, the President and Congress would already have weighed the extent of these operating difficulties in deciding how wide the employment and consumer spending bands ought to be. Secondly, Congress might very well agree that employment and consumer spending could, without any presumption of mismanagement, stray outside their "allowable" bands briefly—say for two or three monthly periods or one quarterly period. Finally, as said earlier, a major undertaking would build up both an adequate reserve shelf of last-resort jobs and the capacity of local agencies to act quickly in starting and stopping those job programs once the signal was given. And the essential local cooperation would also be prearranged for quickly activating the consumer spending adjustments.

EPI AND INFLATION CONTROL

To hold inflation down by letting unemployment rise is morally wrong, difficult anyway because of the alternative income provided by unemployment compensation etc., and impossible beyond a point because of public opinion. Realistically, inflation requires altogether different and to some extent independent treatment.

Scarcities of natural resources are the element hardest to deal with. Even temporary bad weather raises prices, and if a world food shortage materializes, chronic inflationary pressure will accompany the mass starvation and death, population control being the only final remedy. As for *nonrenewable* resources like oil, shortages cannot be overcome directly but must be evaded by discovering substitutes.

Energy, which can also be used for transforming minerals and other substances into those most needed, is at the center of the resources picture in every respect. No doubt the best hope of overcoming the energy crisis lies in drawing more on our relatively abundant nonrenewable resources, such as coal in place of oil, as an interim measure, and moving as rapidly as possible meanwhile toward permanent reliance on various ways of using renewable and nonpolluting solar energy. Even then, however, some energy-caused rise in the general American price level seems highly likely in the years ahead. Dollar depreciation from massive oil imports can be stopped and hence also the rise in import prices generally and the consequential administered price hikes by domestic producers (e.g. Ford because of Toyota); but upward pressure from the cost of producing energy itself, and products embodying substantial amounts of energy, may well remain.

By contrast, the inflationary pressures that come from *other* cost-push factors and from the *demand-pull* side can be dealt with more swiftly. Let me list the specific contributions that EPI itself could make to a program to control those inflation forces.[14]

(1) EPI would effectively prevent excessive demand pull. Because consumer spending would have a pre-set ceiling, the familiar price spiral would be cut off at the final demand end. (Thus, making the government the employer of last resort would *not* unleash an inflationary flood of spending in private markets. For if those last-resort government-derived payrolls did threaten to raise total purchasing power above target, a standby tax of a predetermined kind would by advance authorization be activated to hold consumer spending down, as previously explained.)

(2) Because of (1), there would be little need for cost-of-living wage boosts.

(3) EPI would also lower unit costs of production in two other ways. Not only does full employment spread the overhead cost over more units of production, but the elimination of business cycles would minimize costs from business and labor efforts to cushion future slumps with special business reserves, job-security clauses in union contracts, etc.

(4) If, as I suggested earlier, the concept of responsibility will never take very firm root with business or labor until the government assumes its own responsibility for holding the economy at a satisfactory level, the converse is probably valid too: once the government *does* assume its own responsibility, why should not industry, labor, and others stand ready to cooperate voluntarily? Industry would be assured of a level of demand adequate to sustain business prosperity indefinitely; labor, of enough jobs to go around. Public opinion, if honestly and thoroughly informed, would recognize that there was no longer any real excuse for anyone's refusal to join in curbing the common enemy, inflation. In short, the whole "chemistry" would change. (There would thus also arise opportunities to review other basic questions of efficiency and fairness that seldom get a hearing today—e.g., how minimum wages should relate to average wages, and poverty-line supports to minimum wages, and how unions and management can do

better justice to all concerned on problems like temporary work and chronic absenteeism.)

(5) Finally, by reason of (1) through (4), EPI would largely end the inflationary *expectations* from which *current* inflation draws tremendous force today.

EPI AND FULL-EMPLOYMENT POLICY AS A WHOLE

The EPI idea is not in conflict with others that aim to make our economic system perform closer to capacity, with fewer fluctuations, and with less inflation. EPI would simply be an umbrella policy, for use in conjunction with all other policies currently in effect, to make sure that the wanted economic stabilization results were in fact obtained. It would do so by assigning responsibility for quantitative definition of the results needed and by arranging matters so that, when events had shown how our economy was actually performing at a given moment, the gap would be filled or the excess trimmed away, if either existed. Thus EPI is not a "special" solution for full employment; it is the "general case" solution.

A thumbnail historical sketch may be helpful. The Classical School held that there was an inherent tendency toward full employment, since supply *was* demand. Keynes found that that was not so, but concluded "that a somewhat comprehensive socialisation of investment will prove the only means of securing an approximation to full employment."[15] In America, Hansen leaned toward the related view that the way to take up economic slack was to expand public investment.[16] Others soon emphasized that slack can be taken up equally well by additional private spending, from tax reduction. So far, so good. But then somehow the pursuit of full employment got lost amid the loud claims of those who *wanted* tax reduction and *opposed* government spending, or the reverse. No doubt this helps to explain why many economists became disenchanted with fiscal policy. Under EPI, however, the tendency toward full employment would be deliberately restored and reinforced, those rival claims notwithstanding.

A final word about full-employment policy more broadly, to show some especially important interconnections.

(1) *Monopolies, oligopolies, etc.* When business or, sometimes, labor organizations with substantial market power choose extortion over moderation in administering their selling prices, they contribute to inflation by keeping those prices up, and to unemployment by holding those outputs down and by leaving the public less money to spend on other things. EPI would allow routinely for the "moderation-extortion ratio" already present in the economy; the lower that ratio, the higher the needed full-employment GNP and the guaranteed rate of consumer spending. Then, if that ratio should fall *unexpectedly* during the year, the effect would be offset by temporarily drawing extra jobs from the reserve shelf. Obviously, however, competition should be promoted and monopolistic restrictions opposed, wherever found. If the remedies discussed above should prove insufficiently effective, then legal price and wage controls might have to be imposed on a limited number of the larger business organizations and unions.[17]

(2) *Investment.* Expanded capital formation is needed to keep the American economy competitive, and also to provide new job openings in the easiest way. If an investment upsurge is imminent,[18] so much the better. EPI itself would powerfully stimulate steady

investment (and so reduce the required consumer spending) by promising sustained future demand for the final goods and services to be produced. In addition, tax policy should favor accelerated depreciation, but with insistence on measures (recycling, etc.) to keep from overdoing the drain on natural resources, since the key problem now is how to focus the wanted investment so as to protect and enhance the environment. Highest priority should be assigned to developing new energy sources, as by government subsidies to OTEC and other promising energy systems, like the subsidies that built our canals, railroads, and roads.

(3) *Structural unemployment.* Much of our worst unemployment is "structural," occurring in decayed inner cities and other areas with a weak economic base, and afflicting groups with limited skills and mobility, particularly black teen-agers. Here special countermeasures are essential: expanded creation of new industries and public job programs and training programs in disadvantaged areas, and probably also wage subsidies to private industry for hiring young workers.[19] Under guaranteed full employment those measures would enlarge the labor force, changing "unable" into "able" workers and attracting other able, previously "discouraged" workers. And they would expand employment, not just by lowering unemployment to the existing "necessary frictional" level but also by easing the frictions and so reducing the amount of unemployment that remained "necessary."

NOTES

1. Our lost potential GNP is estimated by the Council of Economic Advisers in *Economic Report of the President* (1978) at about $330 billion in 1972 dollars during 1974–77; by Keyserling (in Senator Muriel Humphrey and Representative Augustus F. Hawkins, *Goals for Full Employment and How to Achieve Them* [Washington, D.C.: February 1978]), at $5.27 trillion in 1977 dollars during 1953–77. The former uses a 4.8–4.9% unemployment "benchmark"; the latter, 2.9%.

2. Emile Benoit emphasized this interconnection between long-term environmental measures and the short-term inflation-unemployment problem. See, e.g., his "Dynamic Equilibrium as an Alternative to Unrestricted Growth," *National Parks & Conservation Magazine* 52 no. 7 (July 1978): 14–19. (Paper presented at a session on Economic Growth Theory and Models of the Atlantic Economic Conference, October 13, 1977.)

3. According to Paul Lewis (*New York Times*, July 5, 1978), an unpublished report by Christopher Freedman for the Organization for Economic Cooperation and Development highlights this danger. Guaranteed-income advocate Robert Theobald stressed the problem at least as early as 1963 (*Free Men and Free Markets* [New York: Clarkson N. Potter]), also claiming it made full employment obsolete.

4. Paul Davidson has sagely remarked (in "Why Money Matters: Lessons from a Half-Century of Monetary Theory," *Journal of Post Keynesian Economics* 1 57 [Fall 1978]) that "Time is a device that prevents everything from happening at once." This is comforting!

5. Sir William Henry Beveridge, *Full Employment in a Free Society* (London: Allen & Unwin, 1944), p. 257.

6. Enactment of the Humphrey-Hawkins bill (Full Employment and Balanced Growth Act) is a hopeful sign. However, all versions of it, excepting the unworkable early plan to have job rights enforced through the courts, have been ambivalent about actually guaranteeing full employment.

7. As cited by Leonard Silk in *The New York Times*, May 4, 1978.

8. My argument does not, of course, depend on retention of this leading national employment index in its present form.

9. See, e.g. Tobin, James, Pechman, Joseph A., and Mieszkowski, Peter M. "Is A Negative Income Tax Practical?" *Yale Law Journal* 77: 1–27 (November 1967).

10. In my "On Underwriting Consumption and Employment," *American Economic Review* 45 (September 1955): 645–47. (See below, pp. 124–26.)

11. Language for this was suggested in my testimony on the Humphrey-Hawkins bill. See U.S. Congress, House of Representatives, Committee on Education and Labor, Subcommittee on Employment Opportunities, *Hearings*, 95th Cong., 1st sess., 1977, II, 473–79. (Included below, pp. 28–33.)

12. And possibly also for half-yearly or even quarterly periods during the transition *to* full employment.

13. E.g., I here arbitrarily assume $50 billion added to GNP for each percentage point subtracted from unemployment.

14. The program must obviously also include other measures not discussed here, such as vigorous antitrust action, reduced Social Security taxes, and perhaps some tax-based incomes policy as variously advocated by Sidney Weintraub, Henry Wallich, Arthur Okun, and others (see, e.g., Laurence S. Seidman, "Tax-Based Incomes Policies," *Brookings Papers on Economic Activity* 2 [1978], pp. 301–48); or as found in President Carter's "wage insurance" plan.

15. John Maynard Keynes, *The General Theory of Employment, Interest and Money* (London: Macmillan, 1936).

16. Alvin H. Hansen, *Fiscal Policy and Business Cycles* (New York: Norton, 1941).

17. As recommended by Galbraith on numerous occasions; see, e.g., his *Economics and the Purpose* (Boston: Houghton Mifflin, 1973), pp. 312–16.

18. As suggested by Walt W. Rostow, "It Will Take Skill to Avoid a Boom," (interview with Leonard Silk in *The New York Times*, January 10, 1978).

19. As recommended by Lester C. Thurow ("For Wage Subsidies to Help Fight Unemployment," *The New York Times*, January 10, 1978).

2

The Terms of a Real Solution for Stagflation

The policy we need would be aimed first at securing guaranteed full employment in the United States; that is, at assuring that everyone who is able and seeking to work will always have that opportunity. This, however, is not something that should or can happen in isolation. The policy must put an end to deflation generally and to the business cycle, must minimize price inflation, and must really favor individual initiative and private enterprise, not just pay them lip service.

What I am proposing is the imposition of control over the level of operation of the economy as a whole, not over the individual producer except as necessary to avoid price or wage extortion in special cases. The new element here is the concept of "economic performance insurance." This would involve guaranteeing bottom and top limits to employment and consumer spending. Once the President and Congress had aligned those two targets for the year ahead, final adjustments of the actual aggregates would be brought about without further Congressional debate if and as current statistics showed them to be required.

This would not present as much difficulty as some might imagine. Everyone knows that a self-sustaining "circular flow" of production and demand at the full-employment level is impossible, in view of monopolistic interferences with the market mechanism and the absence of any special reason why intended savings and actual investments should add to the same total. But what counts today is that we could reinstate that Classical idea in a practical way by constantly attending to the two aggregates, employment and consumer spending. Each of them would then strongly reinforce the other, leaving the final adjustments to be rather small, as long as the rest of our economic and social policies were in reasonable balance.

This summary dates from May 1978.

The guaranteed minimum of consumer spending would be calculated from estimates of necessary over-all demand and its other GNP components, and so it would essentially solve the Achilles heel problem of our kind of economic system—the problem of markets. Industry would always be assured of an adequate market for which to compete. Policy makers in government would feel economically safe in making the right decisions on issues like foreign trade and the environment, because the needed totals of demand and jobs would be protected in any case.

At the same time the inflation spiral would be checked by the prearranged top limit on consumer spending, taken in conjunction with whatever action was really called for to control the "cost push." The substantial savings in production costs inherent in assured full employment—savings from spreading the overhead and from not needing to cushion future slumps—should certainly be reflected in the final prices concerned. Given the favorable new conditions, this could probably be arranged through voluntary cooperation. The oil problem and other natural resource scarcities are open to inventive solutions, too, but would of course remain as a somewhat longer-term part of the price-level question.

3

The Central Question
and the Needed Concept

The economic concept makers are gone. Loyal bands of their followers battle over questions such as whether monetary or fiscal policy is more important, whether the structural approach is the one that really makes sense, whether everybody is a Keynesian now or Keynesianism is dead. Congress and the Administration find the range of conceptual options uncomfortably narrow as a basis for action.

The nub of the problem is that none of the concept makers has squarely faced the question that, in our time, needs to be put first. That question is: *how can we have permanent full employment in the United States, and have it without inflation, by means that won't weaken but instead will strengthen the private enterprise market system?*

Full employment *is* the key to the answer. Some of my fellow economists avoid this conclusion by taking refuge behind the idea that unemployment and price inflation are locked into a trade-off (the Phillips curve), so that one has to go up if the other comes down. Some others who do envisage economic stabilization at full employment seem to think that it can only be approached indirectly—by tackling a series of other, mostly egalitarian, social goals directly and then (if successful there!) extracting full employment as a sort of by-product. It is as though they were a little ashamed to advocate full employment head-on, of treating it as worthly of their determined effort in its own right.

This attitude is very puzzling. I share their view that goals such as equal opportunity and reduced inequality of income are a fine thing. A guarantee of the opportunity to work (with no inflation or impairment of our traditional system) will nevertheless have to be accomplished independently, and it will moreover be the finest thing of all—finest as a paramount objective in itself, a powerful help in achieving those other goals too, and a means whereby our economic future will come to the aid of our economic present by multiple feedbacks via good anticipations—as I propose to make clear.

This unpublished article, originally titled "For Guaranteed Full Employment," was completed early in 1978.

18

How does one convey the *intrinsic* significance of full employment? One can try by stripping away common misconceptions. Full employment does not mean forcing any man or woman to work, or providing jobs for people not able to work or not honestly seeking to. Nor does it mean having nobody unemployed at all, since obviously in any dynamic society some designated small percentage of "frictional" unemployment is necessary to accommodate labor turnover. But it does mean having no more unemployment than that, so as not to have people up against a blank wall. Surely, if the pursuit of happiness is meant to be for everybody, we must abolish involuntary unemployment and have full employment for its own sake!

But we need assured full employment to help us achieve other major goals as well. The elimination of poverty in the United States is a prime example. Even though many people will never be earning money because they cannot and should not work, ending poverty would be enormously simplified by the expanded income from continuous full employment—because of the increased amount of paid labor and the lessened chances for certain employers to exploit workers by paying substandard wages.

Another prime example is discrimination. How can the drive for equal employment opportunity, let alone affirmative action programs, hope to succeed in the absence of continuing full employment? The answer is that they can't, beyond a certain point. The efforts must be pursued anyway, but the condition for full success is that the amount of opportunity must be large enough to encompass everyone.

Or take our self-evident need for big investments in city rehabilitation, mass transport, conservation, energy research, low-cost housing, education, and health. Think how the wastes of *non*production are limiting what our society can afford to undertake (whether on a private, government-assisted, or government-sponsored basis) in these and other important fields. Quantitative estimates here will depend on the particular assumptions, and will vary widely. What matters in any case, however, is not the exact numbers—which are astronomically large over the years by any calculation—but rather the point that combating underemployment of resources would help to avoid such wastes in future, and that the largest waste avoidance would occur under continuous full employment.

This point is more or less familiar. What has been much less widely noticed *in discussions of public policy* is the feedback effect of uncertainty about future prosperity on the state of the economy today. Considering the amount of time and talent now devoted to forecasting the ups and downs of our economy, and the amount of talk about the need for business confidence, this again seems surprising. The clues are everywhere. After all, a market-oriented economic system is a dynamic complex heavily dependent on anticipations. Why not, then, start controlling the anticipations that can be controlled and are strategically the most important?

Business investment depends on expectations concerning markets for final products in future years. The wage increases and fringe benefits sought by trade unions reflect not only the current state of the economy but the very fact or existence of the business cycle, since that is what necessitates the construction in good times of all sorts of buffers against bad times to come. Consumers' decisions to spend or to save change markedly with cyclical swings. And these are only the most obvious examples of how the expected future always influences—and often disrupts—the economic present.

Some other major illustrations will apear later. But enough has been said already, I believe, to suggest that a new economic strategy is needed, and that the distinguishing feature of such a new strategy must be the inclusion in it of not just a set of goals as usual, but also a limited number of *binding promises.* A goal is not a promise. In the individualistic and hard-nosed world of the marketplace, anticipations cannot be counted on to respond satisfactorily to mere public *goals.*

*   *   *

Because reaching and then permanently keeping full employment is the heart of the economic problem, it follows by definition that the way to solve the problem must be to take out a kind of "insurance policy" for the American economy. The Humphrey-Hawkins bill would carry us a long way forward from the Employment Act of 1946, but would not—in either its present or any earlier form—achieve this goal. Specifically, I propose a pair of guarantees to be given by the federal government on a year-by-year basis: first, a guarantee of the level of employment itself, and second, for reasons to be made clear, a guarantee of the level of consumer spending. This combination I call "economic performance insurance" or EPI for short.

EPI would be only part of a total full-employment policy, obviously. It would be the new element needed to provide decisive "measures of last resort" for use as actually required, and thus also to provide a solid basis for good anticipations. With it should go a well-considered battery of "measures of first resort" (structural, fiscal, monetary, etc.), both in order to meet the specific purposes of those measures themselves and also to put less strain on the guarantees.

For example, I cannot imagine a total policy for full employment that would not put heavy emphasis on special programs to get young blacks into jobs, and strong action against monopolistic restrictions, and reforms aimed at spreading purchasing power by making the tax system as a whole more progressive. Neither can we afford, I think, not to encourage initiative and risk-taking more than we do, especially innovation along ecologically sound lines, such as the development of new energy sources. Here a case in point is the OTEC system—solar energy via ocean temperature differentials—which can be tested properly only on a large scale, and which to my mind is especially worthy of risking government subsidies on.

The reader can amplify these last paragraphs to suit himself or herself. My own purpose in digressing was merely to avoid possible misunderstanding by making clear that the EPI proposal is *not* offered in isolation. Rather it is conceived of as an umbrella policy, needed to make sure that the sum of our economic policies—not those merely advocated but those *adopted and in effect*—will always give the stabilization results that the nation wants.

To go back to the levels of employment and consumer spending to be guaranteed under the EPI system, these "levels" would actually be ranges or bands between a floor and a ceiling. That would be important for administrative feasibility and inflation control. In his annual Economic Reports the President would recommend a numerical floor and ceiling for total employment and a numerical floor and ceiling for total consumer spending. The employment floor would express his view of full employment, i.e. it would in the President's opinion allow only the necessary small percentage of frictional unemployment, except that he would have to set lower floors for several years first, while the economy was recovering from its present condition.

The President would also recommend specific measures of last resort to go into effect if either employment or consumer spending started to drop below its floor or exceed its ceiling. (Seasonally adjusted figures are published monthly for civilian employment, quarterly for personal consumption expenditures.) The Congress would then approve or amend the President's recommendations, both on the numerical targets themselves and on the standby measures to be used, when necessary, for final adjustments to keep the economy within the targets.

The simplest procedure would be for Congress to make the final decisions. If this were objected to, a procedure involving the possibility of Presidential vetoes and Congressional overrides could be used instead. But in any case, and this is the essential point, the annual process would have to end with *definite, unambiguous decisions on these particular questions.*

After that the Executive Branch would be obligated to carry out those decisions without further Congressional mandates. The guarantees would be in place. The intended stabilization results would follow without any need to keep on legislating to offset earlier wrong predictions about economic trends.

What would those standby measures of last resort consist of? For employment they undoubtedly would involve accelerating or else decelerating certain kinds of public works and services. It would hence be necessary to develop and afterwards maintain an ample reserve shelf of such projects (expansions of existing programs plus some totally new ones), together with unprecedented arrangements for quick reserve-shelf withdrawals and replacements. For consumer spending there could be numerous options, but all of them would involve the principle that consumer purchasing power would (if or when necessary for honoring the guarantee) be enlarged or reduced by tax or transfer-payment adjustments. For example, the vehicle for these final adjustments could well be the personal income tax, with a negative tax feature added so as not to omit low-income groups. Or it could be a new federal sales tax made reversible into a sales bonus, using income-booster coupons or "I.B.s", when consumer spending was below target and needed to be raised.

Some readers, accustomed to thinking that having enough jobs will in itself create all the buying power needed, may wonder why a separate guarantee of consumer spending should be proposed at all. The answer is that enough jobs will not necessarily create enough *spending*, because of the possibility of oversaving in relation to investment. Similarly, enough spending will not necessarily generate enough jobs in return, because of the possibility of increased monopoly or oligopoly restrictions on production and employment.

It may be remembered that the Classical School of economists held that full employment tended to occur automatically, with supply and demand reciprocally sustaining each other. In this belief they were wrong (since they ignored the savings-investment problem and the problem of imperfect competition). They were not so far wrong, however, but that it is possible to create by means of a system of prearranged, minor, contingent adjustments at *both* ends of the production-consumption process a practical modern analogue to the unreal abstraction they had in mind.

That the guarantee of demand should be applied to *consumer* spending rather than to the total of *all* spending on goods and services (gross national expenditures, equivalent to GNP) comes about because the other components of total demand just do not lend themselves to this treatment. Nothing is lost, however, since all of the other components would be used to calculate the particular level of consumer spending to be guaranteed. (To speak technically for a moment, adding the expected amounts of (1) government purchases at all governmental levels and (2) gross private domestic investment and (3) positive or negative net exports, and then subtracting this sum from the GNP thought to be needed for full employment at anticipated price levels, would give the necessary— operationally speaking—consumer spending. Thus the smaller the estimated total of other demand, the larger the consumer guarantee.)

And here we see clearly why EPI would strengthen the private-enterprise market system. Last-resort government jobs would not threaten to have to grow and grow, since EPI would assure manufacturers, farmers and other producers of goods and services *that they would always have a big enough market to compete for.* The federal government's demand—used, as just explained, in calculating the to-be-guaranteed consumer demand—would include all of the items wanted by the President and Congress for their own sake, but not any others, so that basically all parts of the full employment not public by choice would be reserved to the private domain. We could therefore always have the GNP level we need without having a public sector level that we as a nation don't want.

*   *   *

Contrary to the common fear that full employment would make inflation worse, the fact is that a system of assured full employment as here proposed would help hold inflation in check.

A distinction has to be drawn, however, between the upward pressures on prices that come from the growing scarcities of oil and other nonrenewable natural resources and those that derive from other causes. In the former case there is clearly no readymade answer, so that some rise in the general American price level seems inevitable in the years just ahead. What can help us here is the discovery of substitute materials and, above all, new power-generating methods, capital-saving inventions, conservation and recycling, and more-explicit emphasis on the *qualitative* aspects of economic growth.

The outlook is far brighter for holding down the inflationary pressures that derive from "demand pull" and from the part of "cost push" not caused by natural resource scarcity. To begin with, EPI offers a fundamental cure for excessive demand pull. Because employment and consumer spending would have their guaranteed ceilings as well as their floors, the price spiral would be cut off at the demand end. For example, making the government the employer of last resort would *not* unleash an inflationary flood of spending in private markets: if those last-resort government payrolls did threaten to raise total purchasing power above target, a standby tax of a predetermined kind would by advance authorization be activated to hold consumer spending down, as was explained earlier.

In the case of cost push, the partial remedies already available would be strongly reinforced by EPI. Conventional kinds of antitrust action can prove very helpful, and some of the special tax inducements or penalties recently under discussion may also be practicable for encouraging wage and price moderation. Beyond that, moreover, there is the insufficiently publicized fact that full employment itself lowers most unit costs because it spreads the burden of the overhead cost. And EPI would certainly lower costs still further if only because the disappearance of the business cycle would limit the need to build "storm cellars" as advance precaution. Corporations could reasonably set higher break-even points. Unions could demand fewer special job-security clauses.

But this is not all. Once our national government stood ready to accept its due economic responsibility by agreeing to maintain prosperity and guaranteed job opportunity, I suspect that business and labor would also accept theirs by agreeing voluntarily on some fair system of guidance for wages and prices. The reason for thinking that this might happen, when it hasn't in the past, is simply that the chemistry of the situation and of public opinion would be basically altered. Certainly, when it came to the test, this might not happen at all. Even so, however, there is everything to be said for seeking voluntary cooperation.

*   *   *

Two other sides of the question need to be briefly mentioned in conclusion. The first is our international relations. Guaranteed full employment would give us an excellent chance to become and remain a good neighbor.

The main issue involved is trade. As was indicated, under EPI the size of the consumer-spending guarantee would automatically rise, other things equal, if an export surplus were expected to decline or an import surplus grow. For this reason we could always pursue our national best interest in trade matters, free from those compulsions that stem from the fear of a shortage of markets. Protectionism would therefore lose much of its force; our liberal policies would be reliable. As far as the Third World countries are concerned, for instance, we would not only extend them economic aid more generously (by reason of being much better-off ourselves) but would also be prepared to help them find export markets and "move from aid to trade" as they became ready for it.

A special angle today is the baleful international trade in weapons. Under EPI it would be impossible to claim convincingly that we need those sales of arms abroad to bolster our domestic economy.

Finally, the twin EPI guarantees could transform the whole outlook of our ecology policies. It is ironical that environmentalists, advocating a course where the stakes are the real quality of our existence and perhaps existence itself, a course which moreover could itself contribute handsomely toward providing the additional jobs that we now need, should be so hampered by fears about the economic consequences of their proposals. But they are. Here I can do no better than quote from a paper presented by Professor Emile Benoit of Columbia University at a recent session of the Atlantic Economic Conference held in Washington.

"It is only," Benoit points out, "if we can recapture the confidence that full employment can be maintained and disemployed people quickly rerouted to new jobs, and that average price levels can be stabilized (by reducing some prices as others go up) that we can realistically expect to embark on the long term environmental programs we need—which will necessarily cause disemployment in some environmentally dangerous or wasteful industries, and require substantially increased costs for new energy sources and antipollution equipment."

4

Some Bids for Wider Discussion and Action

SOLVING THE MARKETS PROBLEM

The Achilles heel of modern capitalism is the constant threat of a shortage of markets. Flora Lewis (IHT, Oct. 9) cites a spreading conviction that the West must look to the semideveloped world for markets to pull itself out of its chronic economic slump. An AP despatch (IHT, Oct. 10) has the Kuwaiti Oil Minister charging the industrialized countries with obstructing OPEC countries that want to make refined oil products and then using quotas and high tariffs to keep their markets effectively closed to those products in any case. More evidence: Other poorer nations are helped to develop (and urged to "shift from aid to trade") but then begrudged markets for industrial products. Arms sales are still growing.

The basic solution lies in the bold step, not yet tried but feasible, of turning the whole approach completely around. Instead of looking to foreign markets to make up for deficient domestic markets, *guarantee* a domestic consumer market that will be adequate in combination with the expected (net) foreign market, private domestic investment and government demand, and *guarantee* full employment too, using some equally convenient statistical definition. The full employment will tend to create the guaranteed consumer demand; this demand will tend to recreate the full employment; and prearranged adjustment devices up and down on a standby basis at either end will complete the picture. The guaranteed *ceiling* on consumer demand and the business cycle elimination will simplify inflation control. Policies to encourage ecologically desirable, innovative investments can meanwhile promote competitive efficiency and qualitative growth.

Details have been published on how this would operate in the United States. Studies might show its applicability in some other countries as well.

JOHN H. G. PIERSON
Greenwich, Connecticut

This letter, addressed to the editor of the *International Herald Tribune* in October 1978, raises the question of the possible applicability of EPI to some economies other than our own.

24

A REQUEST FOR DISCUSSION

I am sending you the attached summary note with a request that you examine the *guaranteed full employment* proposal and analyze it in your columns. Whether the Humphrey-Hawkins bill is enacted or not, I believe that adoption of my suggested "economic performance insurance" approach is the logical next step.

The proposal is not at all in opposition to more familiar measures (fiscal, monetary, structural, etc.) for improving economic stability. It merely calls for adding an umbrella policy to make sure that the sum of all measures will always give the stabilization results we want.

Details have been circulated quite widely in Washington, in Congress and the Administration, and will be gladly mailed to you on request.

Sincerely,
John H. G. Pierson

Guaranteed Full Employment via
Economic Performance Insurance

It is possible to guarantee the chance to work, and furthermore do so in a way that will strengthen the position of private enterprise and stop inflation.

The guarantee aspect is central. Everyone's chance to work is something we need to make sure of. Not only that but our system is one in which economic health depends on confidence in the future. Knowing that we were going to achieve and then maintain full employment and control inflation would help enormously from that point on. We would reach our target more quickly and stay there more easily.

The position of private enterprise would be strengthened. This proposal would certify that business would always have a big enough market to compete for. Total consumer spending would be guaranteed, as well as total employment. The Federal government's demand used in calculating the to-be-guaranteed consumer demand would include only items wanted by the President and Congress for their own sake, so that basically all parts of the full employment not public by choice would be reserved to the private domain. We could therefore always have the GNP level we want without having the public sector level we don't want.

"Full employment" would similarly be a number selected by Congress in the light of the President's annual recommendation. It would be based on the rate of frictional unemployment viewed as unavoidable at that time, a rate that can obviously be lowered in due course by attacking structural rigidities.

To honor the guarantees, the President would have contingent authority (mandatory, not discretionary) to do two things: accelerate or decelerate public services and public works, to adjust total employment; and modify designated taxes and/or transfer payments (e.g., the income tax with a negative tax supplement, or a new Federal sales tax/sales bonus), to adjust total consumer spending.

Holding consumer spending on target would in itself greatly simplify doing the same for employment, and vice versa; the "insurance" would *reduce* the need to use the contingent authority. Of course, to *minimize* that need, other things would be required as well—strong action against monopolistic restrictions, special programs to get young blacks into jobs, and tax reform, to name three.

The effect on inflation. Even temporary full employment lowers unit costs; antitrust is in the spotlight again; new anti-inflation devices are being explored—*and* the following circumstances, peculiar to "economic performance insurance," could be expected to clinch the matter: (1) Employment and consumer spending would have guaranteed ceilings as well as guaranteed floors, thus cutting the price spiral off at the demand end. (2) The disappearance of the business cycle would let business and labor stop demanding extra cushions that the cycle necessitated in the first place. (3) The Federal Government's acceptance of its due responsibility for the economy would be a publicly understood signal that business and labor should also accept theirs and agree voluntarily on some fair system of guidance for wages and prices.

Note finally that the consumer spending guarantee would provide a specific adjustment device enabling America to have an equally adequate total market with either an export or an import surplus. We could therefore view our national best interest in trade matters (as also in disarmament, or in ecological policy) freed of those compulsions that stem from the fear of a shortage of markets.

This note was circulated in late 1977, mainly to newswriters and other publicists.

FOR A NEW START

The thing we need most in this country is a policy that guarantees full employment and checks inflation. This would also be the best pivot for all other true forms of economic and social progress, it would let us come to the right terms with the natural environment, and it would contribute to solving international problems as well.

Many people mistakenly say that a policy of guaranteed full employment without inflation is an impossible dream. That's simply wrong. I have studied this question for a long time. I know how such a policy can be built and operated, and besides that I know that our private enterprise system need not be hurt—indeed, it can be considerably strengthened—as a result.

The real question is whether a political movement can take shape to get that policy established. I hope that President Carter with the support of like-minded members of Congress from both parties will see to that. If not, then somebody else should take the lead.

But first there needs to be publicity. Nothing gets done nowadays without publicity. So I ask this question: who is going to provide the publicity for a drive to give America guaranteed full employment without inflation?

This note was privately circulated in September 1977.

IN THE SPIRIT OF '76

Life, liberty, and the pursuit of happiness . . . in 1776 the purpose of government was said to be to make such rights secure. But you can't pursue happiness very far if you need a job—for the money or the independence of it—and there's no job to be had.

I'm John Pierson. I've studied the question of full employment for many years. I want to see the Employment Act of 1946 amended and strengthened so as to make it guarantee jobs for all who are "able, willing, and seeking to work."

That can be done, and I can tell you how. I am asking people to join with me in an effort to see that it does get done.

We can't legislate happiness, obviously. But we can, and I say we should, put into the law a solid pledge of work opportunity for every American, and this will bring the right to the *pursuit* of happiness down to earth.—In the spirit of '76.

This was written in early 1976 as part of an exploration of the feasibility of establishing a Center for a National Full Employment Policy.

5

Testimony on the Humphrey-Hawkins Bill

Mr. Chairman and Members of the Committee: I appreciate very much the opportunity to testify before this Committee on H.R.50/S.50, the Full Employment and Balanced Growth Act of 1977. This is a landmark bill. I wish to urge its enactment and suggest certain amendments to facilitate that and increase its effectiveness once enacted.

It would be almost impossible to overstate the importance of the core idea in this bill, that every American who wants a useful job should always be able to find one and receive fair pay for doing it. This touches the very heart of our country's basic philosophy. The pursuit of happiness is virtually out of the question for most people if they don't have a real chance to work.

The bill presents a number of other good reasons why full employment should be permanently maintained in America, and involuntary unemployment permanently banned. I want to cite two additional reasons. First, not only do recessions and the fear of recessions make equal employment opportunity almost unattainable, as this draft says, but they often impel powerful organizations in business, labor, and agriculture to push their financial claims too vigorously, so that special interests find themselves in conflict with the general interest.

Second, recessions also heighten the pressure to adopt restrictive foreign-trade measures. And those measures, while they may in some cases produce a net gain in domestic jobs, undermine the larger national interest by sacrificing vital opportunities for international cooperation.

In terms of dynamics, these two bad effects of our economic instability—both of them easily observable today—are among the strongest arguments for adopting this bill that

This was submitted in writing to the Subcommittee on Employment Opportunities of the House Committee on Education and Labor on April 18, 1977. (Printed in *Hearings*, 95th Cong., 1st sess., Washington, D.C.: GPO, 1977, II, 473–79.) A shorter note dealing just with the last two amendments advocated here had been addressed to the sponsors of the bill a year earlier.

could be found. Of course, they can be stated positively instead, to make them more palatable. By assuring the maintenance of prosperity and full employment we can create conditions for a more cooperative, public-spirited approach to our common domestic problems. And by not having to rely for that assurance on export surpluses, we can set the stage for building the kinds of relations that will serve us best abroad.

Although my main concern here, Mr. Chairman, will be with trying to improve this bill further, I do want first to mention some of its many excellent features. One of them is its firm emphasis on nondiscrimination. Another is its pioneering effort to provide for a continuing assessment of national priorities, tied in with a kind of long-range planning that will help the country without hurting individual enterprise. A third is the attention it gives to the regional and structural aspects of unemployment.

The bill is also very helpful in emphasizing that our income maintenance programs should be integrated with our full-employment policies. Obviously valuable too are the latest drafting changes that sharpen the working definition of full employment and the intended target and timetable. These particular clarifications, taken in conjunction with the proposed permanent, comprehensive youth employment program, should remove some honest doubts that constructive critics had previously expressed.

Finally, I believe that the rules for Congressional action on the President's annual economic recommendations, including rules to govern the Joint Economic Committee's preparation of a concurrent resolution with assistance from a new Division of Full Employment and Balanced Growth in the Congressional Budget Office, come close to creating a practical operating set-up.

*   *   *

Now I turn to my suggested amendments. First and foremost, I urge that the language be clarified to indicate that, under this law, full employment would be not just a goal— surely, it has been a *goal* for a long time!—but an actual *promise* to the American people.

I use the word "clarify" advisedly. The bill's position on this cardinal point is not clear now. There are passages where one senses that what is intended *is* a promise—and, personally, that is what I believe the sponsors would prefer if a practical way can be found. On the other hand, in many other places the bill seems to settle for naming a high goal but not undertaking any firm commitment to achieve it.

Examples of this ambiguity could be spelled out at considerable length if time permitted, but I will only summarize. In the Declaration of Policy (both (a) and (b) of an amended Section 2 of the Employment Act of 1946); in Section 108, on the duties of the Council of Economic Advisers; and in 206(d), on the reservoirs of last-resort employment projects—here we find language that seems at first glance to convey a promise.

But elsewhere—in sections 2(c), 106, 202(b)(1), and 202(b)(2)(H), for example—we keep bumping up against the idea of "high unemployment due to recessions," "cyclical movements in the economy," and "periods of substantial economic slack." Here, in passages like these, we are not just being reminded that we have a long way to go from present unemployment up to full employment. No, what these phrases tell us is that the employment goals are not expected to be realized fully even when that interim period is over.

What is one to think? How is this ambiguity to be clarified?

Obviously the drafters of this law will be obliged in the end to do one of two very different things: either get rid of the pessimistic clauses that imply a continuation of business cycles as usual, or else tone the language down wherever it seems to suggest a promise.

Historically we have taken the latter course. I well remember what happened to the proposal to "assure . . . continuing full employment" that was in the bill that became the Employment Act of 1946. After various vicissitudes and re-drafts it was found at one point that the policy statement, being still keyed to the idea of the right to work, was too vigorous for the watered-down operative clauses. So Congress clarified the intention by toning down the policy statement.

Mr. Chairman, I believe it is a matter of the utmost importance that now, on this second time around, the opposite course be taken. I respectfully suggest to this Committee that the thing for Congress to do is not tone down once again the clauses that sound like a promise but rather tone up the bill wherever it now seems to be talking about an unattainable goal.

I am entirely aware of a belief in some quarters that anyone asking for a real *promise* of full employment is well-intentioned perhaps but certainly impractical. It would of course be nice, say some of those people, to have the bill even stronger than it is—to have it actually embody "economic performance insurance"—but the bill's sponsors are up against enough opposition already and cannot afford any more. The clear premise in this kind of thinking is that strengthening the bill would automatically strengthen the opposition to it as well.

That premise will not stand up. How many of those same people, one wonders, feel the slightest surprise if they read of some new man-made material that is stronger than steel but lighter? Or were they ever skeptical when they heard that the latest generation of computers could handle more work than the previous generation even though smaller? It would seem that only in a field like political economy is it unthinkable to them for a new approach to be more effective and more widely acceptable both at once.

But in fact this is just what a new approach could be. I am sure that the Full Employment and Balanced Growth Act can be amended to have it actually promise full employment and yet be more widely approved (and textually simpler too) than it is now.

In various sections of the bill—most importantly 103 and 303, dealing respectively with the President's recommendations in his annual Economic Report and the Congressional review of those recommendations—the present draft calls for setting "annual numerical goals for employment, production, and purchasing power." This represents a great advance over past practice but is still not adequate. What is needed to make it adequate is the insertion, after that phrase, of the following additional words: *"including the minimum and maximum levels of employment and consumer spending regarded as acceptable."*

(I do *not* suggest setting minimum and maximum levels of *production*, the other item in that familiar sequence carried over from the 1946 law. Specific levels cannot be promised for all three magnitudes simultaneously, and in any case production, or its rate of growth, only needs to be still a *goal*.)

What my proposal would accomplish would be to have the President, and then in the last analysis Congress, assume responsibility for setting lower and upper limits to total employment (or civilian employment, or it could at first be the employment of civilians 20 years of age or more, whichever statistical target was preferred) and to total personal consumption expenditures as well. I mean that the final decisions arrived at after Congressional review would represent a real commitment to the country—a commitment that the stated limits would be defended by varying the last-resort job programs and the designated tax-and-transfer-payment rates up or down as needed.

This should be perfectly workable. To avoid undesirable rigidity, the spread between bottom and top limits could be as wide as was felt to be necessary. To avoid having the execution of the policy upset by leads and lags and occasional erratic movements of statistical indicators, it could be agreed that employment, or consumer spending, might without prejudice sometimes stray outside the "acceptable" band for brief periods while corrective action was taking effect.

But, with those minor qualifications, this proposal would definitely hold employment at the intended levels, during the transition stages up to full employment as well as afterwards. In other words, the attainment and the subsequent maintenance of full employment, as defined in quantitative terms in advance, would be a promise and not just a goal, and the text of the bill could be altered wherever necessary so as to reflect that critical difference. In the Declaration of Policy, for instance, the conditions to be fostered would not merely "promote balanced growth and useful employment opportunities" but rather "promote balanced growth and *assure* useful employment opportunities"—one important word added.

And yet—here is the other half of my point—this stronger wording would surely heighten the positive appeal of the bill and leave less room for opposition. There are several reasons for this. The first is that the establishment of a framework and procedures to *assure* continuous full-employment prosperity in future would in itself create much of the confidence that producers and consumers need. Investment would be stimulated. Our economy would arrive at full employment more quickly and stay there more easily.

Secondly, that confidence would be further strengthened because there would be a much greater prospect of achieving the anti-inflation goal. The concept of a trade-off between inflation and unemployment would be simply irrelevant here. On the demand side of the picture, the proposal would minimize the risk of inflationary spirals by setting top limits to employment and consumer spending, not bottom limits alone.

Meanwhile on the supply side, it would help hold costs down by eliminating the need for management and labor to build up various sorts of expensive cushions against recessions. On top of that, the Federal Government's assumption of due economic responsibility would create a moral climate in which there would be unprecedented opportunity for avoiding excessive price and wage increases on a cooperative, voluntary basis.

Thirdly, this approach would specifically assure the country that the maintenance of full employment would not be accomplished at the private sector's expense. Section 102 now guarantees that the Act will not change historic ratios of private to public civilian employment, let alone lead to governmental control over private production. To include such reassurances is very likely a good idea, and it may sound well too when Section 206(d), for example, reiterates that private job opportunities "are the first and major purpose of this Act." But when it comes to fulfilling this aim *and at the same time really maintaining full employment*, nothing could be more effective—because nothing would improve the "economic environment" in a more practical way, or in other words be more *genuinely* reassuring to private enterprise—than a straight guarantee that the overall demand for the products of private enterprise will always be adequately high.

I will conclude on this proposal by pointing out that there is no conflict between it and the spirit of the present bill. Quite to the contrary. The Declaration of Policy calls for "expansion of conventional private jobs through *improved use* of fiscal and monetary policies and other policies." (My emphasis, as also just below.) Section 202(b) requires the President within ninety days after enactment to send the Congress a comprehensive proposal, with legislation, to "establish on a permanent basis the range of supplementary employment policies and programs *necessary*." And the next subsection, (c), goes on to state that the President's proposal shall "provide for an *automatic trigger* or set of coordinated triggers that would implement . . . and phase out the program."

This language would certainly permit a later consideration of the very suggestion I am making here. But if that is the case and if the idea is a good one, why wait? I respectfully ask why the Congress should not do what is necessary now, in its own bill, rather than depend on receiving exactly the right message from the White House ninety days after the law is enacted.

*   *   *

I can be briefer in presenting my two other amendments for strengthening this bill.

One is concerned with meshing the operations under this bill with those under the Congressional Budget Act in 1974. Legislation to assure full employment should obviously not contravene the essential purpose of the hard-won Congressional Budget Act, which is to enable the Congress to take orderly, responsible action in controlling Federal budget receipts and expenditures. Neither should the latter Act be capable of being so construed as to deny the assurance of full employment. The two aims are complementary, not antagonistic.

H.R.50/S.50 as now drafted takes a good step forward by calling for amendments to the Congressional Budget Act that would incorporate the "numerical goals for employment, production, and purchasing power" in the annual concurrent resolutions on the Budget. For reasons partly but not entirely explained already, however, this wording does not go quite far enough.

To complete the explanation—the annual budget resolutions should be clear about permitting advance approval by the Congress of certain *contingent changes* in the agreed-upon total of Federal expenditures and receipts. Not any and all manner of changes, of course, since that could largely defeat the main aim of the law, but those occasioned by last-resort actions that may later be shown to be necessary to honor the full-employment commitments. In other words, changes that will result from the mandatory activation of designated standby measures *if*, in the course of the year, the designated employment and consumer spending series show that such activation is needed.

The way this point could be met would be by rephrasing the amendment that Section 303 now seeks to introduce into the Budget Act. First, Section 301(a) of the Budget Act would be amended a little differently than is now proposed. (I have some suggested wording here but won't read it out because the points are mostly secondary and are hard to follow besides unless one has both texts handy.*) Then—and this is the heart of the matter—a new 301(b) would be inserted in the Budget Act (with present 301(b) becoming 301(c)), this new subsection to read more or less as follows:

(b) CONTINGENT MODIFICATION OF BUDGET OUTLAY AND REVENUE TOTALS.—The concurrent resolution shall indicate that the necessity to hold total employment and total consumer spending within their limits as given under (a)(6) above is paramount, and that the levels of budget outlays and Federal revenues referred to in (a)(1) and (a)(4) are subject to upward or downward adjustment if that proves necessary to keep those limits from being transgressed.

*   *   *

The final amendment I am proposing relates to 304(f), at the end of the section concerned with Congressional review of the annual full employment and balanced growth plans.

Probably the greatest single weakness in the Employment Act of 1946 is that it gives the Congress no opportunity and no responsibility for concerted, conclusive action on the President's annual economic report, and so leaves the really critical questions without final answers. Here again H.R.50/S.50 in its present wording goes a long way toward correcting the fault. But again, in my estimation, it fails to go far enough.

According to Section 304(f), once the annual concurrent resolution on the Plan has been adopted, Congress is to transmit a copy of it "to the President ... for such actions as the President deems appropriate." In the matter of assuring full employment—which should be, and I assume is intended to be, covered here too, along with the less quantitative aim of achieving balanced growth—this is really insufficient. What I suggest is that the final sentence of this subsection, containing those words, should be re-drafted at slightly greater length to read more or less as follows:

A copy of the concurrent resolution shall be transmitted to the President by the Clerk of the House of Representatives or the Secretary of the Senate, as appropriate, so as to indicate the action (including the use of standby measures if necessary) that the President is requested to take to maintain total employment and total consumer spending within their respective limits as approved by the Congress, and for such other actions as the President deems appropriate.

The purpose of this rewording is to make clear the intention of this legislation that the annual economic exercise as a whole must arrive at definite, action-shaping conclusions on the essential points, and that the Congress should play a major part in defining those conclusions.

*The wording might be:
(b) Section 301(a) of the Congressional Budget Act of 1974 is amended—(1) by inserting ', subject to contingencies specified in (b) below,' after 'appropriate level' in clause (1) and again after 'recommended level' in clause (4); (2) by striking out ', for contingencies,' in clause (2); and (3) by inserting after clause (5) (and consequently redesignating present clause (6)) the following new clause: '(6) numerical lower and upper limits for total employment and total consumer spending; and'.

6

An Explanation of
Economic Performance Insurance

To understand "economic performance insurance" or EPI, think of our economic system as driven by two engines: production, which provides the jobs and generates income, and spending (consumption and investment spending), which motivates production and employment by providing a current and prospective market for goods and services. Each engine pumps out to the other and each depends for fuel on what the other pumps out. All this is familiar, of course. So is the fact that the system doesn't tend to keep running at a full-employment rate automatically, as the Classical School assumed.

What is not so familiar is the idea that a balanced circular flow at the full-employment rate, while it won't come about naturally, can nevertheless be created artificially by tuning both engines occasionally so that each reinforces the other with optimum support. Once they are revved up by stages to the right pitch, neither one can easily get very far out of line, and comparatively minor tuning should then suffice. Furthermore, the system's chronic obstructions and leaks will then be considerably easier to identify and correct; hence a prospect of still less tuning. This in essence is the EPI idea.

EPI would *not* rely on trying to find remedies after something important has gone wrong, or do the opposite and set about filling "prospective gaps" glimpsed in forecasts, or pay attention to just one engine and let the other take care of itself. Instead, EPI would have our government, year by year, prescribe an operating rate for each engine separately. It would equip our system with two throttles, one on each engine. And it would issue standing orders for each throttle to be opened or closed a little whenever that engine would otherwise fail to hold to its prescribed operating rate.

Translating this: the government would annually set an employment level (bottom and top limits) and also a consumer spending rate (bottom and top limits) to be adhered to throughout the next year; would decide in advance on the means to be used—the

This paper dates from February 1977.

34

kinds of public works and services to be accelerated or decelerated, the kinds of taxes and/or transfer payments to be varied—when or if necessary for keeping the actual trends within the pre-set limits; and would designate the agencies responsible for both kinds of contingent action.

(Total spending—the GNP—would not be targeted and held in line, as the analogy might suggest, but consumer spending would be, in order to avoid unsuitable restraints on business or the government itself. Secondly, the *top* limits on employment and on consumer spending would be a good reason why EPI would help check inflation; others would be the elimination of the costs of cushioning management and labor against recessions, and the psychological dividends from the government's own assumption of due responsibility.)

The principles here summarized could, if desired, be written into the Humphrey-Hawkins bill.

The EPI regulators should clearly not be submitted to constant strain. In the analogy, engineers should be out on the lines finding ways to improve the flow in both directions and so reduce the need for throttle adjustments at either end. Visualize here the enactment, over time, of tax reforms and other measures that spread purchasing power and boost consumer spending, plus steadfast help to competition and vigilance against monopolistic restrictions, to keep increased spending from lifting prices instead of production and employment.

We are usefully reminded now and again that some employer interests are adamantly opposed to full employment on any sustained basis.[1] Whether effective full-employment legislation can be enacted in the face of that opposition may not be clear. The EPI approach should, however, improve the chances that it can be, because the employment level chosen as corresponding to "full employment" (the prescribed speed of the first engine) would reflect the judgment of the President, as modified by the Congress in its review of the President's recommendations, concerning the amount of "frictional" unemployment essential for proper mobility in existing labor-market conditions. Advocates of a 3 percent allowance, or 4 percent, or any higher or lower figure would all presumably have some influence on the final selection.

It is also said that actually *guaranteeing* full employment would force expansion of the public sector at the private sector's expense, whether intended or not. That would be untrue under EPI, however, because of the method of deriving the guaranteed consumer spending rate (the prescribed speed of the second engine) from the total market estimated to be necessary.

The key quantity subtracted from that "needed" GNP—along with anticipated private domestic investment, state and local government purchases, and net exports—would be a federal government component made up of items that the President and Congress concluded should be in the budget for their own sake, not just to fill gaps. Although the public jobs throttle would at times still have to be opened or closed a little, because of net error in the various advance estimates, what this approach means is that basically all parts of the full employment not public by choice would be reserved to the private domain.

---

1. See, e.g., Robert Lekachman's article, "The Specter of Full Employment," *Harper's*, February 1977.

7

Why Economic Performance Insurance

Consider not just the best combination of tax cuts and new government spending for recovery now, but a more fundamental issue. I am suggesting that today the key question is whether to take out an "insurance policy" on the U.S. economy, in support of all other remedies for unemployment, inflation, and the cycle that may be adopted, and that the right answer to this question is yes.

I am an admirer of something that I will abstractly call the Walter Heller and Arthur Okun brand of economist, or Heller/Okun for short—no offense intended. (I don't mean to sound personal, or suggest that their views are always the same, or imply that other economists are not as good.) As I see it, Heller/Okun has the technical *expertise* and the values needed to move us in the direction of full employment and inflation control, with a fairer distribution of the benefits too.

But my admiration has limits. Heller/Okun has been conscientiously avoiding discussion, let alone acceptance, of a concept that in my view is clearly required to make good Heller/Okun policies work decisively better. I refer to a proposal that has been in the literature since the early forties and has come to be called "economic performance insurance."

For those who are unfamiliar with this concept and proposal, let me quote the shortest summary I have been able to devise so far: ". . . under that approach the Federal Government would state in advance each year (a) the minimum and maximum levels of employment, and (b)—so as to assure private business of a continuously adequate total market—the minimum and maximum levels of private consumer spending, that would without fail be maintained. The government would then use accelerations and decelerations of public services and works as necessary for honoring its commitment under (a), and changes in consumer taxes and/or transfer payments on some predetermined basis as necessary for honoring its commitment under (b)." (From a letter

This was addressed as a memorandum to "Those concerned with the problem of full employment" and was circulated rather widely in Washington in January 1977.
36

inserted by Senator Ribicoff in the *Congressional Record* of July 26, 1976, in his "Comments on Inflationary Impact of Full Employment Economy.")

This statement leaves a lot to be said, I know, but space is limited and I think I have answered many of the questions elsewhere. Hence with due apology I turn immediately to the elaboration of what I find missing in Heller/Okun.

The nub of it is simply that Heller/Okun proposals could never, without the addition of economic performance insurance (EPI), give us the same *assurance* of continuous full employment without inflation that they could with EPI added. And we need, I contend, that assurance. We need to be *sure*. Both for the future's sake and for the help that such assurance about the future would give us in solving our immediate problems now.

Insecurity is basic to life, of course. Individuals and the individual firm should expect to remain insecure (although with society contriving forms of readjustment aid and other mitigations). What is extraneous, however, is the *added* insecurity that is needlessly caused by the constriction and instability of the general economic framework. Needlessly, because a more mature organization of our economic affairs can in future eliminate it, thereby saving us in America incalcuable human grief, directly and indirectly, and senseless waste, and serious damage to our international relations besides.

Coupled with this will be the good feedback effect obtainable from the expectations. By assuring that our economy is going to reach and thereafter maintain full employment and control inflation, we will enormously benefit our economy right away from that point on. We will get to noninflationary full employment more quickly and stay there more easily.

A market-oriented system like ours practically runs—or it stalls—by its anticipations. Confidence makes all the difference. "Those who blame inflation on the incurable wickedness of Big Business or Big Labor or both," I wrote in another place, "often seem unaware of how far the behavior of both has been caused by the malfunctioning of our economy—its cyclical instability combined with secular weakness—the inevitability of which is precisely what needs to be denied."

As long as the malfunctioning is expected to persist, it will continue to tempt our most powerful business and labor organizations to raise their selling prices an extra notch in order to accumulate reserves against a coming slump. And consumers will keep altering their spending/saving behavior, to the confusion of arguments over the likely effect of anticyclical tax changes.

When Arthur Burns told the Senate Banking Committee recently that "in today's environment of deeply ingrained inflationary expectations" the Keynesian devices for increasing total demand are risky medicine for curing unemployment, the reactions varied, but not because anyone doubts the potent effect of inflationary expectations. Or of deflationary fears. What we need is not only to steer clear of deflation and inflation "when the time comes" but to be sure in advance that we are going to.

Why can't we get these results from Heller/Okun, including the predictability? Of course the first reason is that Heller/Okun may not always be listened to anyway. Different administrations prefer different configurations of economists, prescribing different economic medicine. Hence, without some better institutional and procedural frame than the Employment Act of 1946 provides—a frame something like what the Humphrey-Hawkins bill seeks to establish—hardly anything can be really nailed down.

But suppose Heller/Okun *were* always listened to. Imagine Heller/Okun as the permanent economic adviser to all administrations. Why is it that, in the absence of EPI, we could still not be sure of having continuous full employment without inflation?

There are two main reasons. First, because Heller/Okun itself does not know exactly what economic results will follow if its proposals *were* adopted. (Just ask Heller/Okun.) Or take a moment to reflect on the extreme complexity of the interactions in our economic system. Change a certain tax on business—a simplified example in unreal isolation—and the ramifications spread in all directions.

Not even the most sophisticated econometric model pretends to incorporate all the significant knowable variables, as I think Lawrence Klein would agree. And then there remain the unknowables—bad weather, wars, concerted foreign action on our oil supplies, etc.—fully capable of upsetting the best calculations.

Yet that is still only half of the Heller/Okun difficulty. The second half is that no President of the United States can expect to have everything that he asks for approved by the Congress in all respects. Grant him the very paragon of an economic adviser, grant him into the bargain the excellent national priorities budget that Leon Keyserling would put together, and the Congress will still want to change things. It may be just differences of opinion over ways of accomplishing the same result. It may be one issue running afoul of another (aid to education versus church schools). Or it may be that major philosophical disagreement is involved over how much the government itself ought to be doing in its public sector. Whatever the combination of reasons, Congress *will* want to amend the President's recommendations in some particulars, and therefore the program nicely tailored by the President's paragon of an economic adviser will emerge from the legislative process with alterations.

Obviously Heller/Okun will have foreseen that outcome. Heller/Okun's hope will not be that there would be no Congressional alterations but rather that those alterations could be compensated for as necessary by means of special counter-measures to be enacted at the right time. But this is precisely what *cannot* be counted on. As anyone who has been paying attention knows, what can be counted on instead is a long wrangle over whether a tax cut (say) is needed for extra stimulus, what kind of a tax cut, and when. In this way the whole idea of making certain to maintain economic stability at full employment finally falls to the ground.

Under EPI it would not fall to the ground. This is so because the basic legislation (say the Humphrey-Hawkins bill, amended) would provide for maintaining the level of jobs and the rate of consumer spending between their predetermined lower and upper limits by predetermined means no matter what happened. In other words, it would provide for *contingent* action to be taken by the President, without any further Congressional debate, as soon as the agreed-upon signals flash the need.

Look at the matter this way: Good economic advisers are not enough without a definite, recurring legislative procedure. Such a procedure is not enough without well-selected targets. Those targets are not enough unless they are firm. Firmness is impossible without contingent arrangements.

It goes without saying that EPI is not a whole policy in itself but must be combined with other elements. Certainly we need *special* cures for special hardship situations; the fantastically high unemployment rate among black teen-agers is an obvious example. And also we certainly need the following: (1) fiscal and monetary measures that will give us roughly the right level of spending (i.e., even before EPI adjustment) when a full-employment level of income is flowing; (2) antimonopoly measures, including effective restraints on excessive price and wage increases, to give us roughly the level of production and employment we have a right to expect in response to adequate spending; (3) encouragement of initiative and innovation along ecologically sound lines.

My (1) and (2) will hold the need for final adjustments under EPI rules to a reasonable minimum. (3) is recommended if we want the best of both possible worlds—plenty of genuine enterprise and a habitable planet. It will afford us a chance, too, to keep the price level from climbing in the face of inexorably shrinking supplies and rising costs of nonrenewable fuels and raw materials.

(1), (2), (3) and the special cures are the common coin of just ordinary good economic and social policy. Fine, let us try to have them! But all of these things, achieved, would still not eliminate the need for EPI. And in the meantime, the stiff battle to achieve them should itself be fought out under the EPI umbrella.

8

Statements for the
Congressional Record

FULL EMPLOYMENT IS POSSIBLE WITHOUT INFLATION

Greenwich, Conn.,
July 9, 1976

Hon. Abraham Ribicoff,
U.S. Senate, Washington, D.C.

Dear Senator Ribicoff: We are continually reminded these days of our historic American dedication to life, liberty, and the pursuit of happiness. Well, you can't pursue happiness very far if you need a job—for the money or the independence of it—and there's no job to be had.

This letter, however, is more specifically in response to your recent communication in which you emphasize that the steps we take to cope effectively with the unemployment crisis must not be allowed to become a factor for more inflation.

I am quite sure that what you say expresses the sentiment of many millions of Americans. Fears obviously persist that adopting a full-employment law would cause—or increase—inflation. Many persons argue, for example, thinking of the Humphrey-Hawkins bill, that making the Federal Government the employer of last resort would have an inflationary impact.

That all depends, however, on the approach taken. *Full employment is possible without inflation.* A program of *guaranteed* full employment based on an "economic performance insurance" approach, as recommended by this writer, would not only *not cause* inflation but actually be the best *cure* for inflation.

Any full-employment program worth considering can be expected to contain certain built-in elements of defense against inflation risk. First of all, a rising level of economic activity will in itself spread the overhead costs of production and so reduce unit costs and

This letter was inserted by Senator Abraham Ribicoff of Connecticut in the *Congressional Record* for July 26, 1976.

40

let prices be held down. Then, to make sure that they *will* be, the full-employment legislation will and must have associated with it a tough policy towards powerful economic organizations that are in a position to administer their prices. An active antitrust administration is needed, and an incomes policy too, with standby authority to impose mandatory price-wage controls.

This counter-argument seems valid but, not surprisingly, it runs up against widespread reluctance to lean as heavily and as permanently on direct controls as the prescription may appear to require. Hence there is occasion to see how the prospects could be improved by introducing "economic performance insurance."

In briefest summary, under that approach the Federal Government would state in advance each year (a) the minimum and maximum levels of employment, and (b)—so as to assure private business of a continuously adequate total market—the minimum and maximum levels of private consumer spending, that would without fail be maintained. The government would then use accelerations and decelerations of public services and works as necessary for honoring its commitment under (a), and changes in consumer taxes and/or transfer payments on some predetermined basis as necessary for honoring its commitment under (b).

(The level—or, more precisely, the range between limits—of employment called for would reflect a policy decision on what would constitute full employment in a practical working sense, with enough but not too much allowance for frictional unemployment. The level or range of consumer spending called for would derive from a technical calculation as follows: dollar value of an adequate total market for the nation's output— full-employment GNP—at expected price levels, minus best-guess amounts for private domestic investment, government purchases—reflecting the prevailing current view as to the proper size of the public sector—and net exports.)

The first thing that this mechanism would do (if embodied in the Humphrey-Hawkins bill, for instance) would be to give our economy two good brakes against "demand pull" inflation. As just noted, neither employment nor consumer spending would be allowed to rise above its ceiling. Thus, making the government the employer of last resort— which is certainly essential—would *not* unleash the widely dreaded inflationary flood of spending in private markets. For if those last-resort government payrolls threatened to raise total disposable personal income too high, a standby tax of a predetermined kind would by advance authorization be activated to hold total consumer spending down.

In addition to these brakes on the demand, there would also be new deterrents to "cost push" inflation, on the side of supply. To begin with, since the new basic law would provide for annually setting satisfactory floors under employment and consumer spending, certain kinds of expense now caused by the anticipation of future recessions would be eliminated. Today, big business and big labor will often make their sales prices and their work contracts provide financial cushions to help tide over bad times to come. That would no longer be necessary; the XYZ Corporation, for example, could set higher break-even points than it can afford to at present. Costs of production would thus be lowered not only by the *currently* high operating rate, as seen above, but also by the disappearance of the business cycle.

The most important change on the supply side, however, would be the moral or psychological effect of the adoption of a policy that really assured continuous prosperity and full employment. As things stand now, there is a general shirking of social responsibility. Government fails to take genuinely significant responsibility in regard to the economy (full employment is called a goal, of course, but is still not a promise) and so business and labor on their part are understandably reluctant to assume much responsibility for acting with moderation in regard to prices and wages. Nor, in the present state of affairs, is the public inclined to blame them very greatly for their attitude.

But the adoption of a decisive full-employment law could be expected to change all that. Why should not business and labor also, then, assume *their* appropriate responsibility? Why would it not be possible to get agreement on suitable wage-price guidelines—more particularly as labor's cost of living would be held down by the ceiling on consumer spending? Here would be a situation made for voluntary cooperation. The standby controls already cited should no doubt be kept available but, given the improved general outlook under "economic performance insurance," it seems probably to this writer that they would seldom have to be invoked.

Sincerely yours,

John H. G. Pierson.

TO ASSURE FULL EMPLOYMENT REALLY

The Classical economists wouldn't have approved of the Hawkins-Humphrey full-employment bill, since the economy in their view tended toward full employment automatically. When one industry lost its markets and declined, others would gain markets and expand. Keynes later explained why this wasn't necessarily so, but he didn't find a good remedy.

In the American system of production for market it would seem likely *a priori* that the remedy would largely consist of finding an acceptable way to sustain the overall market (total dollar value of demand for goods and services; GNP expenditures). Solve it, in other words, by maintaining deliberately the principal condition that the Classical School wrongly supposed would maintain itself automatically.

Expectations would be enormously helpful. Assuming the market can be maintained, we could guarantee to maintain it. Then business and labor and consumers would know that no recessions or runaway booms lay ahead, and their confidence in tomorrow would make them act in ways facilitating full-employment maintenance today.

This in essence would be Economic Performance Insurance. This proposed system would hold employment and also consumer spending (explanation below) between pre-set, guaranteed lower and upper limits. The government would adjust disposable income up or down whenever the income flow under full employment failed to bring the promised consumer spending, and would adjust employment up or down whenever the production-inducement effect from that spending needed reinforcement or counter-action.

This concept raises three important questions in principle and three more on practical application. All are answerable. First of all, does such emphasis on the demand side make sense today, when demand so often has its effect blunted by monopolistic restrictions on the side of supply? Yes, it does, because policies to maintain demand aren't supposed to be a complete solution. To assure full employment by such means alone would burden the taxpayer too much. Antitrust policies in the wide sense must provide support—enforcement of competition wherever it can exist and curbs on restrictions wherever monopoly is inevitable.

But is there any consensus for closing all gaps with extra government demand? The answer is that this misconceives the proposal. There's always some level of Federal Government spending for goods and services that sentiment in Congress will support. Adding that estimated amount to expected State and local government spending, private domestic investment, and net exports, and subtracting that sum from the GNP thought to be needed for full employment at anticipated prices, gives the "necessary" (operationally speaking) consumer spending. This last is what is proposed to be guaranteed, besides employment. Only when extra employment was still needed would the government as last-resort employer increase its market demand marginally. It would also sometimes have to act to raise consumer demand, to honor that second promise. But sometimes too it would have to reduce its market demand, or take more from (give less to) consumers.

That leaves one basic question—inflation. However, the supposed "trade-off" between unemployment and inflation (Phillips curve) is dangerously oversimplified, as many writers have shown, and it's almost totally irrelevant here. First, consumer spending and employment would both be under ceilings as well as over floors; hence no runaway spiral. Second, the cost of living being thus held down, labor needn't press the same wage demands. Third, full employment always permits considerable price moderation by spreading the overhead costs, and continuously guaranteed full employment would go farther and make it unnecessary besides for large monopolistic organizations to amass financial cushions against a future recession.

What counts, of course, is not that moderation could be practiced but whether it would be. My own view here is that big business and big labor would by and large cooperate voluntarily to hold prices down once government on its part was ready to assure the demand. But that's an opinion, not a certainty, so that direct controls over some prices and some wages—Galbraith's proposal—may possibly be needed, even under guaranteed full employment.

Bear in mind that Economic Performance Insurance as such is concerned with assuring that last-resort balancing measures will be used as required. Clearly we also want first-resort measures capable of keeping the need for those final adjustments reasonably small. Strong antitrust action, as already said; tax reform for a better distribution of purchasing power; encouragement of initiative and innovation (along ecologically sound lines); other measures.

Now for the practical application. (1) Is it possible to legislate such a system? Clearly it is. The procedures already in force under the Employment Act of 1946 can be strengthened so that the President each year proposes the targets and standby adjustment methods for employment and consumer spending, and Congress makes final decisions on those targets and methods, and the President executes those decisions.

(2) How can the government control the level of consumer spending, which depends on individuals' decisions about whether to spend or save their income? Practically speaking, it can do so through income-tax adjustments, with a negative-income-tax feature incorporated to include low-income groups. Or it could institute a two-way tax-or-bonus scheme at consumer sales points (described by me elsewhere but too much to explain here), which would be totally effective when restraining consumer spending and virtually so when raising it.

(3) Can the government really accelerate and/or decelerate public services and works whenever the statistics show that final adjustment is required at the job total end? Yes, this is feasible, in spite of our poor record with half-hearted efforts to date. But there's no escaping, here, a major new undertaking. A permanent "reservoir" or "reserve shelf" of such jobs has to be built up and kept up nationwide, and unprecedented arrangements have to be developed for its speedy activation for either expansion or contraction.

The Hawkins-Humphrey bill in its successive versions seems to be almost coming to embody an Economic Performance Insurance system. (The latest draft—Full Employment and Balanced Growth Act, H.R.50 and S.50—continues also to stress planning.) Major improvements include the abandonment of an unworkable earlier definition of full employment and the addition of rules designed to assure timely and budget-connected Congressional action on the President's annual economic recommendations. In my view, however, the current bill still suffers from fiscal policy ideas only incompletely assimilated to an insurance approach—the language is full of references to cyclical downturns, recessions, periods of high unemployment—and suffers, in addition, from giving too little responsibility to Congress. It could be simpler and stronger.

Representative Richard Bolling of Missouri inserted this article in the *Congressional Record* on June 21, 1976.

9

Letters to *The New York Times*

FULL EMPLOYMENT: THE CRUCIAL GUARANTEE

To the Editor: Recent Washington discussions on the latest revision of the Hawkins-Humphrey full-employment bill (H.R. 50) appear to show heavy concern over the "timetable" issue—whether to promise to reduce unemployment to 3 percent in eighteen months or three years or even four years. This is understandable because we should waste no unnecessary time in curing the miserable unemployment conditions that exist today.

But timing is less important than enacting a full-employment-guarantee law that really does guarantee. The central issue for the drafters of the new law has to be this: once we reach full employment, reasonably defined, the provisions must assure us of maintaining it permanently thereafter.

Luckily, that assurance would be the one thing that would also help most to get us up to full employment quickly to start with. Since all of us (businessmen, workers, consumers, even government officials) respond tremendously to economic expectations, the real assurance of continuous prosperity at full employment hereafter would of itself greatly stimulate the economy in the present. In an "economic performance insurance" approach, the "insurance" is not window dressing; it is of the essence functionally.

Inflation would be provided against, too, under such a policy. This means that special measures to expand private and public activity today would be less risky than they would be without that overall context.

In particular, this sort of legislation must require that a nationwide reservoir of public-service and public-works jobs be prepared and kept permanently up to date (in addition, of course, to those under regular appropriations, not standby). Once that perspective has been assured, the extra public-service jobs that need to be activated now can be more readily accepted by all schools of thought. They can also be more efficiently designed and scheduled once that kind of economic machinery is seen as a permanent feature of the landscape—machinery that, however, the legislation will authorize to be used only when, as and if actually necessary.

John H. G. Pierson
Greenwich, Conn.,
March 6, 1976

TOWARD GUARANTEED FULL EMPLOYMENT

To the Editor: In view of the dismal unemployment picture and the welcome introduction of the Hawkins-Humphrey bill (H.R.50), allow me to restate briefly the special advantages of the Economic Performance Insurance approach to guaranteed full employment. (This new "insurance" approach is only partly visible in H.R.50 now.)

1. The act of assuring continuous prosperity—the assurance as such—would yield certain benefits that present methods cannot. Recession being ruled out in advance, business and labor would have a new confidence enabling them to do without charging extra in good times to cushion bad times to come. Consumers could spend and save with greater confidence and regularity. And since the Government would be committed to taking the agreed and specified final-balancing action, but only when the necessity as defined in advance arose, the whole stabilization process would be freed from the guesswork, confusion and delay that beset it now.

2. Neither an elaborate planning system nor a proportionally bigger public sector would be required. The merits of those changes can (and should) be debated separately; no need to delay full employment while waiting for a clear outcome from difficult confrontations.

3. The traditional division of responsibilities between the Executive and Congress would be easily maintained. The President in his annual Economic Report would propose the targets and the final-balancing methods; Congress would decide conclusively on both; and the President would carry out those decisions.

4. Control of inflation would be simplified. As regards demand pull, top as well as bottom limits would be set to employment and to total consumer spending. As regards cost push, lower unit costs at full production and elimination of the need for cusions against recession would permit lower pricing, and the Government's own new commitment would justify business and labor in noting that possibility and cooperating freely.

5. Foreign policy would be enormously assisted. Enough total demand would be assured regardless of the state of our trade balance. This would virtually end the temptation to adopt restrictive foreign trade measures—measures that may generate additional domestic jobs but only at the expense of the larger national interest, since they sacrifice vital opportunities for international cooperation.

A final point: Economic Performance Insurance is an "umbrella" policy and requires no abandonment of doctrinal loyalties by anyone who wants full employment (that's the acid test). Many arguments dear to economists would continue under the umbrella. Anyone could propose additional stabilization measures. Good ones if adopted would help reduce the frequency and extent of the final-balancing action needed.

John H. G. Pierson
Greenwich, Conn.,
Dec. 26, 1975

10

How to Get Economic Performance Insurance Started Now

The key to practical application of the Economic Performance Insurance (EPI) idea is in the interplay of three elements—public service[1] jobs, consumer spending maintenance, and assurances. The heart of EPI, and the real novelty, are in the assurances. Since they would guarantee continued, noninflationary prosperity, the assurances would make business, labor, and consumers confident and the economy buoyant. Since they would certify what steps the government would take when (but only when) a defined-in-advance need to use one of the final balancing devices arose, they would transform the whole stabilization process, freeing it from the guesswork, confusion, and delay that beset it now.

This note will speak first of the above three essential elements, before going on to suggest how to get EPI started.

THE ESSENTIAL ELEMENTS

1. *Assurances.* It would have to be enacted into law that the Federal Government would from then on guarantee and maintain (i) total employment and (ii) total consumer spending at economically "right" levels. Some elaboration is called for here:

"Right" levels means full-employment levels—the goal is stabilization at full employment—except that there has first to be a step by step (quarter by quarter) progression up to full employment, in view of present heavy unemployment.

The guarantees have to be quantified—there must be advance commitment in terms of officially recognized indicators, i.e. government statistics, of (i) persons employed[2] and (ii) dollars of personal consumption expenditures.

The "levels" here discussed are really "bands." That is, in order to guard against inflationary overheating of the economy, ceilings (maxima) need to be set on employment and on consumer spending, as well as floors (minima). The distance

---

This note was privately circulated in March 1975.

48

between floor and ceiling should in each case be what is administratively reasonable considering, e.g., the time-lag problems.

2. *Public service jobs.* Public service jobs ought to be greatly expanded today quite apart from any question of EPI. EPI's added requirements are: (a) a permanent "reserve shelf" of such jobs to be built and thereafter maintained on a scale that would always enable employment to be held at its guaranteed level; (b) unprecedented arrangements for quick reserve shelf utilization, i.e. quick expansion or contraction of public service employment whenever up- or down-adjustment may be called for to honor the employment guarantee.

3. *Consumer spending maintenance.* Almost all analysts agree that tax cuts to boost the purchasing power and spending of consumers are needed now. For purposes of EPI—in order to be able to maintain employment without relying (or risking the need to rely) on public service jobs to an excessive extent—the added requirements are: (a) a particular method, or several alternative methods, of lowering or raising tax rates on consumers and/or raising or lowering transfer payments to consumers[3]; (b) to provide for introducing such changes in taxes etc. by Executive action, without further Congressional debate, so that consumers' disposable income will be promptly boosted or lowered whenever one or the other adjustment is required for honoring the consumer spending guarantee.

HOW TO GET STARTED

1. *Enact amended full-employment legislation.* EPI assurances, and the resulting favorable expectations and orderly stabilization procedures, must await improvement of our permanent legislation relating to full employment.

What this legislation needs to do is to spell out procedures to be gone through each year, to the following effect: (a) The President's Economic Report would make a point of including specific recommendations on (i) employment and (ii) consumer spending. (b) Congress would have a broadened policy-making role, taking on an entirely new responsibility for the final decisions on acceptable levels of (i) and (ii) and on the standby means for maintaining them both. (c) The President without having to obtain further approval would do the necessary maintaining.

This legislative basis could be achieved by incorporating certain limited amendments—a rather simple matter textually—in the Employment Act of 1946.[4] There is also a bill in Congress, sponsored originally by Representative Augustus Hawkins and Senator Hubert Humphrey, entitled the "Equal Opportunity and Full Employment Act of 1976." Finally, the new Congressional Budget and Impoundment Control Act of 1974 needs to be kept in mind when the drafting is done, since its provisions do not explicitly allow for the possibility of authorizations of Presidential action on a contingent/mandatory basis, such as would be called for under EPI.

As to timetable: although the President has already issued his Economic Report for fiscal year 1976 (beginning July 1975), this need not prevent EPI from getting started under the requisite permanent legislation even during FY1976. Evidently, however, the first cycle of steps (a) to (c) according to the outline given above could only apply to FY1977.

2. *Build a nationwide "reserve shelf."* EPI's most laborious undertaking would be the construction of a reserve shelf of public service employment. In addition to its

necessarily large total extent, this roster of available extra jobs would also need to have the following characteristics, among others: (a) It must obviously have nationwide coverage; thus the cooperation of State and local authorities all over the country would be involved. (b) It should only include works and services that are intrinsically valuable, i.e. accelerations of activities already being carried out for that reason, plus new projects clearly useful too in improving the quality of life. (c) It should include a wide spectrum of "industry" fields and occupational skills. (d) It should be able to be started functioning and tapered off quickly, and hence should avoid undue dependence on kinds of equipment that have inflexible delivery or operating schedules.

A satisfactory reserve shelf has not existed so far and will presumably remain an unrealistic objective up to the time when the intention to enact EPI legislation becomes clear. At that point its construction would become an urgent matter.

3. *Establish price and wage guidelines.* Another preparatory step of major importance would be the holding of discussions on anti-inflation policy with representatives of business and labor. As already noted, price spirals would be checked, under EPI, by having ceilings on employment and on consumer spending. In addition to those controls on the "demand pull," however, something should be done to moderate the "cost push" pressures toward higher prices. Much would be accomplished here if the government's own assumption of new responsibility for the economy were matched by business and labor commitments to support a reasonable set of price and wage guidelines. Talks looking to such undertakings by business and labor should be started while the new full employment legislation was still under debate.

4. *Conduct technical studies.* In implementing EPI a certain number of technical (statistical and economic) studies would obviously need to be made. None of them should prove unduly difficult or time-consuming if tackled with the staff resources available to the President's Council of Economic Advisers and/or the several interested committees of Congress (Joint Economic Committee, Congressional Budget Office, etc.).

One quantitative study that would claim high priority, to get the assurances started off on a realistic basis, would be an assessment of the various stages envisaged leading up from present recession to full employment. Special emphasis would need to be given to estimating an optimum quarter-by-quarter succession of employment and consumer spending levels (the latter calculated, of course, in the context of overall demand or GNP projections). This study would probably follow the common practice of spelling out the considerations for and against faster and slower alternatives, so that informed policy choices could then be made.

NOTES

1. "Public service" here includes conventional public works (construction etc.) as well as a much wider range of activities requiring skills at many different levels.

2. Or, alternatively, percent unemployed.

3. Such methods certainly can be found. Two examples of instruments convenient for the purpose: (a) the personal income tax with a negative tax feature added; (b) a new federal sales tax reversible into a sales bonus.

4. Minimum essential amendments are suggested in my statement printed in the *Congressional Record* for March 1, 1972 (see pages 32–33).

11

Eight Radio Broadcasts

I

Economic policy proposals are having a field day. But let us go a little deeper. I want to explain in a series of talks that we can have continuous full employment under the American system without inflation. The secret lies, I will show, in *adopting a kind of insurance approach to economic stabilization.* This proposal is rather conservative really but it involves one or two unfamiliar concepts. Maybe there *is* something new under the sun.

Sometimes a negative idea seems to paralyze the imagination. The theory of the trade-off between unemployment and inflation is a perfect example. This theory tells us our system has awful limitations. We are stuck forever with inflation or unemployment or some mixture of both.

Now that, I submit, is wrong. We don't have to choose between those evils at all. The time has come to face up to an agreeable fact. The best cure for inflation isn't high unemployment, it's guaranteed full employment.

If this seems to be standing things on their head, the reason is that too many experts have been looking too long at statistics and have missed the essential new point. They have given no thought to having a policy in which full employment would be actually *guaranteed.* But they should.

Let me sketch such a policy. Call it, for convenience, Economic Performance Insurance.

The idea behind Economic Performance Insurance is to get away from reacting defensively to every happening and take to offensive instead. Stop trying to guide the economic ship by point-to-point navigation. Downgrade forecasts. Keep things generally loose but have the President and Congress use their rightful powers to take out a firm national insurance policy on the key things that really matter.

This series of broadcasts was delivered February 3–11, 1975, from Station WGCH of Greenwich, Connecticut under the general title "Permanent Full Employment Without Inflation."

What are those things? The opportunity to work is one. Another is acceptance—will people accept the guaranteeing of employment opportunity in a private enterprise system? That hinges, I would say, on assuring the continuous adequacy of the national consumer market (consumer spending) as well as the job level itself; but I will have to explain this another time.

Why would guaranteed full employment restrain inflation rather than make it worse? Because, firstly, we would not only have floors under employment and under consumer spending but ceilings over both as well. We could not have deflation or recession because of the floors. Because of the ceilings, an inflationary spiral could hardly begin.

The second reason is psychological. By acknowledging its own due share of responsibility our government would be setting an example that business and labor would want to copy. What's more, they could afford to, and public opinion would know it. Full production spreads the cost; besides which, with recessions abolished, those reserves considered necessary against recession would have become *un*necessary. Wage and price guidelines would certainly make sense in that psychological climate, altogether different from the past.

A decisive, moderate policy like this could begin to help us immediately. Economic behavior depends on expectations. To damp down inflation we have to kill off inflationary psychology. Washington should start now to frame the rules for a system of Economic Performance Insurance to come into effect later. Given a new prospect like that, it would be much easier to use direct controls, if we have to, as a temporary measure today.

II

Many people think that the price of full employment would be more inflation, or a less free functioning of the private enterprise system. Some seem to feel, on the other hand, that a full-employment policy has to wait for the right tenant to inhabit the White House. Luckily those objections don't take into account how a system of Economic Performance Insurance would work. I have already shown this in regard to inflation. Now I come to the mechanism for regulating the job level itself.

Once full employment is explained as (of course) allowing some so-called frictional, or between-jobs, unemployment, not many people are against it. Admittedly certain sweatshop-minded employers of labor are; so are some traders who specialize in the wide market swings; some economists whose "thing" is the cycle too; a few others.

Obviously, though, the problem in establishing a permanent full-employment economy lies elsewhere. Among people, for instance, who regard full employment as desirable, but . . . "But unfortunately it cannot be achieved," they say, permanently, except by paying too high a price in inflation and in damage to our free enterprise system. Or else they may feel, as members of the Democratic Party, that nothing as basic as this can be done until they can take over the Presidency.

In between our recessions some people have also suggested that the full-employment issue is out-of-date, and not important enough to make a fuss over. This, however, is usually a misunderstanding over words, and probably the other objections need to be taken up first.

All three of them—the inflation objection which I answered last time, the free-enterprise objection, and the partisan political objection ("let's get our person in the White House first")—involve misconceptions not over words but substance. People who express those views just don't understand how a system of permanently assured full employment would actually work. Further clarification is needed.

The starting point is that such an economy would behave, overall, quite differently from the fluctuating economy we know. Economic Performance Insurance would stabilize it. That is, stops would be set, by Presidential recommendation and Congressional final decision, both below and above the performance levels considered satisfactory.

Stops on what? Performance of what, exactly? First of all, of course, employment itself. Total employment would not be allowed to drop below a level decided upon in advance as being required to meet the full-employment concept. But neither would it be allowed to rise above a slightly higher level, also set in advance, for fear that overemployment would overheat the economy.

For control like that to be possible, the government would clearly have to stand ready to step in as employer of last resort; or to step out, when necessary—as what you might call disemployer of first resort. The mechanism to permit that would be a nationwide reserve shelf of additional public services and public works.

This mechanism would be inherently flexible. Its use would be contingent on events but then mandatory—that's the point. The extra projects, and expansions of existing ones, would be activated only if, when, and as long as needed for keeping total employment within its previously decided limits.

Here we have the employment regulator, familiar in concept although never properly tried. My next subject will be the consumer spending regulator.

III

Last time I discussed the employment regulator—expansions and contractions of public services and works. This device is familiar but is only used in a half-hearted manner; take this winter, for instance. Now I will talk about the need to regulate the size of the private consumer demand too. Floors and ceilings on consumer demand are something hardly ever mentioned but actually they are crucial for a system like ours in which production follows the market.

In 1968 the Democratic Party platform promised that "For those who cannot obtain other employment the federal government will be the employer of last resort, either through federal assistance to state and local governments or through federally sponsored projects."

This idea of filling employment gaps from a reserve shelf of public works and services has been around a long time. It is a very good idea. Why isn't it used more? Why aren't the reserve shelves of projects even there? Why does a promise to really use this device as needed only serve to widen the credibility gap?

The reason is not unlike the reason a bird cannot fly on one wing. The employer of last resort is an excellent wing, but the other wing is missing. Private enterprise needs also to be assured that the final market for its products will always be adequately large to enable a full-employment volume of goods and services to be sold.

This is not double-talk or misunderstanding. The economic case against one-wing flying is fundamental. Certainly employment creates income to spend; however, even assuming we had full employment to begin with, no one could say how long the final demand would keep up adequately. Sluggishness—oversaving, if you like—could always appear in the economy, causing demand to turn down, and then employment too unless last-resort jobs were multiplied progressively.

In short, adequate employment cannot be trusted *entirely* to sustain necessary demand, any more than adequate demand can be trusted entirely to sustain employment. The reciprocal feedbacks are there but they are only approximately reliable. So, both key elements must be kept at their right levels independently. Our economy needs two independently strong wings.

Now a little reflection will show that the final market for purposes of size management has to be the *consumer* market. Not only is this by far the biggest part of the total—over 60 percent—but private investment ought not to be handled that way in any case; investment needs to be free to respond to anticipated consumer, government, and foreign demands in future. And those two other GNP components—government expenditures for goods and services, and net exports—rule themselves out for equally obvious reasons.

How would a guaranteed level of consumer spending be maintained when it failed to maintain itself? By adjustment of consumer taxes or of transfer payments (social security benefits and the like). One excellent mechanism would be the personal income tax if it had a negative income tax built into it as an anti-poverty measure.

For technical reasons a reversible federal sales tax/sales bonus at the retail level might be even better. The bonuses here would operate through stamps convertible into cash— "income boosters" or "I.B.s", they might be called. Or some other option could be chosen. The important thing is not the precise mechanism but its mandatory, prompt use whenever the official indicator showed that that was required for honoring the guarantee.

IV

In my previous talks I examined the inflation and private-enterprise objections to full employment. As I have shown, both of them fall to the ground if full employment is guaranteed. Basic to that conclusion are the firm floors and ceilings that would be set to consumer spending and to jobs. Now I want to sketch the governmental procedures for managing such a policy—the role of the President in it and the greatly enlarged responsibilities of the Congress.

Some people blame the Administration for our inflation and unemployment problems. Well, Presidential leadership is vital, of course; but, for maintaining permanent full employment, the fact is it is Congress that needs to assume a new, continuing responsibility under law. Hence Congress has reason too to initiate the needed legislation—even more so than when the Senate took the lead in this field thirty years ago.

Under that Employment Act of 1946 the President's annual Economic Report, with his recommendations for action, is referred to the Joint Economic Committee of Congress. The Committee studies this and issues its own report on it. But then the whole process breaks down. Congress is not obliged to act on the matter in any concerted way. The Committee's report simply goes to the other interested committees of Congress to use as they may see fit. The economic stabilization thrust, no matter how good, is dispersed in thin air.

What is clearly called for is an amendment requiring Congress as a whole to take certain definite decisions by joint or concurrent resolution. Congress should each year either accept or modify the minimum or maximum employment limits and consumer spending limits that would be proposed by the President. Second, it should ask the President to hold total jobs and total consumer spending within those approved limits. Third, it should specify the standby measures—the kinds of public works and services, and of consumer taxes and transfer payments—to be used when and if found needed for a final adjustment.

Then the Executive Branch, without interference, should execute the decisions of Congress on the President's original recommendations.

Here in a nutshell is the operating rationale for guaranteed full employment. Nothing about it would require Congress to rubber-stamp the President, or to give him undue discretionary power, or infringe on the legitimate powers of Congress' own committees.

This approach separates the non-controversial goal of stable prosperity from the controversial question of how big a public sector we want. Whenever Congress disagreed with the President's annual federal program proposals, the resulting change would be a change of proportions only. Government spending would go down or up. But overall GNP demand would remain at the full-employment level through an offsetting change in the guaranteed rate of consumer spending.

In *my* view of our national priorities, much larger expenditures are clearly needed— by government and business both—for the environment, housing, mass transit, other city services, health, education, backward rural areas, and so on. Meeting those social needs would also provide more jobs per dollar, and more useful ones, than other kinds of expansion could.

Yet to say that some particular program along those lines is essential to get full employment as a by-product is, I am sure, simply wrong. Congress might settle for a less liberal policy than the President had recommended; but the super-priority, full employment, would be achieved all the same—under my proposals—only with a somewhat different job mix.

V

In earlier talks I explained the concept of Economic Performance Insurance; the regulators or balancing devices needed for keeping employment and also consumer spending from either falling too low or rising too high; and the way the President and Congress could readily make this system work. Now the question arises: why is an *insurance* approach necessary? Can't we get the same results without it? This talk will be addressed to that question.

The first great advantage of an insurance approach to economic stabilization is simply that the human stakes are high and it would be good to be sure. We don't need inflation and unemployment. There are enough other painful problems.

Who would dream of flying in an airplane certified to be unsafe? Nobody. Why, then, should two hundred and more million Americans continue to be entrusted to a chronically unsafe economy, when there is a way of avoiding it?

The second big advantage of the insurance approach follows from the first. If people could be sure, they could have confidence in the future, rather than fears, and that would make the economy function better in the *present*.

Private enterprise would be encouraged because it would be assured of an ample market for which to compete. Individual businesses could operate at higher "break even" points with lower prices, because good times would not be leading to bad. Unions with strong bargaining power could skip the part of their demands meant to cushion future layoffs. Consumers would not have their saving and spending patterns distorted by the cycle.

But that is not all. Ideologically—and here I address myself especially to my fellow economists—Economic Performance Insurance is an "umbrella" policy, not a contender against the New Economics, the Old Economics, or any other. It offers no threat to any other economic views. No loyalties need be abandoned on its behalf. All the old arguments can go merrily on under the umbrella.

Let me explain that. Domestic economic policy proposals usually aim either at creating a greater measure of social justice or at improving our economic stability.—Or, indeed, at both, since victories for social justice often promote economic stability too, particularly by spreading purchasing power, the life blood of the system.

Yet once we define stability in practical, measurable terms, and guarantee it, most stabilization measures—basic fiscal policy changes, week-by-week adjustments of money by the Federal Reserve, or others—turn out to be *first-approximation* stabilizers only. Final balancing devices will still be needed.

So, if employment and consumer spending are chosen as the magnitudes to which the guarantees are going to apply, then the extra-public-works-and-services regulator and the consumer-tax-and-transfer-payments regulator become those final balancers. They put the latch on the door.

This detracts not at all, of course, from other measures in which economists of different schools are interested and on which dozens of committees of Congress work. In many cases those measures can help give our economy better first-approximation stability, and so limit the need to use the final balancers.

Two examples will show this relationship. If tax reforms are adopted that help the low-income groups, we can anticipate less need to use the consumer spending regulator as final booster. If the antitrust campaign is pushed hard, monopolies will not raise their prices as much. In this case, the guaranteed level of consumer spending will more easily induce expanded production and so sustain full employment without needing help from the government employer of last resort.

VI

My talks so far have dealt with the mechanics of how to get rid of unemployment for good without letting ourselves in for some other things we don't want either, including inflation. I am now going to go back and nail down the point that full employment can be not only reasonably but unmistakably defined. And I will also comment on the question of first things first, or how this issue stands among the other great issues of the day.

The full-employment goal is often misunderstood. Sometimes the words themselves are thought to mean that everyone has to work. Or else people just take too narrow a view of what is at stake.

Full employment actually has nothing to do with obliging people to work but only with giving them a chance to work if they want to. The aim is well stated in the Employment Act of 1946 as "useful employment opportunities, including self-employment, for those able, willing, and seeking to work."

By common consent full opportunity to work admits of some "frictional" unemployment—persons changing jobs or seeking their first job. The question is, how much? Three percent of the labor force? less? more? Here opinions differ.

Under Economic Performance Insurance this question would get a definite answer. The President would annually recommend, and then Congress would decide, and so give the country the working definition for the year ahead. Maximum and minimum limits would both be set. Very likely the statistical reference point would be the national employment series published each month by the Labor Department, with allowance for seasonal variation and labor force growth trend.

Let me now turn from definitions to what is really at stake. In the first place, involuntary unemployment is destructive of personality. And as our bicentennial draws near, we might pay particular attention too to life, liberty, and the pursuit of happiness. In 1776 the purpose of government was said to be to make such rights secure. But you can't pursue happiness very far if you need a job—for the money or the independence of it—and there's no job to be had.

Second, assured prosperity at the full-employment level would weaken the antisocial compulsions of business, labor, farmers, and other interest groups. These compulsions divide us today and they feed the fires of inflation. Count on them to be with us until the cycle is tamed.

Third, racial peace is impossible in this country without universal employment opportunity. Nor could anyone but a wild optimist expect to see an end to the alienation of youth, or the bitterness of older people pushed into early retirement.

Fourth, getting rid of poverty would be greatly simplified as a result of the cash income effects of continuous full employment. There would be more paid labor and less chance to exploit labor by paying substandard wages.

In the fifth place, we just cannot afford the extravagance of nonproduction—those $100 billion or so of annual lost output. Think how that wasted wealth is needed to help meet the problems of the cities, of our rural Appalachias, and the environment generally, if for nothing else.

In this too-short list of reasons why full employment is essential, I have here spoken only of the domestic scene. But the international aspect is now equally compelling. I will take that up next time.

VII

I have described a technique of Economic Performance Insurance that would keep all the freedom of our present economic system but also give us full employment permanently, and practically rule out inflation. Last time I reviewed some of the far-reaching implications here at home. Now I will talk about something that is often overlooked entirely—why we need assured full employment for our international economic relations too.

The man from Mars would be amazed to see so many countries all trying to use each other as an economic crutch. Each striving for an export surplus by boosting exports and cutting imports, as a way to gain markets for its businessmen and jobs for its workers.

"Your economy has a neurotic personality," he would be strongly tempted to say if asked. But that could be wrong, of course, for two good reasons. Everything would depend on what the conscious motivation was, and the capability.

Maybe this was the old combative world in which it was not neurotic at all, but healthy, to win out by beggaring your neighbors. Or even if it wasn't—suppose conscious motivation was now shifting toward accommodation, friendship, some sense of world unity—a country might still be too small or too weak to do anything significant internationally.

This little fable leads back to Economic Performance Insurance. I think that the American impulse to be a good neighbor has always been genuine, and that cooperation is clearly dictated by enlightened self-interest too. What is needed, however, is a system assuring permanent full employment without the necessity of export surpluses, so that our policies on trade and on aid will, not in theory only but in fact, gratify our friendly impulse and serve our own self-interest.

With foreign aid, the point is that our prosperity would make us feel able to be more helpful. With trade, the point is the spectacular one that the technique of Economic Performance Insurance would, by the very way it was set up to work, abolish for us the age-old fear of a shortage of markets.

This is so because net exports—whether plus or minus—would be one of the elements counted when determining the proper amount of consumer spending. Mathematically, the level of consumer spending to be guaranteed would equal the total market or GNP believed needed for full employment at expected price levels, minus three things: (1) intended government spending for goods and services, (2) expected domestic investment, and (3) this expected difference between our exports and our imports.

We would have a *high* volume of trade, let us hope, in *both* directions, but we would not any longer be trying to take more markets away from foreigners in order to secure our own full employment. Instead, we would be adapting the size of the domestic market to what was necessary for full employment, given what the net balance in our foreign market could reasonably be expected to be.

Our friends in Western Europe are once again deeply fearful of what our recession may do to their export sales. As far as the Third-World countries are concerned, they have for years been telling us that they want to move from aid to trade as soon as possible. We applaud that sentiment. But will we buy enough from them to help make the transition possible?

Good will is involved and a lot else besides. We are going to be negotiating with the Third World from now on, in the United Nations and other forums, on a wide range of subjects, not excluding policies on oil and on other raw materials vital to us.

VIII

As I end these talks, it looks as though the idea of guaranteed full employment may be coming alive in Washington. Bills entitled "Equal Opportunity and Full Employment Act of 1976" have been introduced in both houses of Congress. If passed in satisfactory form, supplementing or amending the Employment Act of 1946 and properly coordinated with the Congressional Budget Act adopted last year, this could mark a giant step forward.

By common consent the heart of our dilemma is the inflation-recession syndrome. The energy crisis hasn't helped, but we had better not blame our economic instability on external factors. The main point is that we need to set our own house in order.

Some analysts argue over whether the problem is inflation *or* recession. Others propose different measures for combatting both at once; that can be more useful, obviously.

Much better still, however, would be to improve the functioning of our economy so that both evils are ruled out. The modern medical treatment for manic-depressive disease is not to doctor manias by one means and depressed states by another. Instead, patients are given a medicine (lithium carbonate) that helps prevent both mania and depression by normalizing the underlying physiological conditions. Could not the same be done for our manic-depressive economy?

I believe the answer is yes—if we adopt the Economic Performance Insurance approach which I have been describing. So far, the idea of insuring our economy has mainly turned up in editorial or political rhetoric. But actually the tools of the political economy trade are better than they used to be, and carrying out this idea seems perfectly feasible today.

In substance the breakthrough would consist of setting guaranteed top and bottom limits to two things, employment and consumer spending, letting other things fall into place. The other new element is procedural: Congress would take firm decisions on the President's annual recommendations as to those two specifics and then give him contingent authority to act.

Guaranteeing consumer spending would make guaranteeing employment a practical proposition—serving everyone's common interest in prosperity in spite of our obviously wide disagreements over government's role in production. Also, as I have shown, it would strongly combat inflation, and would leave us genuinely free to follow a good-neighbor policy in trade.

Such a program would not necessarily involve large costs or unbalance the budget. *Recession always* generates big deficits because tax revenues go down and various relief expenses go up. We see again today that budget balance doesn't depend on whether the government does something about the economy or sits on its hands; it depends on whether the economy is sluggish or buoyant.

That, in turn, will of course partly depend on *what* the government does. By supporting business markets, Economic Performance Insurance would offer ideal conditions for economic buoyancy. But budget predictions are not to be trusted;

certainly, big import surpluses or other developments could lead to deficits.

We also cannot go from heavy unemployment to full employment overnight; but we *could* immediately set firm performance targets that would get us ahead step by step— quarter by quarter. Then too, by adopting the insurance approach, we would benefit immediately from all the effects on expectations. This is why we might reach full employment sooner than most of the experts have said we can.

12

The Employment Act Revisited

The candidates are setting their economic sights too low. When the Democrats fault the administration for giving us inflation and unemployment both at once, and promise to do much better themselves if granted the chance, that is not enough. Also needed—and also possible—are some solid assurances or guarantees.

The American economy can no longer afford the luxury of reacting defensively to every inflationary of deflationary pressure that happens to develop. Without forcing the economy into rigid controls, it is possible to devise a system of "performance insurance" procedures to maintain guaranteed full employment without inflation.

Such a system could be built around annual estimates—submitted by the President and legislated by Congress—of acceptable ranges of total employment and consumer spending for the next fiscal year. The procedures that could be established to carry out such a system would control the overall amount of economic activity while in general leaving the individual producer free.

Certainly this proposal does give conventional thinking a wrench. Some of our institutional machinery would have to be strengthened to put it into effect. In short, it raises several practical problems. Why not? For this is not a question of patchwork but of shaping the economic core for the social regeneration of America that is now, one hopes, on the way. The main point is that an approach is possible with, not against, the grain of tradition, so that under good leadership the practical problems raised can perfectly well be solved.

NEW GROUND RULES

A full-employment guarantee is perhaps implicit in what some presidential candidates have sometimes proposed. Thus, Sen. Edmund Muskie has said: "It is time to commit our nation to the right to a job." Sen. George McGovern: "If I were President of the

Reprinted by permission from *The Washington Post*, where it appeared May 14, 1972 under the title, "Full Employment without Inflation: A Proposal."

United States, I would set as the first order of business the creation of a decent job for every American." Sen. Henry Jackson: "As far as I am concerned, the Employment Act of 1946 means what it says . . . that the Federal Government under any administration, Republican or Democratic, must be prepared to use all the powers at its command to see that people have work." Sen. Hubert Humphrey: "Employment is a right for every American—like freedom or due process. Government has an obligation to fulfill that right as the first matter of policy."

Such statements would, I believe, be more frequent and more explicit if it were wholly clear how a guarantee of the chance to work would really, if given, be implemented. Some will recall that the 1968 Democratic Party platform promised that "For those who cannot obtain other employment the federal government will be the employer of last resort, either through federal assistance to state and local governments or through federally sponsored projects." But without an explanation of how it can be accomplished this does little more than widen the credibility gap.

Once the focus shifts from merely reducing unemployment to actually guaranteeing full employment, without going against the grain of tradition, some new ground rules have to be observed.

The first rule is that the approach must not threaten to have the public sector undermine private enterprise. An ironclad governmental pledge to serve as employer of last resort up to full employment might be construed as posing such a threat if offered all by itself. Such a pledge is indeed essential, but it needs to be supported by a further pledge that the market for the output of private producers will be sustained at a level high enough to maintain full business prosperity and preclude excessive reliance on the last-resort work programs.

This is one side of the question. Yet a basic problem in our society today is its obvious need for greatly expanded services (and capital investments) in the public sector, to counterbalance our overemphasis on the production of gadgets for the more or less surfeited rich. Both our cities and our backward rural areas cry out for attention. Health, education, low-cost housing, anti-pollution, mass transport—the fields starved for funds are well known. Those expenditures, partly governmental and partly private, should be made for their own sake, and clearly some intiative must come from Washington. An extra advantage is that many of them would produce more jobs dollar for dollar, especially jobs for less-skilled and less-educated workers, than would additional private spending.

In this sense the government should, as Michael Harrington recently put it, serve as employer of first, not last, resort. There is an imperative to so reorder our national priorities—a social imperative, like the need to narrow rather than widen further the income gaps between our rich and our poor. But the necessity for the government to serve as employer of last resort is also there, and this—the stabilization question—is essentially an economic matter. Two different issues, separate but complementary, are thus involved. Strong action of the first, socially motivated kind would undoubtedly reduce the need for the second, the stabilization action, but the second too is indispensable, like a latch on the door.

A PLEDGE ON SPENDING

As for maintaining the market for the output of private business, the government should also guarantee an appropriate rate of aggregate consumer spending. Calculating this is a technical matter, for the President's Council of Economic Advisers is the first instance. However, what is essentially involved is: (a) to estimate the total overall expenditures for goods and services (GNP) necessary to justify production at the full-employment level; and (b) to subtract the anticipated government and business and (plus or minus) net export components. This gives (c) the rate of consumer spending to be announced and pegged.

The second ground rule is that guaranteed full employment must also not heighten inflation. Here we should distinguish between the grave dangers of inflation and whether full employment should be cast in the villain's role. Unfortunately this subject has been much obscured by preoccupation with the concept of an inevitable trade-off between inflation and unemployment, based on the "Phillips curve." Serious inflation can obviously occur far short of full employment. On the other hand, no modern government is going to use unemployment for really keeping inflation stopped, because the extent of unemployment, misery and repression required would be utterly out of harmony with present ideas of social justice. In short, a different, positive approach is needed—one in which some sort of incomes policy has a big part to play.

But luckily, that is not all. Actually, a program of guaranteed full employment would not feed inflation but could greatly help in the control of inflation. The mechanics of such a program would halt upward spirals, since ceilings as well as floors would be set to employment and to consumer spending. Thus "demand pull" would be kept in check, as would much of the "cost push" that stems from workers' efforts to keep up with a rising cost of living. Besides that, with the government at last assuming its proper responsibility for underwriting the continued health of the economy, the psychology would be right for business and labor leaders to agree to cooperate by abiding by some reasonable set of price and wage guidelines and thus minimize the need for measures of compulsion.

The third main ground rule is that guaranteed full employment must not be sought by means that disregard the traditional relationships between the President and Congress. There could be little future in any plan that expected Congress either to rubber-stamp the President's program or to grant him unduly broad discretionary powers.

THE ROLE OF CONGRESS

Let me now show specifically how the Employment Act of 1946 could be amended so as to guarantee the opportunity to work to all Americans. The act provides that the President, guided by his Council of Economic Advisers, shall each year by Jan. 20 transmit to the Congress an Economic Report; this report is now required to include a statement of the levels of employment, production, and purchasing power needed to carry out the policy of achieving "useful employment opportunities, including self-employment, for those able, willing, and seeking to work."

That passage should be amplified by addition of the words "including specifically the minimum and maximum levels of employment recommended in the light of that policy, and the minimum and maximum rates of aggregate personal consumption expenditures deemed consistent with that policy in view of the program of Federal Government purchases of goods and services recommended to be undertaken and the anticipated other demands on the national product." The point is to tell Congress how the President proposes to define full employment and in what proportions he recommends having the country's economic activity divided between the private and public sectors.

It is in section 5(b)(3) that we are brought face to face with the basic weakness of the act. At present the Joint Economic Committee, after it has studied the President's Economic Report and reached its own conclusions, is merely required "as a guide to the several committees of the Congress dealing with legislation relating to the Economic Report . . . to file a report with the Senate and the House of Representatives containing its findings and recommendations with respect to each of the main recommendations made by the President in the Economic Report." But surely the annual economic exercise should not end by disappearing this way in thin air. Rather, the JEC should be empowered and required to file its report "together with a draft Joint Resolution for the consideration of the Congress as provided for in section 6."

This new section 6, presumably entitled "Congressional Action on the Report of the Joint Economic Committee," could for brevity be phrased approximately as follows: "Sec. 6. As soon as practicable after the filing of the report of the Joint Economic Committee, the Congress shall by joint resolution of the Senate and the House of Representatives set forth its decisions with respect to: (a) the minimum and maximum acceptable levels of employment throughout the year in question; (b) the minimum and maximum acceptable rates of aggregate personal consumption expenditures throughout the year; (c) the preventive action to be taken by the President if employment should at any time tend to fall below its minimum, or rise above its maximum, acceptable level as defined in (a); and (d) the preventive action to be taken by the President in case personal consumption expenditures should at any time tend to fall below their minimum, or rise above their maximum, acceptable rates as defined in (b)."

HOW IT WOULD WORK

What this means is, first of all, that full employment would have a clear-cut statistical definition which would change from year to year. From the estimated labor force must always be subtracted some amount of unemployment deemed reasonable in the light of production shifts, manpower policies, and labor mobility at the time (the allowance for "necessary frictional unemployment"). Having considered the various factors, the President might in some year—this is simply an illustration—propose a minimum of 86.5 million jobs in terms of the seasonally adjusted monthly total reported by the Labor Department. He might also state that, in his view, anything over 87.8 million jobs would represent too tight a situation in the labor market, with too much upward pressure on pay scales and on total income payments. (Some such "band" between minimum and maximum is necessary—how wide is another question, not dealt with here—to keep from having to balance the economy on a razor edge.) Congress on its part, acting under the proposed new section 6(a), could disagree quantitatively on various grounds if it wanted to—technical estimating grounds or a difference in point of view about the percentage of unemployment consistent with "full" employment. But in any case it would have to assume the resonsibility of arriving at definite decisions of its own.

Suppose then that, in spite of a favorable general outlook buttressed by the assured maintenance of enough consumer spending, employment as reported by the Labor Department started dropping below its congressionally established floor. What would be done? Obviously the government would have to step in as employer of last resort, accelerating some ongoing public works and services and taking other projects off the reserve shelf. Congress would have written the specifications for this under section 6(c)—what sorts of works and services were to be included (federally financed state and local government projects would certainly be, but could private nonprofit projects qualify?); the formula for apportionment by states; and so on. Execution would rest with the agencies designated by the President.

If an opposite situation should arise, with employment going through its ceiling, projects would be decelerated or discontinued entirely and put back on the reserve shelf, again under rules laid down by Congress in section 6(c).

ADJUSTING CONSUMER SPENDING

In the case of consumer spending, the proposed procedures would, to begin with, resolve the impasse that occurs now when Congress is less impressed than the President is with the need for new governmental leadership in social programs, or vice versa. Suppose that the President, keen on reordering the nation's priorities, were to recommend a number of spending programs that would, in sum, raise the percentage of GNP represented by the government's own purchases of goods and services. The majority in Congress might agree, or go even farther. On the other hand, perhaps the majority would favor maintaining the existing GNP ratios instead. Thus, to illustrate, Congress might some year decide—under 6(b)—that the acceptable limits to consumer spending would be $765 billion and $780 billion, whereas the President, with different GNP proportions, more heavily weighted on the government side, in mind, had recommended a range of only $745–760 billion.

Suppose this time that it was consumer spending, in terms of the seasonally adjusted annual rates reported each quarter by the Commerce Department, that tended to get out of line. In spite of continuous full employment it might do so, in either direction. What would be the remedy? In making the applicable rules for this eventuality, under 6(d), Congress would have had numerous options. It might have decided that any necessary adjustments should be made through variations in the personal income tax and the addition or termination of certain payments to low-income households. Or, if welfare reform had led to the adoption of a plan guaranteeing a minimum income to all households as a matter of right, and of a negative income tax as the pay-out mechanism, Congress might have accepted a presidential recommendation that the income tax itself (positive and negative) should be the only instrument used.

Or perhaps congressional economists would have concluded that spending by consumers might still (even with booms and slumps ruled out) fail to respond sensitively to adjustments in their disposable income, brought about by methods like those just mentioned. In that case Congress could choose a method that would cut direct to the goal, such as a federal sales tax/sales bonus at the retail level, with the bonuses operating via stamps convertible to cash. During periods when the tax aspect had to be called into play to keep consumer spending from going too high, this tax would automatically lower the amount received, net, by business, that being then designated the amount required to be held below the established ceiling.

SELF-SUSTAINING SYSTEM

Under the approach proposed, since our whole forward-looking system is geared to expectations, consumers and producers would behave in ways tending to make the economy inherently more self-sustaining. Gone, for example, would be such deflationary influences as the oversaving and overpricing due to the fear of the loss of jobs and income in a future slump.

The regular committee system of Congress would function as it does now. Tax reform decisions in the Ways and Means Committee, for instance, would not clash with the standby tax adjustment mechanisms, but would only—since they would alter after-tax income and its distribution—affect the likelihood that those mechanisms would have to be called into play. In fact, considerable legislative feedback could be expected. An unduly large or frequent need to use adjustments for shoring up employment or consumer spending would spotlight the urgency of improved legislation relating to distribution of income, enforcement of competition and/or regulation of monopoly, or other factors strategically affecting the self-balancing capacity of the economy.

The "automaticity" of this approach would certainly not eliminate the need for good operational judgment, especially in deciding when to start and when to stop taking compensatory action. Gearing up for fast action would certainly be required, and agreement on how long employment or consumer spending could without prejudice remain at "unacceptable" levels, outside the prescribed band. The preparation of an adequate reserve shelf of public works and services would be a major task but not as difficult by any means as it always has been in the absence of a firm national commitment to, and understood means of maintaining, full employment.

How does this bear on the immediate problem of reducing unemployment from close to 6 percent? If the proposed plan with its built-in restraints on inflation were already on the legislative drawing boards, unemployment could probably be brought down to 3 percent—or to whatever other level Congress would want to stipulate—more quickly than discussions today suggest. But there is no point in attempting the impossible. In the transition period it might well be decided to move up to full employment in a series of quarterly steps and reach it, say, in the second year.

One of the especially striking advantages of the proposed plan lies in the area of foreign trade policy. An increase of net exports, through import restrictions and other means, has often been sought in the past as a solution for our unemployment, even though other countries might suffer from the action we took. That indeed is exactly the escalating danger today. The approach here proposed would turn the relationship around and call for an expansion of the domestic market (via consumer spending, which would be pegged higher) when the foreign market (net exports) was projected as declining. Consequently this approach would allay fears of a shortage of markets in the overall sense, and so would help to maintain a liberal foreign trade policy based on the widest interpretation of national self-interest. The less-developed countries, for instance, could then be extended a generous helping hand in their efforts to move "from aid to trade."

Foreign trade; society's claims vis-a-vis those of business, labor, farmers, and other interest groups; the problems of blacks and other minorities—these and other basic issues of the times all show that what is really needed is not just less unemployment but full employment on an assured basis. The opportunity to work is fundamental in America and in a real sense it is necessary to sustain all other forms of opportunity. Certainly even a reduction of present unemployment would be very welcome. The extra wealth from the extra production could then—together with any resources shifted from defense to peace—be devoted to making more rapid headway in fighting poverty and rescuing the environment. But we can do much better than that. The candidates are setting their economic sights too low.

13

Completing the Employment Act

In the twenty-six years since the Employment Act of 1946 was signed into law, the country has experienced five recessions. Even when business has prospered, the central aim of this Act—useful employment opportunities for all those able, willing, and seeking to work—has seldom been brought within sight, let alone achieved. Only for three years, in the Korea war boom, has the official unemployment estimate averaged below 3.5 percent of the civilian labor force (dropping to 2.9 percent in 1953 and to 2.5 percent, in seasonally adjusted figures, that May and June). In as many as eleven years it has stood above 5 percent (rising to 6.8 percent in 1958 and to 7.5 percent that July). Earlier bench marks, not entirely comparable, were 24.9 percent unemployment in 1933 and 1.2 percent in 1944 under wartime price controls.

In the long absence of recessions after 1961 the unemployment rate finally dropped to 3.5 percent for 1969 (touching 3.3 percent momentarily early that year), but the statistics somewhat overstate the actual improvement since stricter definitions of unemployment were used as from 1965 and 1967. Then in 1970 the jobless percentage jumped to 4.9, and in 1971 it hovered around, and averaged just under, 6 percent.

Six percent unemployment now means more than 5 million persons. Even 4 percent—sometimes treated as though it were an acceptable goal—would still leave some 3½ million persons in this country looking for work and unable to find any. Moreover the published unemployment total understates the real extent of involuntary idleness at virtually all times and especially during recessions. One reason among several is that some persons who want to work full-time can only get part-time jobs. Some others eventually become too discouraged to keep on looking and are then no longer counted as part of the labor force; and so—except for less frequent and less reliable estimating—they slip through the statistical net altogether.

A list of the legislative measures enacted or proposed since 1946 to try to cope better with our national economic problems would be long indeed. Many amendments have

This article appeared in the *Congressional Record*, March 1, 1972, inserted by Representative Patsy T. Mink of Hawaii.

been offered to the Employment Act itself, keyed mainly to three objectives: (1) Repeated efforts have been made from the outset to have the Act not only promote employment but also restrain inflationary price increases. (2) Lately, since about 1960, it has often been urged that this law should concern itself with our balance of payments as well. (3) There have also been attempts to go back to the more formal kind of "national full employment budget" planning which was originally suggested in 1945–46 but rejected by Congress at that time.

No amendments other than technical or housekeeping ones have ever been adopted, however, and some of the reasons are easily imagined. Many proposals were addressed to section 2, the Declaration of Policy.—Why load the Act with further policy objectives when its first objective was still not being achieved? Again, the "national full employment budget" concept was originally framed in a way that automatically aroused strong opposition by failing to safeguard the private enterprise interest. And all else aside, tinkering with an Act so broad in scope would have seemed like opening Pandora's box.—Where would the modifications end if once begun?

But are the reasons for standing pat still good enough? The need to have our economy function properly is as great as ever. The quarter-century record of failure of the Employment Act as written is more obvious today than before because of the length and peculiarities of the present slump. Indeed we now have not only the doctrine that full employment and price stability cannot be achieved simultaneously but the experience of the simultaneous nonachievement of both. Meanwhile in engineering, for example, scientifically-minded practical people are every day making progress by simply asking "what would be the conditions under which X" (some desired result) "would be achieved?" and then proceeding to construct those very conditions. Certainly the question must be raised whether the arguments against changing the Act are still convincing.

The answer to this must depend at least partly on whether amendments can be framed that will once and for all complete the Employment Act—make it do what it should, ideally speaking, have done from the start. Can it be strengthened to guarantee jobs to able job-seekers, while at the same time staying clear of irrelevant matters? (To keep full employment from itself causing inflation is of course anything but irrelevant.) Can these things, moreover, be done without prejudging the handling of a touchy public-versus-private-sector issue; or changing the traditional relationship between the President and the Congress (as by expecting Congress to rubber-stamp a Presidential spending program or to give the President unduly wide discretionary powers); or interfering in the legitimate concerns of Congressional committees?

It is here submitted that all this is possible, and textual amendments to the Act are offered below to illustrate how. Much the most important amendment and the key to the others is the addition of a new final section 6 to vest appropriate responsibilities in Congress as a whole. However, for the sake of clarity, this discussion will proceed straight through the Act from the beginning.

*   *   *

First, however, a word is needed about what is really at stake, because the arguments over the full-employment issue are often pitched on altogether too narrow ground. In briefest summary: (1) Involuntary unemployment is destructive of personality. (2) An assurance of continuous prosperity and full employment would weaken the antisocial (usually inflationary) compulsions of business, labor, farmer, and other interest groups. (3) Racial peace seems impossible in this country without universal job opportunity— the present lack of which is also partly responsible for the alienation of youth, not to speak of the helpless bitterness of many older people. (4) Getting rid of poverty would be greatly simplified as a result of the cash-income effects of continuous full employment (more paid labor; less chance of exploiting labor by paying substandard wages). (5) The extra wealth (GNP) which would be created under those full-activity conditions—the staggering amount now wasted through avoidable non-production—is needed to help finance programs to meet the problems of the cities, backward rural areas, and the environment generally, including again problems of poverty but not limited to them. (6) Internationally, that extra wealth would confirm our ability to extend more generous aid to the world's less developed countries. (7) More (and more fundamental) than that, confidence in our ability to maintain a market adequate for our own full-employment prosperity through domestic policy would substantially deflate our fear of imports and our exaggerated preoccupation with export markets and export surpluses; thus it would enable us to be a "good neighbor" that encourages and helps the less developed countries to shift "from aid to trade" as they become ready for it.

* * *

Section 1 of "AN ACT to declare a national policy on employment, production, and purchasing power, and for other purposes" (60 Stat. 23) (Public Law 304—79th Congress) (approved February 20, 1946) merely states that the short title is "Employment Act of 1946."

Section 2

Section 2 is the "Declaration of Policy." This has received so much attention that it will be quoted here in full, with proposed additions to the text *italicized* (as also subsequently) and proposed deletions placed within square brackets:

Sec. 2. The Congress hereby declares that it is the continuing policy and responsibility of the Federal Government to use all practicable means consistent with its needs and obligations and other essential considerations of national policy, with the assistance and cooperation of industry, agriculture, labor, and State and local governments, to coordinate and utilize all its plans, functions, and resources for the purpose of creating and maintaining, in a manner calculated to foster and promote free competitive enterprise and the general welfare, conditions under which there will be [afforded] *the assurance of* useful employment opportunities, including self-employment, for those able, willing, and seeking to work [, and to promote maximum employment, production, and purchasing power]; *and opportunities for training, to improve employability; and healthy growth of production, with full, non-inflationary employment and purchasing power.*

COMMENTS: (1) It is necessary to include an assurance of employment opportunity, since that is the heart of the matter. (The rather profuse introductory language of this

Declaration might perhaps be pruned a little too without sacrificing vital safeguards, but that is not essential, and the changes suggested here are purposely held to a minimum.) (2) The concept of "maximum employment . . . " has been a false lead from the beginning. Maximum purchasing power is inflationary. Maximum employment is either inflationary or simply weak ("let's do the best we can"). And maximum production is now more than ever open to challenge as a national objective, both psychologically and ecologically. Hence there is much to be said for rewording the final clause.

(3) The Employment Act is not the place where training programs should be spelled out. As far as policy is concerned, however, there is or should be a national purpose not only to provide employment opportunities for all those able, willing, and seeking to work but also to fight against so-called unemployability; that is, to help anyone, "willing" and "seeking" but not as yet "able," to overcome his or her inability. Hence the end of the Declaration could well refer to that issue too, as here suggested.

Section 3

Section 3 deals with the "Economic Report of the President." Additional language is proposed for the first subsection in order to give special emphasis to certain recommendations, not now debarred but not explicitly required either, which the Economic Report definitely needs to include:

Sec. 3.   (a) The President shall transmit to the Congress not later than January 20 of each year an economic report (hereinafter called the 'Economic Report') setting forth (1) the levels of employment, production, and purchasing power obtaining in the United States and such levels needed to carry out the policy declared in section 2, *including specifically the minimum and maximum levels of employment recommended in the light of that policy, and the minimum and maximum rates of aggregate personal consumption expenditures deemed consistent with that policy in view of the program of Federal Government purchases of goods and services recommended to be undertaken and the anticipated other demands on the national product*; (2) current and foreseeable trends in the levels of employment, production, and purchasing power; (3) a review of the economic program of the Federal Government and a review of economic conditions affecting employment in the United States or any considerable portion thereof during the preceding year and of their effect upon employment, production, and purchasing power; and (4) a program for carrying out the policy declared in section 2, together with such recommendations for legislation as he may deem necessary or desirable.

COMMENTS: (1) The proposed minimum level of employment (in terms, presumably, of the seasonally adjusted monthly national total reported by the Department of Labor) would reflect the President's view of the correct statistical definition of full employment for the year ahead. This quantity would be derived by estimating the civilian labor force and subtracting the amount of unemployment that seemed to the President reasonable in the light of production shifts, manpower policies, and labor mobility at the time (the allowance for "necessary frictional unemployment"). Apart from labor-force growth due to the changing size and age-composition of the population, an effective full-employment policy would no doubt also bring into the picture at the beginning many persons previously not even on record as wanting to work. No need, however, to attempt the impossible. In the transition period from our present excessive unemployment, the President could if he thought best propose moving up to full employment by stages and reaching it in, for example, the second quarter of the second year.

(2) A maximum limit on employment is needed too, as a safeguard against inflation. (Purely as illustration, if the President in some year proposed a minimum of 86.5 million jobs, he might also state that anything above 87.8 million jobs would represent over-employment—too tight a situation in the labor market, with too much upward pressure on pay scales and on total income payments.)

(3) Key importance attaches to also setting limits to personal consumption expenditures (as compiled quarterly, at seasonally adjusted annual rates, by the Department of Commerce), and to deriving this target in the manner indicated. In the first place, since the President would of course state that any expansion or contraction of his recommended government program would imply an opposite change in needed consumer spending, this approach would eliminate the fear that a government commitment to serve as "employer of last resort" might lead to a degree of expansion of the public sector that was unacceptable to Congress. Such a government commitment— such underwriting of the job market—would still be essential, of course; and some consequent manipulation of the level of employment on public works and services would result, in compensation for net "error" in estimating other forms of demand and the employment-generating effect of a given demand. But there would be no inherent one-way bias toward government expansion, no greater probability (if the mid-point between the employment floor and ceiling were aimed at to begin with) of a need to accelerate public works and services than of a need to decelerate them. Hence this approach would remove a basic obstacle to the solution of the problem of making continuous full employment possible in practice.

This approach would also greatly help to remove the second basic obstacle, which is the fear of inflation. While that subject can best be viewed in a comprehensive way at a later point in this article, it is evident that a firm ceiling on consumer spending (mentioned here, explained in due course) would act as a powerful brake against inflationary demand spirals, especially when coupled with the proposed ceiling on employment.

To return to the computations envisaged. First of all, all the statistical series needed are continuously available. Second, while all the components of gross national expenditures, or GNP, would be used for deriving the needed consumer spending, there is no proposal here that the GNP itself or any of its components except consumer spending should have lower and upper limits set. The suggested procedures do not imply control over private investment decisions, for instance. (Given the permanently high final-product markets implied by the policy, private domestic investment could be expected to continue reasonably high also, with its cyclical swings damped down considerably. In estimating it for the purposes here in view, there might be advantages in choosing a mid-point figure on the diminished investment cycle rather than an actual forecast figure. This would look toward having fluctuations in private construction offset by opposite *ex post* fluctuations of public works rather than by opposite *ex ante* fluctuations of private consumer spending.)

This much having been said, the technical estimating procedure may be clarified, at least in outline. Other things (specifically, the sum of State and local government purchases of goods and services, gross private or business domestic investments, and net exports of goods and services) being equal, the needed total of (a) private consumer spending and (b) Federal Government spending for goods and services would remain constant too. ("Needed" here translates into required for a full-employment level of GNP, at a given level of prices.) In point of fact, other things cannot be expected to be quite equal if the ratio of (a) to (b) changes. In particular, certain common types of government spending yield more employment, dollar for dollar, than does more private consumer spending. A substantial program of public service employment would, moreover, have the great advantage that it would help to ease the disproportionately high unemployment among less-skilled and less-educated workers. But differences such as these can all be roughly estimated, just as can the other components of the GNP. Thus, the President would add his optional items to the relatively fixed or unavoidable ones already there and would state what total volume of purchases of goods and services he wanted the Federal Government itself to undertake. He would then specify the level of private consumer spending that in his view would be required to be associated with that much Federal Government spending in order to have, at the price level which he anticipated, an aggregate market capable of sustaining full employment as he had defined it. And no doubt he would also suggest—without needing to have the law say so—a scale of variations of the consumer component that would be appropriate in case Congress introduced variations of the government component.

Here also appears the third major advantage from pegging consumer spending. An increase of net exports has often been sought in the past as a solution for our employment, even though other countries might suffer from the action we took. The proposed approach would turn the problem around, calling for an expansion of the domestic market (via larger consumer spending) when the foreign market (net exports) was projected as declining. Consequently this approach would allay fears of a shortage of markets in the overall sense, and so would help us to maintain a liberal foreign-trade policy based on the widest interpretation of national self-interest.

(4) Part (4) of the subsection asks the President to set forth his program and, if necessary or desirable, recommend new legislation. Although the text here probably needs no formal amplification, the President would clearly be concerned—under this proposal—not only with legislative and administrative measures directly or indirectly affecting the performance of the economy on a continuing basis (welfare reform and antitrust action, for instance) but also with special compensatory measures. The latter would be for use only when that might prove necessary to keep total employment, total personal consumption expenditures, or both from straying outside their specified limits. The subject of contingent, compensatory measures is, however, reserved for later discussion.

Not to overlook the regional aspect of the employment problem—the President's program would certainly not limit itself to questions of national averages. Also dealt with in his recommendations would naturally be the continuing special needs of the country's Appalachias, as well as any unusually severe local job shortages of a more temporary nature brought about, say, by technological change or import competition.

No comment is required on the remainder of section 3. Subsection (b) authorizes the

President also to transmit supplementary reports to Congress. Subsection (c) states that the Economic Report and any supplements shall be referred by Congress to its Joint Economic Committee.

Section 4

Section 4 of the Act deals at some length, in six subsections, with the "Council of Economic Advisers to the President." The functions of this three-member Council, established in the Executive Office of the President, are essentially those implied by its title.

Section 5

Section 5, the last one as the Act now stands, brings us to the "Joint Economic Committee." Here again the text deals largely with matters outside the scope of the present analysis, such as the Committee's composition (ten Senators and ten Members of the House of Representatives, with the majority party represented by six members in each case), the holding of hearings, the appointment of experts, consultants, and other assistants, the procurement of printing and binding, the authorization of necessary appropriations, and so on. Subsection (b), however, one of the five subsections, is concerned with the vital issue of what happens to the President's Economic Report, and here a brief amendment needs to be incorporated, consequential on what comes later. With the proposed addition, this subsection would read:

(b)   It shall be the function of the joint committee—

(1) to make a continuing study of matters relating to the Economic Report;

(2) to study means of coordinating programs in order to further the policy of this Act; and

(3) as a guide to the several committees of the Congress dealing with legislation relating to the Economic Report, not later than March 1, of each year (beginning with the year 1947), to file a report with the Senate and the House of Representatives containing its findings and recommendations with respect to each of the main recommendations made by the President in the Economic Report, *together with a draft Joint Resolution for the consideration of the Congress as provided for in section 6;* and from time to time to make such other reports and recommendations to the Senate and House of Representatives as it deems advisable.

COMMENTS: (1) The process which the Act has caused the President and his advisers to initiate each year by preparing the Economic Report should no longer be allowed to disappear in thin air at the end. Rather, if there is to be the practical possibility of assuring continuous full employment, it is essential that Congress as a whole should also assume appropriate responsibilities. Everything hinges on that.

(2)   A procedural problem arises at this point because the Joint Economic Committee, in spite of what the law says about its powers to recommend, is not regarded as having the authority to recommend "legislative" action to Congress as a whole. Logically speaking, this Committee, with its detailed understanding of the subject, is clearly the one to prepare the annual draft joint resolution. As an interim measure it

might if necessary work with one or more of the other, legislative committees in preparing the resolution for submission to Congress as a whole.

Section 6

We come now to the decisive amendment that would complete the Employment Act by making provision for nearly all the action required to assure continuous full employment from that time on. This proposed new section 6 would presumably be entitled "Congressional Action on the Report of the Joint Economic Committee," and could for brevity be phrased approximately as follows:

Sec. 6.   As soon as practicable after the filing of the report of the Joint Economic Committee, the Congress shall by joint resolution of the Senate and the House of Representatives set forth its decisions with respect to—

(a) the minimum and maximum acceptable levels of employment throughout the year in question;

(b) the minimum and maximum acceptable rates of aggregate personal consumption expenditures throughout the year;

(c) the preventive action to be taken by the President if employment should at any time tend to fall below its minimum, or rise above it maximum, acceptable level as defined in (a); and

(d) the preventive action to be taken by the President in case personal consumption expenditures should at any time tend to fall below their minimum, or rise above their maximum, acceptable rate as defined in (b).

COMMENTS: (1) In adopting this amendment Congress would obviously not be committing future Congresses on the substance of their decisions on the four indicated subjects but only on always reaching some definite decisions on them.

(2)   Congress would always have the option to agree with or differ from the President on the minimum and maximum acceptable levels of employment, or in other words on what "full employment" should mean for operating purposes. It might take a different view, for example, of the size of the labor force (the Joint Economic Committee has the help of its own staff experts); or of how much frictional unemployment was acceptable (the President might have considered, say, 3 percent unemployment as tantamount to full employment, whereas Congress preferred 3.5 percent, or 2.5 percent); or of how wide a gap should be allowed betweeen minimum and maximum limits.

(3)   The decision on acceptable rates of aggregate personal consumption expenditures would above all settle the public-versus-private-sector issue in the way Congress wanted it settled at the time. Suppose that in some year the President's program if adopted would go so far in reordering the country's priorities as to increase not only the overall emphasis on social welfare fields (health, education, low-cost housing, anti-pollution, and so on) but also the percentage of GNP represented by the government's own purchases of goods and services. The majority in Congress might agree—or go even farther. On the other hand, perhaps the majority would favor maintaining the existing GNP ratios instead. Thus, to illustrate, Congress might some year decide that the acceptable limits to consumer spending would be $765 billion and $780 billion, whereas the President, having different GNP proportions (more heavily weighted on the

government side) in mind, had recommended a range of only $745–760 billion.

(4) While decisions under proposed clause 6(b) would thus clearly imply a certain general view of the government's economic role, they would not tie the hands of the Committees on Appropriations, let alone exert any refined degree of control over the elusive question of how much the Federal Government would in fact spend before the year was out. As already noted, the purpose of the pre-announced limits to consumer spending would be quite different: first, to separate the "big government" issue from the full-employment issue; second, to provide, by way of the maximum limit set, a brake against any inflationary upward spending spiral; and third, to make it possible to accept a reduction in our traditional export surplus—since our ability to maintain adequate total markets for domestic output would remain unaffected.

(5) Fundamental to proposed clauses (c) and (d) is that both provide for action that would be made contingent on the showing of the chosen indicators and mandatory in application when one or both of those indicators began to move outside the Congressionally predetermined range. In other words, as far as these compensatory adjustments are concerned (other sorts of economic legislation are dealt with just below), Congress would begin making the rules in advance and would have a more basic policy-making role.

(6) Under clause (c) Congress would be writing the specifications for a government commitment to serve as employer of last resort. Broadly speaking, that commitment would necessarily entail contingent accelerations and decelerations of public works and services. What would be up for decision would be such things as the exact content of that category for the purpose in hand (with reference, for example, to Federally financed State and local government projects and perhaps private non-profit projects); how to secure an adequate, ready reserve shelf of suitable projects; and the best formula for apportioning accelerations and decelerations by States.

(7) Under clause (d) Congress would have a wide range of options. It might, for example, decide that, when and if adjusting aggregate personal consumption expenditures should prove necessary, this would be done by temporarily reducing or increasing personal income taxes—and (on the "up" side, at least) by taking some other fiscal action that would comparably benefit low-income groups not liable for income tax. Or, if welfare reform had led to adoption of a plan guaranteeing a minimum income to all families and single individuals as a matter of right, and of a negative income tax as the pay-out mechanism for this, then Congress might decide that the income tax itself (positive and negative) should be the vehicle for all the necessary adjustments. The allowances or negative taxes would in that case be raised, and the positive income taxes lowered, when necessary to increase consumer spending, and conversely the positive income taxes would be raised, and the allowances lowered (but never below their base level), when necessary to decrease it. On the other hand, Congressional economists might consider the variations in consumers' saving could still—even in the absence of booms and slumps—partly frustrate any effort to control their spending by merely controlling their disposable income. In that case Congress might decide on a more direct procedure.

(8) For example, Congress could enact a Federal sales tax/sales bonus which would be put on a standby basis to be used only for lowering or raising consumer spending to hold that aggregate within the stipulated limits. As a bonus, when spending was running too low, it would work like a (universal) stamp plan: all buyers of goods and services at

retail would during pay-out periods receive stamps convertible (unlike food stamps) into cash at a bank or post-office if promptly presented. As a tax, it would automatically lower the amount of consumer expenditure received net of tax by business, that being then designated the amount required to be held below the established ceiling. Consumer spending could thus beyond any doubt be restrained to any desired extent, any "stubbornness" in spending or saving propensities (and any reluctance to regulate consumer credit) to the contrary withstanding; or alternatively, it could be given a very powerful incentive for expansion. (This fiscal device was first proposed in my communication "On Underwriting Consumption and Employment" published in *The American Economic Review* in September, 1955.)

(9) To see, finally, how this proposed unified action by Congress as a whole would mesh with the normal functioning of the Congressional committee system, let us suppose, for example, that the House Ways and Means Committee took up again the general subject of tax reform. While such tax changes as Congress ultimately adopted would no doubt alter the distribution of the tax burden and probably also the level of tax revenue, neither the target-fixing under section 6(b) nor the choosing of a contingent compensatory formula under section 6(d) would be affected. What almost certainly would be affected is the actual (preadjustment) rate of consumer spending and its likelihood of falling within the acceptable range "of its own accord";—and hence also the likelihood that the President would actually have to apply the contingent adjustment measures provided for under 6(d).

(10) Incidentally, there would be some presumption that by a kind of feedback effect any unduly large or frequent need to take either type of compensatory action (to adjust consumer spending or to adjust employment) would lead to the sponsorship and passage of improved legislation relating to distribution of income, enforcement of competition and/or regulation of monopoly, or other factors strategically affecting the self-balancing capacity of the economy.

*　　*　　*

The above-described actions required to effectuate this proposal—first, the enactment of certain amendments to the Employment Act; second, the annual sequences of steps by the Council of Economic Advisers, the President, the Joint Economic Committee, and Congress as a whole—would of course need to be supported by operational actions. The proposed approach is broadly describable as Economic Performance Insurance, and the country is taking out that kind of insurance policy could expect to see an "automatic" response to the key signals. But it is important to realize that this "automaticity" could not eliminate the need for decisions at the operating level. On the contrary, judgment would be called for not only in the recurrent formulation of terms and procedures but also in the execution process.

The agencies to be designated by the President to operate under this law need not, it would seem, be specified in the Employment Act. The only two statistical indicators required to serve as primary action signals are currently prepared by the Departments of Labor and Commerce, as already noted. Perhaps the Labor Department would also be given broad responsibility over accelerations and decelerations of public works and services. Meanwhile the Internal Revenue Service would have a major part to play in administering the contingent adjustments in consumer spending or disposable income, but would work, presumably, in close collaboration with the Department of Health, Education, and Welfare and other agencies of the Executive Branch.

Timing would present the big challenge. Postponing all action until the employment level or the rate of consumer spending was already too high or too low to be "acceptable" would breach the continuity of the system before correction could take hold. Then again, after any correction was made, the question would arise as to just how soon (at what point within the acceptable performance range) the use of the compensatory device should be terminated.

At present the seasonally adjusted monthly employment totals are published some three weeks after the statistical survey—in the early days of the next month; and preliminary quarterly personal consumption expenditures data, at seasonally adjusted annual rates, are published seven weeks or a little less after the end of each quarter. Those time intervals could perhaps be shortened somewhat; in any case, government experts with access to the data can certainly see trends emerging before the results are published. Nevertheless, there must also be considered the further time lag between ordering a compensatory measure instituted and having it put into effect. For example, an immediate acceleration of public works and services is hardly possible on a geographically widespread basis. In signing a $1 billion appropriation bill to create emergency public service jobs President Nixon said on August 9, 1971 that the first group of unemployed should be at the new jobs by Labor Day—nearly a month later. Of course, however, we neither have nor have had anything approaching either an adequate reserve shelf of public works and services or an adequate system of getting ready to use it; to remedy those deficiencies would be a major project to be undertaken concurrently with amending the Employment Act itself.

The best answer to problems of timing would thus probably combine at least the following three elements: (1) Congress might agree that employment and consumer spending could without prejudice be at "unacceptable" levels briefly—say, for a single reporting period. (2) Substantial effort and expense should be undertaken to build up an adequate reserve shelf on a nationwide basis, and also to give local organizations the capacity for swift action in carrying out Washington directives in regard both to "last resort" employment and to the fiscal means chosen for adjusting consumer spending. (3) The Federal agencies in charge should probably issue an "alert" before employment or consumer spending actually went beyond an upper or lower limit, if it seriously threatened to do so. Their staff economists would thus be expected to use a fairly wide range of data and forecasting procedures. Moreover some wrong guesses would inevitably occur, so that some expense would be incurred throughout the country in mobilizing forces to meet contingencies that failed to materialize. Reimbursing such expenses would simpy be, then, one of the financial costs of maintaining a full-employment system.

*   *   *

A concluding word about inflation. If full employment were, as so often alleged, bound to generate inflation, amending the Employment Act to give it real teeth might have little point. But two recent developments have brought that gloomy thesis into the most serious question—first, the ample demonstration that inflation now tends to occur even without full employment, and second, the not unrelated shift of informed public opinion into favoring an incomes policy of some kind to help maintain price stability.

Thus full employment need no longer carry such burdens as do not, properly speaking, belong to it.

More than that, however, it is here submitted that a program of guaranteed full employment along the lines suggested would not only not feed inflation but actually be the best cure for inflation. This is asserted for two reasons in combination. First, the ceilings on employment and on consumer spending that would be imposed under this approach would choke off upward demand spirals almost entirely. That is the built-in "mechanical" aspect. It would limit "demand pull" directly, as already emphasized, and indirectly it would also moderate the wage-demand side of the "cost push" by holding down the prices that make up the worker's cost of living. Second, there is the psychological point that cannot be proved but that should appeal to common sense—a point that would arise from the very fact of the government's readiness to commit itself in this unprecedented way. An agreement on the part of the government to assure a total market adequate for business prosperity, and to assure continuous full employment for labor, should be enough to persuade business and labor leaders to agree to abide by some reasonable set of price and wage guidelines.

Those who blame inflation on the incurable wickedness of Big Business or Big Labor or both often seem unaware of how far the behavior of both has been caused by the malfunctioning of our economy—its cyclical instability combined with secular weakness—the inevitability of which is precisely what needs to be denied. Once the government stood ready to assure continuously adequate total demand for products and for workers, (1) all businesses would have more chance to spread their overhead costs and hold prices down; (2) management in areas of administered pricing could logically give up planning for extra profits in boom times to cushion losses in future slumps; and (3) union leaders would feel less pressure to demand extreme hourly wage rates on the one hand, or annual pay guarantees on the other, to fortify their members against the return of unemployment.

To put this in context—as these words are being written, the country is deep in President Nixon's economic Phase II. Whether this experiment with a Wage Board and a Price Commission will be followed soon by selective permanent legal controls or by some other incomes policy is impossible to say. But what the government commitments proposed in this article would in any case contribute, when it comes to resolving the ultimate hard-core part of the "cost push" phenomenon, is to open the door as wide as possible to achieving essential results by voluntary cooperation.

14

More Newspaper Letters and Articles

INSURING A STABLE ECONOMY

The problems that by their and our very nature hold our attention are not economic (technical)—they are social (human and moral): how to preserve our planet and live in decent friendship and cooperation with our fellow men of every age, race, and creed. Ecology, Vietnam, racial discrimination, poverty, the revolt of youth.

Nevertheless, we have to solve the problem of economic performance—which we are obviously failing to do at this time—in order to gain even the chance to solve some of our most pressing human problems. We have no choice but to attend to the economic foundations of our social structure.

An approach has been developed which does—that is, would—solve the problem of economic performance in this country and also as far as the economic relations of America with the rest of the world are concerned. This approach I will call "Economic Performance Insurance" (EPI).

Economic Performance Insurance would prevent recessions and would also prevent inflation. On the one hand, it would guarantee the continuous maintenance of full employment—no unemployment in excess of the amount decided on in advance by reasonable men as constituting "necessary frictional unemployment." On the other, it would rule out spiraling prices by curbing both demand-pull and cost-push inflation.

Excessive demand-pull would be checked because the EPI mechanism would set not only floors but also ceilings to aggregate employment and to aggregate consumer spending. Excessive cost-push would cease because the government's commitment to EPI would provide a sound basis for reasonable counter-commitments on their pricing policies by business and labor. (In short, in this kind of "incomes policy," the responsibility would be mutual, as it should be.)

Some corollary benefits would be: restoration of opportunity for all as a cardinal American principle; help in solving the race problem by making equal employment

---

Reprinted by permission from the *Honolulu Advertiser*, August 14, 1971.

opportunity efforts able to success; help in eradicating poverty, both by increasing the amount of paid labor and by creating labor market conditions that would tend to wipe out substandard wages; help in having good-neighbor economic policies, especially by establishing that export surpluses would no longer be needed as a condition for our own domestic full-employment prosperity.

The key to the feasibility of instituting EPI lies in the fact that this approach responds to the existing division of economic powers between the President and Congress and to the existing division of views in the nation on the public-versus-private-sector issue. The noncontroversial problem of maintaining the right level of operation of our economy would be kept quite separate from the ongoing struggle to decide on the size of the government's own program.

In terms of legislation what is required is a comparatively simple amendment to the Employment Act of 1946 which would establish a clear congressional responsibility in this field, to be exercised year by year in specific terms after Congress has received and studied the President's proposals as set forth in his Economic Report.

REMEDY FOR THE NEW MERCANTILISM

To the Editor: Congratulations on your July 29 editorial on "The New Mercantilism." America has, as you point out, become a "mature creditor" nation—one that receives a large and growing return flow of interest and dividends from past foreign loans and investments, while the traditional surplus on merchandise trade declines. This in principle need not be as frightening as many congressmen of both parties have reportedly found it.

Basically, as you say, our response should not be to adopt "mercantilist" subsidies for exports or protectionist measures such as import quotas. Instead we should learn to avoid damage to the American economy as these fundamental international shifts occur. It is stronger domestic economic measures against unemployment and inflation that offer the right solution.

The crux of the problem, however, is this: how can we in fact avoid damage to our own economy as our export surplus shrinks or even vanishes? One must answer this question.

In general terms the answer is that we must learn to control the aggregate of the huge domestic components of total expenditures for domestic output, and purposely move that aggregate up (or down) as the relatively tiny export surplus goes down (or up). In practice this means that the personal consumption expenditures component of G.N.P. needs to be so adjusted; the other two components—private domestic investment and Government purchases—are bound to obey other laws.

Aggregate consumer spending can be perfectly well controlled and adjusted to the needs of full employment in the light of the trend in the export balance (and the current view of the desirable size of the Government's own role). This is so because Congress can, by slightly amending the Employment Act of 1946, assume the responsibility of at last going beyond mere criticism of the President's annual economic report and can decide each year at what level consumer spending, as well as employment itself, is to be held.

This approach also clearly brings inflation control within reach, for two reasons. First, it envisages ceilings to employment and consumer spending as well as floors.

Second, such an assumption of responsibility by the Government is the natural psychological precondition for expecting business and labor to act responsibly on prices and wages. If that sounds unrealistic, let me phrase it differently: this approach will minimize the element of compulsion in the "incomes policy" of which we undoubtedly now stand in need.

John H. G. Pierson
Washington, July 29, 1971

FULL EMPLOYMENT NEED NOT GENERATE INFLATION

The confrontation between fear of inflation and fear of unemployment ought to be resolved before it fires up racial conflict and youth revolt to destroy our society.

We are told that there has to be a "trade-off": if we want greater price stability, we must put up with more unemployment. When rising demand has squeezed most of the slack out of the goods and labor markets, business and labor have the power to make prices and wages spiral upward.

In this spiral, profits and prices tend to rise first, while union wage demands often far exceed productivity increases. The whole process bristles with warranted recriminations.

Many people wonder, since there's so much that obviously needs doing (take pollution control, urban redevelopment, low-cost housing, health, education, municipal services), why intelligent social planning under government leadership couldn't solve the whole problem. Workers would have the jobs. And if prosperity were definitely here to stay, big business could charge lower prices because excess profits would no longer be needed against future recessions. Government revenues would soar even if tax rates were lowered.

Doubtless the main obstacle to acceptance of this approach has long been—and may still be today—a fear of a creeping-socialist effort to take the economy over on the pretext of keeping it going.

Be that as it may, our experts consider the trade-off as axiomatic, and focus on what sort of trade-off to make and how to maneuver. Some economist may advise stopping inflation at any cost. When seeking election or re-election, one probably thinks first about stopping the rise in unemployment.

Now a narrow political view of this matter could be tragically inadequate. That sort of compromise won't do at all. Even to attain full employment is not enough; its continuation has to be assured. What we need is a policy that guarantees that everyone seeking and able (or trainable to become able) to work will hereafter always have that opportunity.

We need this because universal opportunity to have a bona-fide life is what America is supposed to be all about. We need it because the racial problem is practically insoluble without it. We need it for ending poverty in this country—the extra wage income, to make cash and food-stamp allowances less expensive, depends on our having full employment to give more jobs and minimize chances of paying substandard wages. (On improved minimum wage laws as well.)

Our international postion, too, is at stake. We need guaranteed full employment to become the good neighbor we want to be. Not only must we feel able to assist poorer countries that ask economic aid, but also be able to stick to liberal trading principles— because assured of a permanently adequate total market for our own products—and help them move "from aid to trade" as they become ready for it.

But what of inflation? Justice to fixed-income receivers demands that we stop inflation, and so does our need to remain internationally competitive, to protect our balance of payments. Is there really a way out of the impasse?

I submit that there is, and that a solution (described in detail elsewhere) can be broadly envisaged along the lines set out below. It would be "economic performance insurance," guarding against both deflation—too little demand for goods and labor—and inflation—too much demand. It would fully support our private enterprise system and the traditional division of powers between Congress and the President. Let me briefly explain.

(1)   Assurance against deflation: Full employment would be defined and guaranteed each year in practical statistical terms. It would then be achieved by in effect pegging total demand (GNP) in advance at the presumptively right level, with the government coming in as employer of last resort (and disemployer of "first resort") to compensate up or down in case of significant net error in the calculations.

(2)   Acceptability to private enterprise: Business would be assured of an adequate market for which to compete, and against unwanted expansion of the public sector at the expense of the private sector. This would result from combining the job-level guarantee with a guarantee of the level of private consumer spending, calculated from the GNP goal after noting how much government spending for goods and services was actually endorsed by Congress. (Also noted would be State and local government spending, private domestic investment, and—with implications already mentioned—net exports.)

If private consumer spending should tend to fall short of or exceed the promised rate, adjustment would be mandatory through taxes and/or transfer payments (social insurance etc.) vis-a-vis individuals. A negative income tax such as could evolve from President Nixon's welfare reform program would provide an especially convenient although not indispensable mechanism.

(3)   Avoidance of inflation: The guarantees of employment and consumer spending would have ceilings as well as floors. Two powerful brakes would thus act against upward spirals. Besides, on the strength of those governmental guarantees, including the brakes, labor and business leaders could be expected to support some system of wage and price guidelines to reduce "cost push" pressure.

My thesis clearly does not depend, however, on the validity of this expectation, which some will consider unrealistic. For an "incomes policy" has to be evolved in any case. Beyond the "quick freeze" urged by a number of Democratic leaders, probably desirable as a temporary measure, we might even need the permanent legal controls on wages and prices which Galbraith sees as essential for non-inflationary "high" employment in future. (I would doubt that need, however, considering the different approach envisaged.)

(4)   The relationship between the President and Congress: No unreasonable element would be introduced. Congress would not be asked to rubber-stamp a Presidential spending program or give the President wide discretionary powers.

The President's annual economic recommendations under the Employment Act would henceforth include: (a) a full-employment target, (b) a consumer spending target consistent with the recommended government spending program, (c) procedures for adjusting the job total up or down if its target was being missed, and (d) similarly contingent methods for adjusting consumer spending. The vital amendment to that Act would be this: Congress would be obligated not to rest content with criticism but to establish final decisions for the year on those same points. The policy being thus set, execution of adjustments (c) and (d), when actually called for by the current showing of the chosen statistical series, would logically rest with the President.

Questions of prerogative are involved but also questions of commitment, and it is commitment—the willingness to assume appropriate responsibility—that is really essential here.

ARE PERMANENT CONTROLS ON PRICES NEEDED OR NOT?

Addressing the Fabians in England, John Kenneth Galbraith stated again the other day that permanent wage and price controls are essential if we are to have high employment without intolerable inflation in future. The key word is "permanent." This is not the temporary "quick freeze" idea advocated by Congressman Henry S. Reuss and others for stopping inflation now.

"There are," says the next president of the American Economic Association, "no alternatives." Keynesian fiscal and monetary management simply cannot stand up any longer against the power of big unions and big corporations. "At any near approach to full employment, unions can seek and win wage increases much in excess of productivity gains, because . . . corporations can retrieve wage increases and something more."

He adds that the necessary "forever" controls are technically feasible in the U.S. because our economic structure is such that "only a few hundred unions and a couple of thousand corporations need be touched."

What about it? Are these conclusions prophetic or premature?

My view is that this positive suggestion is much to be preferred to the fashionable negative opinion that there is just no way of having full employment and price stability both (the "trade-off" philosophy, sanctified statistically by the "Phillips curve"). Galbraith may be right, too, that legal controls are the only answer. Certainly this cannot be disproved as of now.

But it cannot be proved yet either. Before we treat it as though it were, I suggest that we first try a different approach: a "quick freeze" now, then the offer of a firm guarantee of permanent full employment, in exchange for which business and labor leaders should agree to abide by some reasonable set of price and wage guidelines.

Under this proposal, which I have elaborated in books and articles, there would also be a further inflation-stopper in the form of a ceiling on aggregate private consumer spending. That is, under an amendment to the Employment Act of 1946, Congress would each year set top and bottom limits to consumer spending as well as to employment itself.

This system of "Economic Performance Insurance" would be politically possible because the public-versus-private-sector issue would be automatically disentangled from it. The current consumer spending target would be set in the light of how much government spending for goods and services Congress actually favored—and also (another story) in the light of an internationally sound policy on imports and exports, so sadly lacking today.

To get our national priorities right we obviously need a big expansion of certain public services; at least I join with Galbraith and no doubt millions of others in so asserting. But if a presidential plan along that line were trimmed down in Congress for any reason, we would still, under my proposal, accomplish the super-priority of full employment (without inflation).

According to Lee Cohn in *The Washington Star* of Nov. 10, Chairman Paul W. McCracken of the Council of Economic Advisers now favors a "social bargain" under which the government would stimulate vigorous economic expansion if labor and business would curb wage and price increases. This sounds like at least a faint echo of the proposal which I have re-stated above.

But why be ambiguous about it? Surely the time for ambiguity or timidity in facing our bigger social and economic problems is now past. Let our national leaders—in one party or the other or both—come out flatly for guaranteed full employment, and negotiate with big business and big labor with that offer as the heart of the deal.

If Galbraith is right, this wouldn't work. Very well; we could then adopt his system of controls. But as things stand today, the burden of proof still seems to be on those who despair of business and labor ever cooperating with society unless literally forced to do so. Let the government offer them a solid commitment to permanent non-inflationary full employment, and personally I think they would want to go along.

Reprinted by permission from the *Honolulu Advertiser*, November 30, 1970.

ANOTHER APPROACH

The current talk about an "incomes policy," just given new impetus by Fed Chairman Burns, clearly assumes—often too smugly, I feel—that business and labor should learn to be responsible to the rest of us or else must be made to be. Period.

Some form of suasion or even outright price and wage control may indeed be necessary to choke off the present inflation. A better answer will be called for soon, however. The real key to governmental leadership on the wage-price front and to curbing the misuse of business or labor market power surely does not lie in either admonishing or forcing business and labor to practice self-denial and responsibility—not in that alone, at any rate—it lies in first or simultaneously assuming the government's own proper responsibility.

That is to say, it lies in having the government guarantee the opportunity to work and the level of aggregate demand for goods and services which is a requisite for that continuous full-employment condition. If the government would in this way do its own part in maintaining a healthy economy, why should not labor and business agree to do theirs?

Those "cost-push" pressures toward inflation would then abate. Not only that but the mechanism essential for continuous full employment in a country with our traditions would provide for ceilings as well as floors on the number of jobs and on the rate of private consumer spending, so that inflation would also be restrained from the side of demand. (These conclusions, of course, run counter to the prevailing "trade-off" theory, that the price of less inflation is more unemployment.)

The political feasibility of giving such a guarantee arises out of the insufficiently appreciated fact that maintaining the right overall rate of operation for the economy, which is non-controversial, can be separated from the controversial public-versus-private-sector issue. If Congress wanted to modify the President's proposed federal spending program it could do so, without sacrificing a full-employment gross national product, by simply moving the consumer spending target in the opposite direction.

John H. G. Pierson
Washington

A letter to the editor of *The Washington Post*, printed May 26, 1970. Reprinted by permission.

GUARANTEED INCOME AND GUARANTEED JOB

Hunger can be ended in America quickly. After that, well within the '70s, everyone's income can be raised above the poverty line. A key move in that direction would be a guaranteed minimum household income. The technical problems have been solved on paper. Politically it could soon be possible.

Nevertheless, to guarantee incomes without guaranteeing the opportunity to work would be a mistake.

President Nixon's welfare program is a big step forward, but it falls short on both of those counts. It does not, as it stands, assure a minimum income to all Americans (with or without dependent children) as a matter of right. It does not make sure that everyone always has a chance for a decent job.

Though the work incentive feature is fine, the work requirement aspect is dated, considering how productive our technology has become. Work opportunity is what should be stressed today instead.

The guaranteed minimum should also, if possible, be set higher than Nixon's $1,600 for families of four, plus his say $720 in food stamps. Even a modest beginning, however, would still permit all incomes to be raised above the poverty line (about $3,600 for families of four) by drawing on other income sources too. Moreover, it is important to keep the minimum allowance in proper relation to minimum wages.

Cash allowances are the main thing. But food stamps should still be continued for as long as the poorest people in the country lack the means to buy enough nutritious food and meet their other basic needs at the same time.

What about those "other income sources?" Many poor persons (the aged or disabled, mothers with young children) obviously cannot or should not work. Nonetheless, work could still be the main source of additional income for the poor as a whole, assuming two things.

First, full employment, for more jobs. Second, higher pay at bottom levels, which can be brought about partly by improved minimum wage legislation and partly, again, by ending job scarcity, the condition which always tends to undermine wage levels, especially among poor, unorganized rural workers.

Besides helping the poor to have more income, guaranteed full employment is needed from a social standpoint to make opportunity real in America, and to reduce racial tensions. For equal-employment-opportunity efforts to succeed, the total opportunity has to be sufficient. "Insufficient but equal" faces a troubled future.

From the overall economic standpoint, guaranteed full employment would make recessions impossible and inflation highly unlikely, paradoxical as that may seem. Internationally, it would enable America to be a good neighbor. First of all, we Americans should and could be generous with aid to the developing countries. But, since our own prosperity would be established as totally independent of export surpluses, we could also buy their goods, including manufactures, to help them make the transition "from aid to trade."

As many people have pointed out, a reordering of domestic priorities is essential today, with emphasis on pollution control and environmental improvement, urban redevelopment and mass transit, low-cost housing, health, education, municipal services. Fortunately, this can also help to secure full employment.

But unfortunately it cannot—by itself alone—actually assure or guarantee full employment. Not because of any lack of things needing to be done, but because of differences of opinion about what should be done (the "creeping socialism" issue, for one thing) and because of the way our national economic policies are formulated and carried out.

Guaranteeing the level of consumer spending—together with the level of employment itself, naturally—would solve that problem. If Congress then wanted to modify the President's proposed Federal spending program, it could do so without sacrificing a full-employment gross national product, by simply moving the consumer spending target in the opposite direction.

Maintaining the right overall rate of operation for the economy, which is non-controversial, would have been cleanly separated from the controversial public-versus-private-sector issue.

Finally, what about inflation? First of all, the employment and consumer spending guarantees would have ceilings as well as floors, to restrain inflation from the side of demand and prevent the price-wage spiral.

Secondly, because the government was offering those guarantees, it would be in a position to persuade business, labor, and farm leaders to agree to follow some reasonable set of guidelines in establishing their selling prices, so that "cost push" inflation would be restrained too.

Here lies the explanation of that seeming paradox—the reason why the outright guaranteeing of full employment, far from representing a "well-intentioned but impractical" goal, would itself provide the best cure for inflation. The implications of this may be startling. It collides with the generally accepted "trade off" doctrine, according to which there is supposed to be an immutable inverse relation between inflation and unemployment. But that is an unduly pessimistic idea. It could and should be forgotten.

Reprinted by permission from the *Honolulu Advertiser*, March 27, 1970.

ECONOMIC INSURANCE

To the Editor: Your May 18 editorial "Dubious Economic Insurance" says that "Insurance against recession is needed, but both the nature and the timing of the President's latest fiscal dividend appear questionable." May I make three observations.

Insurance against recession is indeed very much needed, not only for domestic prosperity and full employment but also as essential support for a constructive United States economic foreign policy on trade and aid. The domestic and the international issues involved are so important that it seems time to stop juggling this (insurance against recession) as a phrase and instead establish it as a system.

Second, your editorial criticizes the nature of the President's latest fiscal dividend (cuts in excise taxes), saying that undue reliance is being put on tax cuts and too little on higher spending. I agree in general with your view but, precisely because we need the economic insurance, I cannot agree unconditionally.

Personally I strongly favor, as you do, meeting those "unfulfilled demands for public services—schools, hospitals, transportation—that only increases in spending can satisfy." This should be done because of the values involved and to some extent also because it is easier to get a quick employment lift that way than through tax cuts, as Leon Keyserling and others have pointed out.

But insured full employment does not depend on getting Congressional acceptance for any particular volume of public works and services. Consumer spending can still be raised by means of tax cuts to fill the residual gap.

Finally, your criticism of the timing of the President's move tends to confirm the great difficulties of economic prediction and hence the desirability of following an insurance approach rather than a forecasting approach. Without going into details here, the distinction would hinge on establishing separate targets for employment and (tied to expected domestic investment and the trade balance) for consumer spending; adjusting taxes—possibly through a reversible sales tax/sales premium arrangement—whenever consumer spending actually misses by more than the agreed margin; and stepping up or slowing down public works and services whenever employment, in spite of the supposedly adequate total effective demand, actually strays from its own target.

John H. G. Pierson
Riverside, Conn., May 18, 1965

Some Guidelines for a Rational Economic Policy

THE GUARANTEED INCOME APPROACH TO THE ABOLITION OF POVERTY

Poverty can be eradicated in America. Not only that, but the time is almost at hand when a guaranteed minimum household income might become a politically possible means towards that end.

The sooner the better. There could be a wrong way to go about it, however, and there is even some danger that we might take too restricted a view of our situation and choose the wrong way. That wrong way would be to guarantee a minimum income without also making the pivotal decision to guarantee the opportunity to work.

Imagine the irony of an America where "opportunity for all" meant you could count on being able to consume but not on having a share in the action of production!

Many people are not of working age and capacity, of course, and some who are quite able to work will still prefer not to. But that does not mean that participation in society's business is unimportant to able-bodied people in general. Who wants only to be kept comfortably alive?

For that matter, who wants to see a permanent division between all those who have sufficient advantages to be able to get and keep jobs and those unlucky ones outside the system who must somehow learn to endure a life on the dole?

There is no real doubt that hunger, at least, can be ended in America quickly, given the political will to do it. Surely we cannot in conscience delay where feeding hungry children is concerned, now that the facts have come to light. Then beyond that, well

---

These four articles are reprinted by permission from the *Monterey Peninsula Herald*, where they appeared originally in a 6-article series, March 2–7, 1970. The last two articles have been omitted since they were essentially an abridgment of Chapter 17. The athor's original headings for these articles have been restored.

within this decade of the 1970s, everyone's income can be raised above poverty levels.

Let it be granted that that will not in itself kill off entirely the sociological and psychological roots of the poverty problem: The folkways and attitudes of poverty will no doubt persist and regenerate here and there to some extent. But that is another story, less interesting at the moment than the income story, especially to those who are most immediately concerned.

The number of Americans living in poverty has been progressively declining—from 39.5 million to 25.4 million between the end of 1959 and the end of 1968 (from 22 per cent to below 13 percent of our total population) according to the official definition and count. This trend was expectable, given a reasonably prosperous situation for the country as a whole.

As our economy has grown more productive, average per capita income has risen, and *some* of the gain has accrued even to those at the bottom. Some poor people have had more work at better wages; others have benefited because our general prosperity (not to mention Michael Harrington's book on *The Other America*, or militancy among the blacks) has aroused our social conscience. Many at the lower end of the income scale have profited from the upward drift in income from Social Security, for instance, even though the insurance benefits go largely to the nonpoor. And the 1964 declaration of war on poverty brought the Office of Economic Opportunity into being to try in various ways to give the poor a better chance to compete.

Real progress has been made, even though many of the escapees from poverty are still "near poor" and many of those left behind are less well equipped to sustain the recent trend.

Richard Nixon will go down in history as the president who gave official recognition to the government's responsibility for eliminating poverty in America. Since urgency is implied, however, that requires an all-out attack, which he has not so far proposed.

He *has* proposed a better attack than we had before. The starting point is the abolition of the main part of our welfare system (aid to families with dependent children) in its present form. In place of that humanly degrading and economically counter-productive system we will soon have quite a different set of arrangements if the President's Family Assistance Program is enacted.

Personal certifications of income supplemented by spot checks will take the place of the indignities of the present eligibility investigations. A work incentive will begin to operate, through "retention of earnings"; i.e., relief payments will no longer be reduced dollar for dollar for income gained by taking a job.

(For the first $720 of earned income no reduction is proposed, then 50 cents on the dollar. Allowances stop at an income level of $3,920 for the customarily cited family of four.) Families will have an incentive to stay together, too, since states will no longer be able to deny relief, as half of them do now, to those dependent poor children who have a visible father as well as a mother.

These provisions should more than double the number of persons able to obtain some money to relieve their poverty. Moreover under this plan the federal government will put a floor under relief payments all over the country—at $1,600 a year for a family of four, higher than 20 states now pay—and so will narrow the unjustifiable differences between life on relief in New Jersey, New York or Massachusetts and in South Carolina, Alabama or Mississippi. This same family could also get $720 worth of food stamps free.

All of these things will unquestionably help. So will the increases in unemployment compensation and in public assistance to the aged, the blind, and the disabled which carry the administration's endorsement, as well as the proposed rise in the level of personal exemptions under the income tax. In short, Nixon's program does promise to speed the antipoverty program up.

But time is passing and it is only sober reporting to say that the total result from what the President has proposed is going to be too small. The program does not measure up either to the practical necessities imposed by rising racial tension or to the idealistic values now coming more into prominence as young people and others take stock of what they want our country to become.

What then is missing? It would be a mistake, I think, to conclude that the inadequacy of this program in its present form could be cured by just upping the payments which it proposes to give to many of the poor—insufficient though those allowances do indeed appear.

Rather, the main problem seems to lie in two limitations stemming from the general philosophy which has so far governed the approach. First, that the program misjudges the spirit of the times and studiously avoids being a guaranteed income program (some press comment to the contrary notwithstanding). Second, that in tackling the neglected problem of the "working poor" it misjudges also the native spirit of America by choosing to combine work incentive with work *requirement* instead of with work *opportunity*.

It is not difficult to see why this has happened. You—or your family provider—must work if you want to eat: at least the Protestant-Judaic ethic says so, and indeed that dictum arises out of practically the whole of mankind's hard struggle to wring a subsistence from nature. Thus in his election campaign Nixon appealed to workers themselves in the following terms:

"Nobody has a greater motive to get the out-of-work to work than today's worker.... One [thing on his mind] is to protect what he has, which is human enough; and the other is to resent the fellow who he believes is taking a free ride on the taxes that he, the worker, pays."

According to this view, we should stay away from a guaranteed income, which rewards nonworkers as well as workers and, in the process, undermines the incentive to work. So President Nixon has been at pains to emphasize that his nationwide floor under relief payments is *not* a guaranteed income plan.

Indeed it is not, though it can be said to point in that direction. Guaranteed income plans give income unconditionally, as a matter of right. This program on the other hand imposes definite conditions. Money is not to be paid to single unhandicapped adults less than 65 years of age; or to married couples with no dependent children; or to able-bodied parents who do have dependent children but refuse to accept job-training or work if suitable jobs are available locally, or transportation to such jobs.

(Mothers of preschool children, however, if they do not want to go to work and use the proposed newly funded day-care centers, can stay at home.)

What is wrong with this, in principle? Not a great deal, I think, except that it looks too much to the past and not enough to the future. But that in itself is a serious shortcoming.

With the onward march of technology, production shortages should continue to recede and the civilian output to rise, the drain from wars and military buildup permitting. So much so that it will be necessary to spread the work by progressively shorter work weeks, longer paid vacations, extended education and training, sabbatical periods, and so on.

Seeing this, some people have tended to push the panic button, envisaging the early displacement of man by machines in all production. According to them, automation has already made the system of income distribution based on contributions to production, and especially on work performed, wholly untenable. "We don't need people as producers," someone said (one wonders about the "we"), "we just need them as consumers."

Drawn in this manner, the picture is undoubtedly overdrawn. The need for continued hard work, not only to create a decent America but also to help raise up the pitifully low living standards in the under-developed parts of the world, is much greater than this view would have us suppose. Let us not, therefore, announce the demise of the present income distribution system too far in advance.

Nevertheless the time is coming when the realities of production will enforce frank recognition of the need for at least a hybrid system of distribution. And leadership in our present time of momentous changes should recognize that fact. Political leaders have to deal with what people really believe and want.

The newer "life style," less addicted to work, is the case in point here. Since this new outlook rests on the underlying changes in technology—whose dependence on past work is, of course, irrelevant—it is solidly based and will not go away. Hence it cannot well be ignored.

THE GUARANTEED INCOME APPROACH (continued)

From technological and sociopsychological facts which are readily available to all observers the conclusion has here, in the preceding article, been drawn that America is basically about ready for a guaranteed income plan. For a system, that is, with built-in financial work incentives as heretofore (you get *more* income if you work than if you stand aside)—but with also a reasonable minimum of income guaranteed to everybody as a matter of right.

Under such a system one can well imagine that the great majority of able-bodied people of working age would still be glad to toil to increase their income in order to partake more liberally of all that the advertising industry suggests that they ought to have.

Some others would not so earnestly care to work but would nonetheless be nudged into working by social pressure.

Others again would refrain from work for extended periods, making use of the bare security provided by their minimum income allowance to think and live creatively and develop their potential. (To them we should be at least conditionally grateful.)

Finally, certain people would successfully resist the idea that they should do anything but have a free ride at society's expense. What of it? Seriously, with a technology as productive as ours, why is their case so important?

If in principle we ought to have a guaranteed income program, in practice we face the two interrelated questions of the level of generosity and the technical formula. As point of departure we have this: The official upper limit of actual poverty, which is calculated by the Social Security Administration on the basis of the Agriculture Department's very tight "economy" food budget (multiplied by three), is now about $3,600 a year for a nonfarm family of four. And the sum of all estimated income deficits below the poverty line for households of all sizes throughout the country is slightly under $10 billion—or was in 1968.

Clearly the answer does not lie, however, in having the government simply guarantee to bring all incomes up to the poverty line. There would then no longer be any advantage at all, if you were poor, in *earning* any income: The less you had to begin with, the more you would be given. Earned income would therefore fall off, allowances would have to increase, and the taxpayer's cost would turn out to be much more than $10 billion.

Yet the addition of a work incentive, say an extra allowance equal to a percentage of earned income, would not be the whole answer either. For this would make some households originally just below the poverty line end up with more income than some just above it.

So, to avoid this other unjust and demoralizing result (which would perpetuate one of the many evils of the present welfare system), the percentage allowance for earned income would need to be graduated and costs raised again a bit more by extending allowances to households with incomes already somewhat above the line.

In other words, care has to be taken in constructing the income guarantee formula. But that is certainly no valid reason for inaction. Various technically sound formulas do by now exist on paper, formulas that would be free of obvious injustices, would largely eliminate disincentives to work or to save or to limit the number of children, and at the same time would leave little risk of an unexpected cost overrun such as we now almost take for granted in military procurement.

James Tobin, for instance, has developed a formula which ties in especially neatly with the positive income tax, and this has been used in one of the Brookings Institution's studies of the subject to elaborate four illustrative negative income tax plans ranging in estimated net cost from less than $5 billion to more than $40 billion a year.

The real issue, then, is not technical feasibility but level of generosity. President Nixon's proposed non-universal guaranteed minimum of $1,600 a year for a family of four, estimated to cost some $4 billion a year near the start, plus food stamps at say $1.5 billion, might politically speaking be considered the lower end of the scale.

The universal guaranteed minimum of $5,500 for a four-member family which was favored by the White House Conference on Food, Nutrition and Health would no doubt be close to the upper extreme if conceived of as applicable immediately.

Sen. Harris and others have now introduced as a Democratic alternative a plan assuring to all families of four a minimum income which would rise to the poverty level ($3,600) after three years, with the allowances set in this case to taper off at the $6,300 income level.

By the third year under this proposal the states would be relieved of all welfare cost, and the federal expense might run, it is said, to $20 billion a year.

There is meanwhile also the Children's Allowance approach, long advocated by Daniel Moynihan and recently brought into new prominence by the chairman of the Senate's Select Committee on Nutrition and Human Needs; according to Sen. McGovern's proposal, payment of $50 to $65 a month would be made for every child in the country. This plan differs from guaranteed income proper in that it misses some people altogether but on the other hand seems to avoid drawing any line between the poor and the rest of society.

Available for consideration too is the $2,400 federal guarantee for a family of four proposed as a first step by the President's Commission on Income Maintenance Programs (Heineman Commission), which was appointed by President Johnson and submitted a thorough report within recent months to President Nixon.

This plan, again, would allow 50 percent "retention" of other income, so that any family of that size with less than $4,800 would get some income supplement. Any with as much as $2,400 of other income—from wages or old-age and survivors insurance or a veteran's pension or workmen's compensation or property ownership or supplementary state relief payments (in the richer states) or any combination of these or other sources— would be lifted above today's poverty line right from the outset.

The total annual net cost of the plan taken by itself would be about $6 billion, with the states saving $1 billion and the federal government paying $7 billion. Later, if that modest beginning were to be made, economic growth would let the allowances be raised with a constant fraction of revenues at the same tax rates, i.e., even without presupposing an increase in generosity on the part of the rest of society.

To a cash scheme at this level could be added a liberal food stamp plan, as was done after due consideration by President Nixon. Depending on the details of the cash plan itself, the stamps might perhaps cost $2 to $4 billion a year additional.

Certainly as a general proposition (admitting of course the necessity for certain exceptions in short-supply fields like housing and medical care) it is better to avoid paternalism and give income supplements in cash rather than in kind or in hybrid form. Hence the food stamps should be phased out as soon as possible and replaced by more generous cash allowances.

All the same, hasty action in that direction could be damaging. In *Let Them Eat Promises*, Nick Kotz has shown how a switch from a surplus commodity distribution program to a generally speaking superior food stamp program can sometimes do more harm than good: When that switch occurred in Mississippi in the winter of 1967, scores of thousands of blacks who had been thrown out of work by a wave of mechanization were just too poor to afford the stamps.

So could a switch from stamps to cash actually tend to increase hunger so long as the poorest people in the country still lack the means to buy enough good food and meet their other essential needs at the same time.

It is certainly tempting to simplify our hodgepodge income-support arrangements. Some writers have urged that a guaranteed income program should be adopted *but only* in place of practically all other transfer payments to individuals, and even some benefits in kind.

That is an attractive idea for the future. A well-integrated approach could lower the costs and increase the returns. But probably we should agree to live a while longer not only with food stamps but with most of the rest of our "crazy quilt" system as well. The real point is not the elegant look of the quilt but whether it keeps you warm.

In short, our income security system as a whole could abolish poverty even if a newly enacted income guarantee by itself alone did not. If a rather modest guarantee plan were to be adopted, some families and unrelated individuals would find that their guaranteed minimum allowances *in combination with* their income from wages, social insurance benefits, or other conventional sources would lift them above the poverty line. Others would still be below it. (Apparently in 1968 about half of the estimated 686,000 poor families of four had less than that $2,400 of "other" income referred to above.)

For them to cross the line too, the existing forms of relief including the food-stamp allotment would need to be liberalized if other income transfers were not, or some new basis for last-resort aid could be created within the relief system if that should be regarded as desirable.

THE PIVOTAL ROLE OF GUARANTEED FULL EMPLOYMENT

The preceding article noted the point that a guaranteed income plan may provide allowances which are insufficient to eliminate poverty by themselves alone. That, in fact, seems rather likely at first, nor should such a start be scorned.

Various nonrelief forms of income will then close the remaining gap for many poor households, and other categories of relief in cash, kind and food stamps can help the rest.

The *main* source of additional "other" income is the increased earnings obtainable by the poor through more job opportunity and a stepped-up campaign against substandard pay. Certainly many poor households have nobody in them who can or should work; indeed, persons 65 years of age and over constitute with their immediate dependents about one-fifth of all our poor, and families headed by the mothers of children under 18 perhaps another one-seventh.

Even so, the poverty gap could be more than half closed if we had (1) the *assurance* of "useful employment opportunities, including self-employment, for those able, willing, and seeking to work," coupled with a strengthened program to help willing but not-so-able persons to become able; and (2) higher pay at the lower levels, both directly through improved minimum wage legislation and indirectly through the influence that the full employment itself would exert on the labor market.

Full employment defined as above admits, of course, of a reasonable minimum of frictional or between-jobs unemployment. It is suggested in the next article that the question of how to construe "reasonable minimum" should be decided by Congress on the annual occasions when it would set up its specific guarantees.

In a report submitted to Congress a year ago, former Secretary of Labor Willard Wirtz urged the extension of minimum wage coverage to some eight million additional workers, largely found in small retail and service establishments, in domestic service, and on farms, and also the raising of all minimum rates to $2 an hour over the next half dozen years.

These measures would tremendously increase the earnings of the working poor, assuming, as seems to be likely, that a carefully phased program along that line would cause no substantial disemployment.

Not as obvious but at least as great is the potential increase in earnings from guaranteed full employment. The disappearance of excess unemployment in the usual sense would of course raise the annual earnings of many more persons than are out of work at any one moment of time.

Also eliminated would be that considerable portion of *part*-time employment (with low earnings) which is involuntary too. There are apparently, moreover, at least half a million other persons in the country who would be counted as additional unemployed today were it not that they have become demoralized by the difficulty of getting a job and have stopped "seeking to work."

(An undercounting of population in the 1960 census may, finally, give our unemployment figures yet a further downward bias.) With continuous opportunity to get a decent job, however, plus a way to train and become qualified for it, most of the now discouraged, ill-equipped people would become employed earners.

In the second place, there is full employment's effect on earnings by way of wage rates: it is much easier to exploit poor and unorganized workers by paying substandard wages when jobs are hard to get than when they are plentiful.

As long as President Nixon's program makes a work *requirement* the basis for relief eligibility without assuring work *opportunity*, it cannot capitalize fully on labor earnings for narrowing the poverty gap. Involuntary unemployment (full-time and part-time) will not be greatly affected by just insisting that people train for jobs, since the main question is in the jobs available once training is completed.

There is also a real danger that the aims of the program may be perverted in some parts of the country in a deliberate effort to hold wages down. By decentralizing of the responsibility for job training to the states and metropolitan areas, local authorities are given the power to decide what constitutes a "suitable" job that must be taken on pain of forfeiting relief.

Experience in other contexts provides ample warning that that power could be used to beat down wages and break strikes, especially among poor minority workers in rural areas.

This discussion shows something that is frequently forgotten, thanks no doubt to what the "new economics" has achieved already in making the return of catastrophic mass unemployment all but impossible.

Even in terms of earnings alone—of what the additional opportunities to work would directly and indirectly contribute toward the raising of money incomes above the poverty level, and so toward the ease and the true economy with which a guaranteed income program could be carried out—an assurance of really full employment would be enormously helpful. But, of course, it would also accomplish far more than that.

One aspect of its basic human importance was mentioned at the beginning of the first article: Any definition of opportunity that leaves out the opportunity to work is simply not good enough to fulfill the promises implicit in the American dream.

Inadequate employment opportunity has furthermore been widening our ominous social divisions. We have all along been suffering, subconsciously at least, from internal strains caused by unduly keen competition for scarce jobs.

The symptoms are familiar: a little too much pressure on older workers to retire before they wanted or could afford to, a little too little consideration for young entrants into the labor market, and above all the fact that blacks have always been the last to be hired in a boom and the first to be let go in a recession.

Today this last phenomenon—not just the fluctuations, but the whole continuing deficiency of Negro, Indian, Puerto Rican and other minority job opportunity—has become so notoriously intolerable that the war against job discrimination has finally begun to be mounted in earnest.

That entire effort for equal employment opportunity is certainly a fine thing. But the fact has to be faced that the movement is bucking a strong current, because the available *total* opportunity is too small.

"Insufficient but equal" faces a troubled future. Only when the day arrives when job opportunity no longer has to be rationed can we know that the most sincere movement for job equality will meet with full success.

The social values to be gained through guaranteed full employment are matched by the economic stability it would provide. Here—in its economic connotations, that is— "full employment" may be after all an inadequate term, since it seems to suggest a rather specialized subject for those interested in labor matters.

Actually, maintaining assured full employment would involve achieving an unprecedented situation in which recessions would be impossible and inflation highly unlikely. That would evidently be in the interests of practically everybody.

Exception should naturally be made of those members of the financial community who make all their money precisely out of the economic ups and downs of the market, and perhaps also for some theoretical economists overspecialized in bravely forecasting business cycles.

GUARANTEED FULL EMPLOYMENT (continued)

Beyond question the bulk of the additional employment needed in this country for years to come should be provided by filling those huge and now widely publicized gaps in pollution control and environmental improvement (conservation and development of natural resources), urban redevelopment and mass transit, low-cost housing, health, education. Undoubtedly this is how we should reorder our national priorities, and many persons have convincingly pointed that out.

Current services are needed as well as capital investment. For example, many municipal services (street cleaning and sanitation, police protection, mail delivery, parks and recreational facilities, clinics and hospitals, etc.) are very much undermanned.

Moreover these services too use a good deal of relatively unskilled labor, the kind whose outlook is the most precarious today.

Much of this socially essential work should be carried out by the private sector, and much of the rest by state and local government, largely with funds obtained on a revenue-sharing basis from the federal government—a highly desirable new method of financing already offered for trial by President Nixon in his antipoverty program. The implied federal partnership and initiative will certainly have to be supplemented, however, by direct federal spending as well.

In fact, it is self-evident that a real guarantee of continuing full employment can be given only if the federal government stands ready to act as the employer of last resort— understanding this phrase to include the possibility of its financing local governments and even perhaps nonprofit institutions to do some of the actual hiring.

Right here lies the crux of the problem of putting full employment on a guaranteed basis. With power at the federal level divided between the President and Congress, and the nation divided more or less between liberals and conservatives, it is not a simple matter to obtain agreement that the government will always step in to support employment to any necessary extent.

The solution of this problem, however, is suggested by the conditions themselves.

To state very briefly some points that will be elaborated in the final article*, the President in his annual Economic Report to Congress should specify not only (1) the level of employment that in his view will be "full," and (2) the federal public program that he favors, but also (3) the level of private consumer demand (based on Gross National

*This article is here omitted.

Product calculations) necessary to maintain full employment if that public program is adopted, and (4) *the degree to which consumer demand should be expanded if the public program is reduced, or vice versa.*

Congress should then go beyond what the Employment Act now provides and should take the final aggregative decisions and give the related final commitments for the year ahead. First, that is, Congress should endorse or modify the President's statistical full-employment definition.

Second, it should decide the basic size of the federal public program it wants. (This may be recognized as a variant of the kind of spending limit already instituted by Congressman Wilbur Mills.)

And third, it should spell out in advance the methods to be used for adjusting total publicly generated employment and total consumer incomes. Reference here is to the methods to be used *if and as* such up or down adjustments are shown in fact (not by forecast) to be required in order to hit the statistical employment target, on the one hand, or the consumer spending target, on the other. Both of those targets, of course, should allow a workable range between bottom and top.

The built-in commitment to adjust *down* in case of either consumer overspending or over-full employment is one of the two reasons why this approach would offer strong resistance to inflation.

The other reason is that a part of the process of undertaking a governmental guarantee of full employment and continuously adequate demand for goods and services in the economy as a whole would logically be the negotiation of a suitable understanding with labor, business, and farm leaders. They should agree to be so guided in establishing their selling prices as to restrain "cost push" inflation.

Such an understanding seems, however, quite out of reach unless the government assumes responsibility in its own proper, overall sphere.

It should next be recognized that the advantages of guaranteed full employment would be not only domestic but international as well. This follows from the fact that our foreign trade balance would logically be one of the factors (one of the components of GNP) to be taken into account in estimating how much consumer spending was required to arrive at a basically adequate total demand for domestic output as a whole.

Hence we would be equally able to maintain full employment with an export surplus or an import surplus. Freed from any compulsive, economic-self-defense need to force our exports abroad or stop imports from coming in, we could begin to use our economic foreign policy much less as a weapon and more as an instrument of good will than we have in the past.

Take for example, our relations with the developing countries. Not only could we (confident of continuing prosperity) easily afford to be more generous to them with well-considered forms of international aid, but we could also encourage them to export more goods to us, including manufactures, as they have to do in order to be able to move "from aid to trade" as soon as they are technically able to make that transition.

Or take trade barrier reduction more generally. Our free traders would still be opposed by protectionists, as usual. But our legislators at least could now resolve the issues on their real merits, with no need to worry any longer about a possibly impending lack of markets and jobs for Americans.

It is hardly too much to say that America would have found the key to the puzzle of how to be the good neighbor it desires to be.

Naturally, all of our main economic policies are interconnected—for better, if we will, or for worse. The relationship between guaranteed full employment and guaranteed income would not be one-sided but reciprocal. The former would help in the attainment of the latter, as has been shown.

The latter, by the very fact that it would regularly channel additional spending money to the poor, would help to keep consumer spending up to its underwritten level without much need for auxiliary devices. Not only that, but it could itself provide a very convenient auxiliary device for use when necessary.

Today a lowering of the income tax will boost consumer spending but obviously not the spending of those too poor to pay any income tax. The other taxes which the poor certainly do pay could nevertheless be rebated to them to a comparable extent on some roughly estimated basis—in periods, that is, when actual consumer spending was falling below guaranteed consumer spending.

Or a reversible sales tax-sales bonus could be instituted at the federal level, and in periods calling for expansion all buyers of goods and services in the retail market would get coupons made redeemable (unlike food stamps) in cash. Possibly the most convenient mechanism of all, however, would be a negative income tax such as might be used for effectuating a guaranteed income plan. Here the allowances (negative taxes) would simply be raised, and the positive taxes lowered, when necessary to increase consumer spending.

Conversely, the positive income taxes could be raised, but preferably without lowering the allowances, when necessary to reduce consumer spending.

Consider, finally, certain parties at interest including the worker who, as President Nixon has suggested, resents having to carry the loafer. The guarantees of income and employment in combination could do a good deal toward sorting out in a natural, individually determined way just where in society people want to belong. True, the minimum income paid for out of taxes would keep nonworkers from starving. It would be up to the democratic process to decide, however, how high in relation to each other the minimum income allowances and minimum wages ought to be set.

At the shop level this sorting-out could continue. Along with strict enforcement of nondiscrimination in hiring, and with a really adequate funded program for upgrading the employability of anyone seeking that help, could go a new insistence that no employer had to hire anyone not willing to do the work and not either able to do it or in processs of training himself so as to become able.

Or take the case of a teen-ager who might work just long enough and often enough to "get by" (by having something more than his minimum allowance to spend)—preferring to do other things than work most of the time. Or the case of an older worker who might have formed the habit of taking extra days off whenever that suited him. Both of them could easily be making the right decisions for them.

At the same time, the new situation would offer an unusually good opportunity for employers and unions to make some adjustments in their rules on temporary work and absenteeism, having in mind both the problems of management and the just claims of the steady, productive worker.

16

A Note on the Budgetary Implications of Guaranteed Full Employment

The writer has described elsewhere[1] a method that could be used to guarantee full employment[2] in the United States. One of the questions of interest to legislators and others is: what would this plan cost?

It would not necessarily cost anything. The proposal is for insurance of the economy by compensatory fiscal action against difficulties that might materialize or again might not, and, if they did, might result in either positive or negative budgetary cost.[3] The factors that would determine the outcome can, understandably, all be subsumed under the savings-investment relationship; for purposes of exposition, however, it will be convenient to distinguish (a) that relationship in purely domestic terms from (b) the effect of the foreign-trade balance, and at the same time to consider both (c) that relationship as calculated in advance and (d) the net result of non-offsetting miscalculations.

The proposal under reference is to the effect that the President should include recommendations in his annual Economic Report, and that Congress should then decide and should give firm commitments, on the following:

(a) that a level of aggregate employment not less than g, or more than g + h million persons (Department of Labor seasonally adjusted monthly figure)[4] would be maintained in the year ahead—any point within this range being officially regarded as corresponding to full employment;

(b) that a rate of personal consumption expenditures (Department of Commerce series) not less than m or more than m + n would be maintained in the year ahead—this being regarded as the adequate, non-inflationary range of consumer spending in a full-employment GNP (in which the proposed government component would be assumed to be determined by considerations partly or wholly independent of employment);

(c) that method (methods) x would be automatically invoked whenever necessary to raise or lower aggregate employment so as to keep it within its target range; and

(d) that method (methods) y would be automatically invoked whenever necessary to raise or lower disposable personal income so as to keep the rate of personal consumption expenditures within *its* target range.

100

A few words of explanation may be added to this summary statement on each of these points.

The numerical employment target in (a) would naturally be meant to provide "useful employment opportunities, including self-employment, for those able, willing, and seeking to work" (Employment Act of 1946, sec. 2); i.e. the intention would be to meet the employment needs of the labor supply in its short-run definition. The proposal also envisages, however, that training programs would stand ready to help anyone to *become* able who wanted to be but at the moment was not. Practically speaking, the President and Congress would be estimating the size of the labor force and deducting what they regarded as a reasonable catch-all allowance for prevailing "frictions" (between-jobs turnover, delays in accommodating new labor-market entrants). Misjudgments would certainly be possible—for example, wrong guesses at the outset as to how many persons would be seeking to work *now* who were too discouraged by lack of job opportunity *before*—but such errors could soon be corrected since the proposal envisages a new quantative definition of full employment each year in any case.

The critical aspect of the estimating called for under (b) would concern the government component of GNP, especially its Federal sub-component. The decisions that establish the regularly approved level of government purchases of goods and services will probably always, under our political system, be influenced by many considerations. Employment itself may be urged as one of the most important considerations at times, but it can seldom if ever be expected to override entirely such other explanations of the final outcome of Congressional debate as differing opinions about the intrinsic value of particular budget items, strong personal biases for or against bigger government or social programs in general (commonly the most important consideration of all), and chance combinations of events. Consequently, whenever— under the proposal—Congress disagreed with the President's recommendations for Federal spending on goods and services, it would be logically obligated to estimate the net effect of its disagreement on the total of government spending for goods and services at all levels of government combined and, other things being equal, adjust the consumer spending target appropriately in the opposite direction. "Appropriately" need not mean equivalently, since the marginal demand for labor might be different (presumably it would be higher) in the public projects in question than in private consumer-goods production.

An estimate would also—under (b)—be needed of business spending, i.e. gross private domestic investment. Although its cyclical swings would be dampened down, or even in the end practically obliterated, by the virtual elimination of fluctuations in the economy as a whole under the continuous full-employment, adequate-demand policy postulated, they might well carry over, diminishing in amplitude, into the early years of the policy. It might thus at that time be thought best, in the interests of stability in the construction industry, to allow for business spending at its anticipated cyclical-average level rather than at the level actually expected in the year ahead. In the former case, that is, the residual private-domestic-investment cycle would be counteracted mostly by means of opposite movements of final, employment-balancing public investment rather than by anticipatory opposite variations in the consumer spending target.

Coming here to (c), it is self-evident that a commitment to hold aggregate employment within a pre-announced range would require the Federal Government to stand ready to act as the employer of last resort, i.e. to hire more workers on its own payrolls or under its own contracts and/or to finance State or local governments (or possibly non-profit organizations) prepared to do that extra hiring. The commitments and action under (c) would thus be within the general frame of the concept of a reserve shelf of public works and services. From this "shelf" additional jobs would be drawn when necessary by accelerating work or starting up new projects, and to it some jobs would be "restored" when necessary by decelerating existing work or suspending or terminating certain projects.

There would be a considerably wider choice of methods under (d) than under (c), since many different ways can be imagined of raising or lowering taxes on consumers and/or lowering or raising transfer payments to them, so as to adjust disposable income *directly*. To the writer it has seemed that a study of the available alternatives might lead to the choice of either (i) enacting a reversible sales tax/sales bonus at the Federal level, or (ii) adding flexibility to a negative income tax plan enacted as the mechanism for giving effect to the guaranteed income proposal. Under (i), everyone buying anything at retail would—in periods calling for expansion of consumer spending—get coupons or stamps that would be redeemable in cash if presented with reasonable promptness at a bank or post office, those agencies being in turn reimbursed from the Treasury.[5] Under (ii), the allowances or negative taxes would be raised, and the positive income taxes lowered, when necessary to increase consumer spending, and conversely the positive income taxes would be raised, and the allowances lowered (but never below their base level), when necessary to decrease it.

Since the proposal envisages two separate operational targets, each of which might tend to be overshot, undershot, or squarely struck, there would evidently be nine imaginable combinations as regards the cost of taking the compensatory fiscal action needed for fulfilling the guarantees once they had been given. Let a minus sign stand for a tendency to create a budget deficit (positive cost), zero for a tendency to create a balanced budget (no cost), a plus sign for a tendency to create a budget surplus (negative cost), C for consumer spending, and E for employment. The alternative conditions and the budgetary results of compensating for the tax changes or government spending changes would then be:

	conditions					results of compensatory action
1.	C	above	target,	E	above target	+ +
2.	C	"	"	E	on "	+
3.	C	on	"	E	above "	+
4.	C	"	"	E	on "	0
5.	C	above	"	E	below "	+ or 0 or -
6.	C	below	"	E	above "	+ or 0 or -
7.	C	on	"	E	below "	-
8.	C	below	"	E	on "	-
9.	C	below	"	E	below "	- -

In short, three hypothetical situations can be distinguished in which fulfilling the commitments would tend to cause a Federal budget surplus; three others in which it would tend to cause a deficit; one in which it would be neutral in its effect on the budget; and two in which the result could go one way or another, depending on the relative weights of the factors involved. That is, in operating a policy of this kind the government might sometimes (in principle, at least) have to expand jobs and cut down consumer spending at one and the same time, or vice versa. (One question would be whether, with employment held on target, consumer spending would tend to stay within the range deemed correct *a priori* and established as its own target; and a separate question would be whether, with consumer spending held on target, employment would tend to stay within the range officially designated as "full.")

But fulfilling the commitments by invoking compensatory adjustments *ex post* would of course be only part of the story. The budget result *in toto* would reflect not only the effects of compensating for tendencies to miss the target, but also the positioning of the targets in the first place. To take an example—the consumer spending target might, in some year, (a) be set high and then achieved by deficit-creating compensatory action which was found necessary *ex post*; or (b) it might be set high and be nevertheless achieved "automatically," thanks to a deficit-creating tax reduction engineered *ex ante* which left more income at consumers' disposal; or (c) it might be set lower, in consideration of an *ex ante* decision to enlarge government purchases of goods and services, a deficit being however created in this case by that new government spending (not financed by new taxes).

Thus, if we try to identify causal relationships, we find ourselves on treacherous ground. Cases (b) and (c) show as much budget deficit, other things being equal, as case (a), but what if the dominant *motive* in (b) were tax reform, and the dominant *motive* in (c) were the conviction that the country needed the new government spending program for the sake of its product, i.e. the resulting goods and services, rather than for the sake of the jobs? Evidently the politically interesting question—"what would the plan cost?"—needs rephrasing into something like "what would be the state of the budget if the plan were in operation?" On this clearer basis a meaningful, even if qualified, answer ought to be possible.

Essentially the answer is that the state of the budget would depend on whether the economy itself was dynamic or sluggish, and *that* would be reflected in the current *savings-investment relationship*. This is not a matter of playing with words. Formulating the problem in such terms is a way of answering ill-considered objections to full-employment policy. If budget deficits were associated with full employment, the blame should be laid on the general tone of the economy at the time, which means on producers and consumers generally; or possibly on the government for hampering producers, i.e. if it did, say by unwise tax policies; but not on the full-employment policy or on the government for sponsoring that policy.[6]

Instead of budget deficits, however, (or, to be sure, the special case of an exactly balanced budget) there might very likely be budget surpluses. There might be, that is, an actualized full-employment surplus—the manifestation of a condition not inevitable or necessarily permanent (as some discussions would seem to imply) but at any rate clearly possible and, in circumstances resembling those apt to be found in the near future, highly probable. Urban rebuilding combined with factors like population growth and mushrooming consumer credit could easily raise investment far above savings. In the context of the present proposal—with consumer spending and employment both held on target—that would mean that the Federal budget when presented on a national income accounts basis would have to run a surplus. The surplus would arise out of (a) decisions that kept taxes above spending *ex ante*, or (b) compensatory action in the form of extra taxes, required to prevent over-shooting of the consumer spending target, or (c) compensatory action in the form of reduced public-works spending, required to prevent over-shooting of the employment target, or (d) the algebraic sum of two or more of those possibilities.

On the other hand, circumstances could also conceivably be quite different, with business depreciation charges, etc., plus undistributed profits plus personal savings exceeding private investment. In that event, the Federal Government would have to engage in deficit financing in its national income accounts budget—in some combination of ways opposite to those just mentioned—to keep consumer spending, or employment, or both, from falling below their target levels.

One possible explanation here might be a general lack of restraint in monopolistic pricing—let us call this a low *moderation-extortion ratio*.[7] Whenever there is little moderation and much extortion, savings will tend to be high as a result of the maldistribution of income arising from the concentrated monopoly profits. At the same time, investment will tend to be low in view of the restrictions on output which represent the other face of the coin of unduly high prices. Thus, under the present proposal, *if* the moderation-extortion ratio were to be low, a consumer spending target high enough to induce full-employment production would tend, other things being equal, to be difficult to achieve without deficit financing, either by prearrangement *ex ante* or by compensatory action *ex post*.

The conventional price-wage spiral would, however, be absent. In this spiral the sequence of events seems usually to have been more or less as follows: (1) as productivity increases, profits rise; (2) administered prices are raised, for still larger profits; (3) workers demand higher wages, in order to catch up—or more than catch up—with the rising cost of living (and obtain a share of the profits announced on the financial pages of the newspapers); (4) the resulting enlarged consumer buying power initiates a rise in competitive prices as well, besides making it possible to raise administered prices again, this time to offset—or more than offset—the higher labor costs; (5) – (n) and so on. Under the proposal, however, the automatic ceiling on total consumer spending— reinforced by the automatic ceiling on jobs, which guards against over-full employment—would at least interrupt this process at stage (4).

Actually, the probabilities are that effective restraint would be imposed not only on the demand factor in price inflation but on the cost-push factor (stages (1), (2), and (3) above) as well. Under the proposal the government would be undertaking to see that labor's most important requirement, adequate job opportunity, would always be met, and equally so the prime condition for the prosperity of industry and agriculture, an adequate total market. Why should not business, labor, and farm leaders be willing, by way of counter-commitment, to accept some kind of reasonable guideposts, guidelines, or frame of reference for the processes that are followed in establishing their selling prices? This point has been dealt with at some length elsewhere. Three propositions are involved: (a) that business, labor, and farm leaders can *not* be expected to show the requisite degree of self-denial and social responsibility merely because of exhortations and the expressed *hope* that full-employment prosperity will be maintained; (b) that they *could* be expected to do so in exchange for firm guarantees; and (c) that they could also be expected to exercise a reasonably adequate degree of control over the pricing behavior of the interest groups they lead.

If our reasoning on this whole aspect of the subject has been valid, we can conclude that the moderation-extortion ratio would not after all be apt to exert much influence in the direction of an excess of savings over investment under guaranteed full employment as proposed. The Government could probably without much difficulty hold the general price level steady (or let it rise very slowly, if that were preferred) and could therefore safely estimate a full-employment GNP, and the derived consumer spending target, on a stable-prices assumption.

The discussion up to this point might to all appearances have been of a closed economy. But *external trade* could turn out to have real budgetary significance under the rules of the game as proposed. In particular a trend away from past export surpluses to future import surpluses could exert substantial influence towards the reduction of full-employment surpluses or the generation of full-employment deficits. Net exports, the final component of GNP to be taken into account (together with government spending and business spending, already discussed) for purposes of establishing the necessary rate of *consumer* spending, will of course always represent an additional market if positive and a subtraction from the aggregate market if negative. Moreover if saving equals income minus consumption, an export surplus can be equated to increased consumption and hence to reduced saving, and an import surplus to decreased consumption and hence to increased saving.

The main practical significance here stems from the fact that the less developed countries will some day have to have export surpluses—through the export of manufactures as well as foodstuffs and raw materials—in order to be able to "move from aid to trade." This implies that the United States, as the leading industrialized country, will have to learn to behave like a "mature creditor" nation and willingly accept import surpluses. The proposal under analysis would clearly permit such a development to occur without sacrifice of American prosperity and full employment, since the consumer spending target would be raised *par passu* with any expected "worsening" of the export-import relationship. There would, however, be a corresponding "deterioration" in the budget position because of that need to assure domestic production of a larger *domestic* market, to compensate for the smaller net foreign market.

Coming finally to the budgetary implications of *miscalculation*—i.e. miscalculation in setting up the consumer spending target—it can be seen that this would not be a factor separate from, or additional to, those already discussed. When a compensatory adjustment was needed to bring consumer spending on target, that could indicate either miscalculation or a deliberate preference for letting the savings-investment relationship (or general tone of the economy) reveal itself instead of trying to guess it too closely in advance. Such a wait-and-see attitude would indeed be quite appropriate, once fiscal management had shifted over from essentially a forecasting to essentially an insurance basis.

Miscalculations could evidently occur in: (1) the size of a full-employment GNP (which would depend not only on the price trend but also on the technological trend, composition of output, and any other factors influencing the labor-capital "mix" in production); (2) the level of gross private domestic investment; (3) the level of net exports; and (4) the level of government purchases of goods and services itself. That is, State and local government spending might add up slightly lower or higher than Federal estimators expected; and the Federal Government's own spending intentions might as heretofore be somewhat unclear at the advance estimating stage, or else, even if perfectly clear then, they might still have to be revised before the year was out.

An unforeseen military emergency, certainly, could make revision necessary. To the extent, then, that a large unexpected increase in national defense expenditure went for the payments to military personnel or to workers in defense plants, the proposed policy could in all likelihood absorb the impact through the prescribed compensatory action (automatic ceilings) on total employment and/or total consumer spending. On the other hand, a very large unexpected increase in military procurement might so greatly expand "guns" production as to necessitate an arbitrary downward revision of the consumer ("butter") spending guarantee originally given, or even suspension of the whole policy—nothing to wonder at, after all, in such a national emergency.

In more normal circumstances, however, the fact that miscalculations would be bound to occur in the course of the statistical exercise by which the consumer spending target would be established should not be considered as constituting a serious problem, whether in its budgetary implications or otherwise. For in the first place, the individual miscalculations would frequently tend to cancel one another out, and it would be only the net miscalculation remaining that would signal the need to take compensatory action. In the second place, moreover, the taking of compensatory action would in any case be a normal part of the system and not an evidence of defect in the system. Putting this differently, the primary reason for including the consumer spending (floor) guarantee in the proposal is not to try to establish that advance estimating has become a science or even a fine art—dubious proposition at best—but rather to make it possible, given the constraints of American political and economic life, nevertheless to reach the goal of continuously guaranteed full employment.

NOTES

1. The citations given in the original article, as written in 1970, are here omitted.

2. Whatever might be the possibilities of achieving a theoretically satisfactory definition of full employment in an imperfectly competitive world, its attainment or non-attainment could be verified unambiguously in practice by having the President annually propose and Congress decide on a level of employment that would be treated as "full" during the ensuing year. See text.

3. Except as otherwise noted, the argument herein can be applied to either the national income accounts budget or the ordinary budget. The broader question of social costs (and benefits) is beyond the scope of the discussion, although that question of course provides the basic arguments against tolerating involuntary unemployment and the attendant under-utilization of other resources.

4. Alternatively it might be decided that the figure for unemployment (or possibly the one for labor force time lost) would be maintained at not more than j or less than j – k per cent of the civilian labor force (or available labor force time).

5. This plan is discussed in some detail in "On Underwriting Consumption and Employment," (see Chapter 20).

6. Indeed—and speaking here more generally—to the extent that government policies are responsible for raising production and employment levels, the government will almost always deserve credit for *improving* its budgetary position, since revenues will rise, with the rising tax base, while added expenditures for public works are likely to be little if any larger than subtracted expenditures for various forms of relief, etc.

7. "Monopolistic" here stands broadly for all departures from pure competition—the whole range of situations in which sellers possess some significant degree of control over selling prices, which they consequently "administer," singly or in concert with others. Use of the pejorative term "extortion" is not intended to deny that there are cases where a departure from the hypothetical results of pure competition is desirable, even essential. (E.g., a labor-saving device may be introduced which, under pure competition, would not only displace workers but have the further short-run effect of forcing certain wage rates below socially acceptable levels.)

17

Best Cure for Inflation—
Guaranteed Full Employment

The "trade-off" is not an immutable law of our economic life. America has not run out of easy ways of doing things. If these are heresies, it can't be helped.

What Chairman Paul McCracken of the Council of Economic Advisers was talking about before the Joint Economic Committee of Congress was obviously not the international political scene (where everyone knows that there have been no easy ways to run out of for many years) but only our domestic economic quandary caused by the rise of inflation. And what I mean as to his comment on that*—and I say this with much respect for McCracken's skill, his values, his tone, and his right to use an expression like that rather loosely in order to make the point that he wanted to make at the time—is only this: that the easy ways that the country may have had of doing things were not doing the thing that was fundamental; that the way of doing *that* is not altogether easy, naturally, but is not so hard either; and that we have not run out of it. But I do mean that much.

The underlying concept of the trade-off came into vogue as the concern over our inflation spread. There is nothing complex about it in principle. Business and labor both like to charge what the traffic will bear, and so the high demand, piled higher for several years by huge military spending, bid up wages and prices. Eventually, in fairness to fixed-income receivers if for no other reason, there had to be a decision to apply the brakes and check the demand—direct fiscal brakes of less spending and more taxing, indirect monetary ones of fewer bank loans at higher rates of interest. But this sort of braking action, while at first it might seem to be having practically no effect whatever, is bound in due course to slow production too in some degree and cause some workers to be laid off. Hence the conclusion is drawn that some sort of trade-off between major *desiderata* is inevitable: if we want more price stability, we must also—so it is said—accept more unemployment.

Reprinted by permission from *The Commercial and Financial Chronicle*, May 8, 1969.

*"The basic fact we find is that the country has run out of easy ways of doing things." McCracken testifying before the Joint Economic Committee, quoted by Hobart Rowen in *International Herald Tribune*, February 18, 1969.

TWO APPROACHES

How much more? Well, figuring out just how much more unemployment we are going to have to have in order to buy just how complete a slowdown in prices how soon is quite another matter. No one really knows the answer, though many feel impelled as usual to act as though they did. (Don't just stand there—forecast something!) McCracken and the Nixon Administration, showing a keen awareness of what is at stake for the disadvantaged groups in our society, have undertaken to apply the brakes as lightly, gradually, and experimentally as may be possible. The other school of thought has all along offered a tougher prescription: if you don't face up to the need to kill off the inflationary psychology and inflation now—and of course that will increase unemployment somewhat temporarily—your softness will most likely bring on a recession that will *really* destroy jobs.

Yet, differ as they do on strategy, there is nothing to suggest that either school questions the trade-off concept as such. Both begin their reasoning by taking it for granted. Economic news writers have made that abundantly clear. Eileen Shanahan for one showed it with particular clarity when she wrote in *The New York Times* (Dec. 8, 1968): "That some sort of compromise must be made between the objectives of full employment on the one hand, and price stability, on the other, is beyond argument. . . . Modern economic theory and policy has yet to find an answer to [render unnecessary] some decision about 'the trade-off.'"

Here I must beg to differ. Economic policy does have, in my opinion, a better answer than that. I also venture to say that it is too late in the day not to use the best answer that we have. But, in order to do that, we will need to discard the whole traditional trade-off approach and embrace a different concept, that of *guaranteeing* the continuous maintenance—paradoxical as this may seem—of full employment.

What is full employment? By my definition it is "useful employment opportunities, including self-employment, for those able, willing, and seeking to work." (Employment Act of 1946, sec. 2). But "those" must clearly mean "*all* those," and in addition—either as an integral part of the definition itself or as an essential accompanying policy: it makes little difference which —people who are willing but not able, and so might be too discouraged to keep on "seeking," must be helped to *become* able. This is where training programs are *especially* important, and our manpower policies generally, including regional programs like Appalachia. This is the main specific remedy for so-called unemployability or true hard-core unemployment.

It does appear that anyone professing confidence in the conventional trade-off doctrine must be a little uneasy. What is the *nature* of all that reasoning about the percentage of unemployment needed to keep the percentage rise in prices within tolerable limits? Speculative in the extreme. What is the *goal* of the policy? Something, I submit, hardly worth the trouble involved in reaching it. Unless, that is, we must pessimistically conclude that in economic policy we lack up-to-date ideas entirely (whatever our ingenuity may be in other fields) and so must be satisfied with inherently very unsatisfying solutions.

HERITAGE OF DEPRESSION ERA

The trade-off is a concept deriving from the days of our great depressions. When one of those "acts of God" occurred (a way of expressing ignorance about the in-any-case frowned-on art of controlling the demand), workers by the millions were thrown on the street and businessmen found their markets absolutely flat. Wages and prices certainly came down. Today, while shunning a return to such conditions, the economic doctors are still preoccupied with the thought that a milder dose of the same old medicine will be just enough to hold prices reasonably steady. Pressure on people but not too much pressure. Just a *slight* twist of the arm. The bull fight without really killing the bull.

But the foundations of that hope are extremely shaky, to say the least. Statistics?—the evidence cannot help but be inconclusive, although the fact that prices continued to climb throughout the recession of 1957–58 while unemployment went up to touch 7.5 percent (seasonally adjusted rate) might be cited as evidence *against* the thesis. Logic?—here the case for the trade-off is especially weak. Why expect our powerful unions to knuckle under in their wage demands if unemployment rises moderately? A response of that kind seems no more probable in the world of today than persistence of upward wage pressure coupled now with rising pressure for more unemployment relief and larger welfare payments. *Ultimately*, to be sure, and *at certain levels* of unemployment and shrunken demand, a real economic squeeze would be bound to produce its intended results, ending the inflation. But what does that mean: hard times of what duration and to what extent—and expectable under what political auspices? Consider also this haunting question: how can anyone say with confidence how much unemployment would still have to be retained as a permanent warning after the shake-down was over?

It only remains to be observed that the effects of even a fairly small rise in unemployment could be dire enough. The mayors of our bigger cities will testify that we will not succeed in creating a better society by going in the direction of making life economically more difficult for Negroes. This point has been made very well by McCracken himself—as, for example, in a speech during late Johnson days to the National Industrial Conference Board, in which he remarked that "Those marginally positioned in the labor force, and therefore the first casualties of unemployment, are also heavily those in the ghettos with whom an awakening national conscience is increasingly concerned. We are not apt to accept many tenths of a percent increase in unemployment to gain ground on the price-level problem." Exactly so.

THERE IS AN ALTERNATIVE

To disparage the trade-off approach to policy would be a great pity if there were no better alternative. Fortunately, however, there is one. That better alternative, I submit, is to grasp the nettle firmly by guaranteeing full employment at all times, meanwhile negotiating a suitable understanding with labor, business, and farm leaders. By "suitable understanding" I mean one in which it was agreed that the *quid* for the *quo* of guaranteed full employment and continuously adequate total demand for goods and services was the acceptance by those leaders of some kind of reasonable guideposts, guidelines, or frame of reference for the processes traditionally followed in establishing their selling prices.

One can hear the objection that such an understanding could not be negotiated, and possibly the further objection that the leaders of labor, business, and farmers could not prevail on their constituents to follow their lead. I firmly believe that the understanding could be negotiated, for reasons to be stated in a moment. As for the second objection, admittedly in this individualistic country the kinds and degrees of influence exerted on their constituents by leaders of farm organizations, trade unions, and the organizations and individual giants of the business world will fit no simple formula. Some of their constituents—one thinks, for example, of the widely scattered craft union locals in the building trades—can probably indeed be counted on to try to be fiercely independent. Nevertheless I believe it is fair to say that, in one way or another, the leaders of our big national economic interest groups (these three groups and also others) could be expected to keep a degree of control adequate for the purpose.

But how can one be confident that an understanding along such lines could ever be negotiated with them in the first place? The answer to this seems to me to be relatively simple: *because* the leaders of the major economic interest groups in our society are, by and large, realists. As realists they must know that the vigor with which their constituents look after their own exclusive interests *can* affect the national interest—that it is even possible for excessive demands for pay or profits to impair the viability of our economy. And, secondly, any realist is bound to recognize that continuously assured full employment and adequate overall demand would be an unparalleled economic blessing.

The assurance of jobs for all those wanting and able to work would obviously solve the problem that is pivotal for *labor*—incidentally in the process doing more to improve race relations than any other one thing at this point in our history could. The governmental policies required for effectuating such an assurance would also be enormously beneficial to *business*, inasmuch as those policies would have to include the maintenance at all times of a sufficiently large market for business output in general. *Farmers* would gain in both ways: many of them as businessmen would be helped to find better markets for their produce, while some others, situated closer to the margin, would see a decent opportunity at last to make a living outside of agriculture.

Notice, however, the catch. It would be only the confident expectation of those results, created by the Government's guarantee, that would make it possible to negotiate the understanding. At least I do not myself see much logical or historical reason to suppose that the leaders of labor, business, and farmers would give their pledge in exchange for a mere hope. It seems to come down to this: if the Government in its proper sphere would undertake to assume the necessary degree of responsibility for our economy, why should they not do likewise?

UNUSED AREAS OF EMPLOYMENT

Evidently, then, the prior issue is whether—and how—a guarantee of full employment could be given and made good. Not in any figurative sense, but really.

Could we, for example, have a plan made up of decently large programs in all those fields where there is wide agreement, backed up by expert analysis, that as a nation we are not doing nearly enough? Let us say in health, education, low-cost housing, urban redevelopment including mass transport, pollution control, conservation and development of resources. Carrying out such programs would be mainly up to the private sector, or to State and local government, but Federal Government partnership and initiatives and Federal spending would be essential too. There is so much catching-up to be done in these areas—and the things needing to be done would furthermore embody such a high proportion of labor, much of it requiring very little training or skill—that an approach like this could, if followed, provide us with a balanced kind of full employment for many years. Comprehensive plans in at least outline form are not lacking either. The National Planning Association, a private organization in Washington, has been publishing such plans for a long time. In 1966 the A. Philip Randolph Institute of New York put out a striking plan along similar lines in a pamphlet entitled *A "Freedom Budget" for All Americans.*

Such an organized, many-sided attack on our "public poverty" would certainly have the enthusiastic support of millions of people, this writer included. If we can have peace in Vietnam, surely the time to launch it will be at hand. Nevertheless a little reflection will show, I think, that this approach *by itself alone* is inherently insufficient as a method of guaranteeing full employment. Why? Not for lack of things needing to be done but because of differences of opinion about doing them and because of the way in which our national economic policies are formulated and carried out.

BYPASSING CONFLICT BETWEEN
THE PRESIDENT AND CONGRESS

The division of powers between the President and the Congress and the cleavage between left-wing and right-wing views—essentially the "creeping socialism" issue—just cannot be left out of account. Let us suppose that President Nixon were to recommend in an annual Economic Report to Congress a section-by-section composite program along the lines just described—one that would, if followed, maintain full employment for the ensuing year. He would plainly not be in a position to guarantee that result, since the various parts of his program might for any number of reasons be cut down by Congress and the resulting gap might not be filled by anything else. Clearly, even in periods when policies and current conditions may be largely favorable to expansion, full employment cannot be actually guaranteed unless the Federal Government itself stands ready to become the employer of last resort. And this is something that, in present circumstances, any President has reason to know that any Congress may very possibly not agree to.

This is why the composite program method, although sometimes advocated as the road to assured full employment, is insufficient by itself alone. Fortunately, however, its limitations can be overcome by broadening the approach. Under a suitably broadened approach, Congress could be enabled to guarantee full employment without having to risk creating a larger public sector than it thought the country should have. And the President, in recommending a series of specific programs, would then not be staking full employment on the willingness of Congress to authorize them all or others of equivalent weight. In short, the issue of public *versus* private activity would have been cleanly separated—by the very nature of the different approach I am talking about—from the issue of maintaining the right overall rate of operation of our economy.

MECHANICS OF SUGGESTED PROGRAM

Since we are now no longer on generally familiar ground, let me take a moment to explain how this would work. (Parenthetically, the enabling amendments to the Employment Act of 1946, though momentous, could be brief and rather simple in form.)

To begin with, the President in his annual Economic Report, prepared as usual with the help of his Council of Economic Advisers, would include *two* proposed guarantees— (1) of the level of employment, and (2) of the level of consumer spending. The level of employment chosen by him as corresponding statistically to the full-employment concept would reflect his judgment of how much unemployment was reasonable in the light of manpower policies and labor mobility at the time. (I would myself suppose that such "necessary frictional unemployment" would amount to 3 percent of the labor force or less.) The level of personal consumption expenditures chosen would be derived by a process of estimating a full-employment level of gross national product or expenditure and subtracting from it its three other components, i.e. estimates of (a) government purchases of goods and services, (b) gross private domestic investment, and (c) net exports.

Two further essentials: First, in order to make the crucial allowance for the possibility that Congress would not agree to all the items in his public expenditure program (a major part of the "(a)"), the President would also indicate, either by means of a series of paired figures or by some more general statement, by how much in his view the consumer spending guarantee should be raised or lowered if that public program were in fact to be reduced or enlarged. Second, in order to minimize the risk of inflation, he would include not only recommended floor levels for employment and consumer spending but ceiling levels for both as well.

Some time after receiving this Economic Report, Congress, advised by its Joint Economic Committee, would agree or disagree with what the President had recommended. In any case, however, Congress would under this proposal be responsible for establishing its own guaranteed levels for employment and consumer spending, and also for deciding in advance what methods of adjustment were to be used when, as, and if those levels proved to be not self-sustaining. That is the crux of the matter.

In regard to the *levels*, Congress might for instance decide that the employment target (floor) during the year in question—in other words, that year's authorized operational definition of full employment—should be 79.5 million jobs, seasonally adjusted, whereas, let us say, the President had proposed 80 million. Or it might trim $10 billion off the President's proposed program of public expenditures on goods and services—but in that case the logic of the situation would require it to raise the private consumer spending target correspondingly. Or if, on the contrary, Congress should decide to increase public spending, it would then be logically obligated to lower private consumer spending.

In regard to the adjustment *methods*, the chief novelty would lie in the devices that might be selected for directly raising, as well as lowering, the level of consumer spending.

(Perhaps it needs to be underscored that maintaining full employment would not always in itself also indirectly maintain the indicated rate of consumer spending, since either too much or too little of that income flow could be channeled into saving.) Two of the most promising available alternatives would probably be the following: (a) A reversible sales tax/sales bonus at the Federal level: in periods calling for expansion, everyone buying anything at retail would get coupons or stamps which would be redeemable in cash if presented within a reasonable period at a bank or post office, those agencies being in turn reimbursed from the Treasury. (b) A negative income tax plan, enacted to give effect to the widely discussed anti-poverty proposal of a nationwide guaranteed annual income: these allowances or negative taxes could be raised, and the positive income taxes lowered, when necessary to increase consumer spending, and conversely the positive income taxes could be raised, preferably however without lowering the allowances, when necessary to decrease it.

TWO IMPORTANT ASPECTS

As to implementation, two aspects will bear emphasizing here. Action would not be triggered by forecasts, since all adjustments of taxes and/or of the "last resort" jobs program would be made only when the accredited national consumer spending and/or employment series of statistics showed that the economy was in fact failing to meet the Congressionally set standards. The adjustments would, however, be made promptly in the prearranged manner then—rather than at the end of the long-drawn-out, uncertain, and partly self-defeating political struggles such as have preceded our compensatory tax changes until now.

Here then can also be summed up the second reason why guaranteed full employment would actually make it *easier* to ward off price inflation, rather than harder. The approach described would automatically call for scaling down consumer spending when the latter would otherwise rise above the level set as its safe upper limit, and would automatically call for putting some public works back on the reserve shelf when total employment would otherwise rise above *its* pre-established ceiling. In other words, in addition to the negotiated restraint on cost-push inflation which was emphasized earlier, there would also be a twofold prearranged check on inflation from the side of demand.

OUR FOREIGN STATUS WOULD BE HELPED

Our balance-of-payments problem, which partly derives from our price inflation but also in large part does not, is beyond the scope of this discussion. I must, however, say something about the way that the burden of this discussion bears upon our position in the world at large. For the advantages of a policy of guaranteed full employment over a policy of trade-off would lie not only in the domestic sphere but also in the sphere of foreign economic relations. In particular, the substantive basis for our policies in regard to foreign trade would be transformed for the better.

The difference would be that the perennial fear of a shortage of markets would be permanently eliminated. That is because one of the elements used in calculating the level of consumer spending to be guaranteed would be, as already noted, our net foreign market or export surplus. Hence whether we faced a continuing export surplus or—in due course, at the right time—a more or less even trade balance, or an import surplus, would not affect our ability to guarantee full employment and a sufficiency of total demand, domestic and foreign combined. Thus we could in particular be more helpful to the developing nations—not only by being generous with well-considered forms of aid but also (since we ourselves could not run short of markets at any time in the foreseeable future) by encouraging them to export more goods to us, including manufactures, so as to move "from aid to trade" as soon as they were ready for it.

Those who speak for liberal trade policies would then still be contending with the inevitable protectionism of certain private interests; but they would not any longer be up against, in addition, the conscience of the legislator who has the public interest at heart and is genuinely worried about an impending lack of markets and jobs for Americans. It is hardly too much to say that America would have found the key to the puzzle of how to be the good neighbor it desires to be.

To return finally to the main thesis of this article, there is the possibility of using full employment itself—rather than unemployment—as a sort of trade-off against inflation. This is so because there is a practical method of putting full employment on a guaranteed basis. If I am right about this, then statements to the effect that we have to compromise between the objectives of full employment and price stability are clearly wrong.

One way to find out if this very different sort of trade-off will work would be to try it.

18

A "Freedom Budget" and Guaranteed Full Employment

It is encouraging that two hundred leaders of civil rights, religious and labor groups and other prominent progressives have endorsed a proposed program under which poverty could be virtually abolished in America in the next ten years. Their call to action appears in the pamphlet, *A "Freedom Budget" for All Americans,*[1] conceived by A. Philip Randolph and shaped by the hand of Leon H. Keyserling. This document deserves many readers, for its panoramic view and its detailed analysis alike. I would only urge the need for a more definitive approach to guaranteed full employment. But I will come to that later.

I

The authors correctly state that abolishing poverty in this country has become a moral problem. Economically, there is no longer any real obstacle. Sociologically, personal deficiencies of the poor or the unemployed should not be mistaken for the main issue, any more than personal weakness would be considered the main cause of fatalities in a shipwreck, especially if too few lifeboats were provided.

The economic point—familiar but crucial, and cogently presented here—is that we are now able to eradicate poverty because of our wealth and our growth potential. By liberating that growth potential and also using the resources idle today, the authors estimate that we could carry out the necessary additional measures and could finance the Federal budget cost ($185 billion in 1964 dollars over ten years) with some room to spare, doing this *without raising tax rates, even if we must continue to enlarge our national defense expenditures substantially at the same time.* Nor need it cause inflation, if we will put first things first and cut only nonessentials. (The same reasoning applies in the last analysis to the balance-of-payments problem, which the authors do not discuss.) In other words, it would be wrong to postpone the war on poverty until the end of the war in Vietnam.

This article was written at the end of 1966.

Skeptics will come forward to attack the basis for this arithmetic. The authors have estimated that our gross national product, which was $663 billion (1964 dollars) in the year 1965, could be raised to $1085–1120 billion by 1975, creating a $2315–2442 billion "economic growth dividend." (By this they mean the excess over what the GNP would hypothetically add up to by remaining constant at its 1965 level.) This growth dividend, enabling us to afford the war on poverty without retrenching elsewhere, presupposes an increase in productivity or output per man-hour in the private sector of about 3¼ to 3¾ percent a year. The result, with a growing labor force, would be an economic growth rate of about 4½ to 5 percent a year, after an initial two years of still faster growth (apparently about 8 percent a year) caused by rapid elimination of the existing unemployment.

Viewed as prediction, this could well be over-optimistic. Yet these growth rates are in line with some other carefully developed estimates of what we could and should aim to achieve. Skeptics and "gradualists" should moreover take note that, while the authors certainly consider such expansion feasible, and strongly urge it—since then *all* income levels would gain—they do not predict it. Instead they say this: should we fail to use our reserve productive powers and our full growth potential, thus diminishing somewhat the extra yield obtainable in future from present tax rates, the war on poverty would still deserve top priority and should in that case be partly financed by raising tax rates and making them more progressive.

To achieve results, their argument continues, we must have time schedules and an integrated, balanced program that will weave together in a mutually reinforcing way (1) the maintenance of full employment, (2) the obliteration of "private poverty," both of workers and of those who, for reasons of age or other valid reasons, cannot and should not work, and (3) the elimination of the "poverty in the public sector." For (2) we need higher minimum and other wages, policies tending toward parity for farm incomes rather than for farm prices, more adequate Social Security and welfare programs, with social insurance also financed in part from general Federal tax revenues, and progress toward realizing the guaranteed annual income concept for all. For (3) we need a great stepping-up of our programs concerned with education, health, transportation, natural resources, air and water pollution, distressed areas, rural communities in general, and above all urban renewal, which should especially emphasize slum clearance and much more construction of low-income housing.

The authors stress that Federal leadership is essential to get the job done, and that the Federal budget is the most powerful single instrument of national economic and social policy. This does not mean, however, that they want the Federal Government's spending to rise at the expense of private enterprise, or of State and local government. On the contrary, the "Freedom Budget" pictures State and local spending as rising more than Federal spending, and the prevailing total-government, private investment, and private consumption shares of GNP as being maintained. (The supply side of the equation is discussed too—or at any rate the structural questions such as what the Office of Economic Opportunity, and training for needed skills, and general education could do to help create a more perfect labor market. But the emphasis throughout is on aggregate demand and its various components, as the subject indeed requires.)

The authors identify full employment—"opportunity for year-round employment to all of those able to work and wanting to work, including those whose abilities need lifting through training and education"—as by far the most important single approach ot the eradication of poverty. Allowing for involuntary part-time workers and also for some who are just too discouraged by scarcity of job opportunity to continue searching for work, they attribute 40 percent of all our poverty directly to full- or part-time unemployment (not counting unemployment's indirect effect in depressing wages), 20 percent to substandard wages, and the other 40 percent to the fact that some households simply do not have anyone in them who could or should be employed. They also consider full employment an imperative end in itself. A guaranteed annual income on a nationwide basis—yes, as a *supplement* to a nationwide full-employment policy. By no means would they agree with the thesis that automation has brought us to the point where the system of income distribution needs a divorce from the system of production and jobs.

II

On pages 4, 12, and 64 of *A "Freedom Budget" for All Americans* it is stated that the Federal Government should "guarantee" full employment. On page 32 an "unqualified commitment" to sustained full employment is advocated. Elsewhere (e.g., page 23) the word "assure" is used. The great majority of the signers must have meant this to be taken literally. My comment, offered in the same spirit, is that the guaranteeing of full employment is essential but is not practicable by the means proposed in this pamphlet. But it *would* be practicable to guarantee full employment if one more element were added—and I hope that the sponsors of the "Freedom Budget" can be persuaded of this.

Let me say at once that for maximizing employment the program as it stands has two great strengths: its size in terms of aggregate demand is auspicious, and its heavy stress on elements like housing construction and slum clearance would structure the employment pattern somewhat away from automation-sensitive kinds of work and toward work that the labor force can do. There are more jobs per extra dollar of final demand in city rebuilding, and in other parts of the proposed program such as resource conservation and replenishment, than in many of the things the individual consumer would buy if he were given the extra money through tax reductions. A massive attack of the kind proposed could contribute enormously to job creation and could certainly create periods of full employment.

Indeed everything coincides to bless a program like the proposed attack on slum ghettos: the fact that it goes to the very heart of our social needs today; the dubious value (stressed by Galbraith, for example) of some of the things that might be done alternatively with the same money, such as produce still more unneeded gadgets for still more affluent consumers; and finally, the excellent employment effect. Surely, that program is a must!

The only trouble is that it and the other good programs proposed cannot as they stand be combined into a total program that *assures full employment*. It might be so on paper, but not in the actual legislative process in which the President in his annual Economic Report or at other times makes recommendations for action to maintain employment, and Congress approves or amends the President's recommendations, or takes the initiative itself. Suppose that President Johnson were to present the "Freedom Budget" as a Great Society program without changing a line of it. Would Congress necessarily also give it blanket approval? To ask this question is to answer it in the negative. Quite apart from such direct opposition as might arise on various points of substance and intent, there are also too many incidental cross-currents. Consider as just one example the religious issue bedeviling Federal aid to education.

Lest this be taken as criticism of Congress, let me ask the signatories of the "Freedom Budget" this question: Would *you* recommend it to the President or to Congress without changing a line of it? You are on record as "in broad agreement with its basic objectives and broad outlines," "while not necessarily endorsing every detail." Fair enough. But where does it leave guaranteed full employment?

Of course the authors do not need to be told that the details will change in the give-and-take of discussion, or that the rate of growth itself will depend on "the feasibility of various ranges of policy endeavors and popular attitudes." What they count on, therefore, is that the Federal Government would "continuously lead in organizing and financing enough job-creating activities to close the gap between full employment and employment provided at other public and private levels. None of the Federally-created jobs, they add, "need to be made-work, because our unmet needs in the public sector are large enough to absorb beneficially this Federal effort." (page 4)

One might wish it were otherwise, but surely there still is good reason to believe that an open-ended commitment to provide jobs on public works and services to those who fail to find jobs elsewhere is impracticable in this country, *unless coupled with a further assurance effectively limiting the weight this commitment might have to bear.* Made-work versus filling unmet needs in the public sector is not the main issue. The main issue is that it would be thought by some to embody too serious a threat to our private enterprise system. This is not a new story. When the Employment Act of 1946 was being drafted and redrafted, the preamble at one stage contained a strong commitment in general terms along the line now again suggested, while at the same time the arrangements envisaged in the operative clauses were strikingly weak. Needless to say, this conflict was resolved by deleting the strong commitment.

But there is no reason for pessimism. I would repeat that full employment can be guaranteed under the "Freedom Budget," in my opinion, by adding to it one element it now lacks. That element is a guarantee of aggregate consumer spending—coupled with the guarantee of full employment itself, which could then no longer be thought by anyone to threaten a possible Federal take-over of the economy. Both guarantees would be given under an amendment to the Employment Act that would call on Congress to express its employment policy year by year in the form of specific commitments. To suggest this approach is not to put more emphasis on private consumer spending and less on slum clearance or on anything else needed to end poverty in the public sector; it should not be so construed. The suggestion aims rather to insure that Congress would not be in the position of chipping away at full employment if it voted against some of the specific items, favored by the author of this note as much as by the authors of the pamphlet, that might be proposed by the President.[2]

In brief outline, this would work in the following manner. Let us say that the President in his Economic Report would present the program of the "Freedom Budget." He would among other things spell out its quantitative implications in terms of a full-employment GNP: (a) so much proposed total government spending for goods and services, (b) so much expected private domestic investment, (c) so much expected net exports (worth separate attention for trade policy reasons, in spite of its small size), and (d) so much private consumer spending needed to round out the total. That amount of (d), and the level of jobs that the President regarded as corresponding to full employment, he would ask Congress to guarantee. But at the same time—and this is the crux—he would point out that, if Congress chose to cut back (a), it would need to increase (d) correspondingly; or slightly more, if (d) would clearly be less labor-intensive than (a).

Congress would then have a choice of proportions between government spending and private spending (which indeed it should have) but not of over-all levels of demand and activity in our economy (which it would not need, full-employment levels having been already called for in principle as far back as 1946). Congress would also give finality to the working (statistical) definition of full employment for the year ahead, and would designate in advance the type of means to be used, without further debate, to raise or lower consumer purchasing power on the one hand or publicly sponsored employment on the other if the official (i.e., Congressionally approved) indexes of consumer spending or jobs strayed appreciably from the target rates. The phrase "raise or lower" is used because, in order to make the system operate equally strongly, and on equally unmistakable signals, against inflation, not only a floor should be guaranteed but also a ceiling—possibly about two percent above the floor. Finally, if Congress remained in virtually continuous session, it could also give the expansion or contraction orders in response to the mandatory signals it had arranged, although surely that task had better be discharged by the Executive Branch.

What means consistent with social justice *could* be specified for raising or lowering consumer purchasing power when necessary, i.e., in those periods when the interaction of all domestic and international events and all the "Freedom Budget" measures and other basic policies currently in effect demanded, by flashing the agreed signal, that type of compensatory action? I suggest three alternative plans:

Plan A. Since income tax variations have already won wide public recognition as a useful tool, introduce the nationwide guaranteed annual income idea in the form of a negative income tax plan that would pay out allowances partly closing the poverty income gap of all poor families and unattached individuals. Then raise those allowances or negative taxes, and lower positive income taxes, when necessary to increase total purchasing power, and raise positive income taxes, preferably without lowering the allowances, when necessary to decrease it.

Plan B. Adopt a reversible or two-way sales tax/sales bonus at the Federal level and use this to achieve the needed variations in purchasing power. Just as most sales taxes are regressive, hurting the poor man most, this particular scheme would be predominantly progressive, and all the more so if sales tax exemptions were granted for necessities in the periods calling for contraction. In the more frequent periods calling for expansion, everyone buying anything at retail would get coupons or stamps which would be redeemable in cash if presented within a reasonable period at a bank or post office, those agencies being in turn reimbursed from the Treasury.[3]

Plan C. Provide for reductions in income taxes for those who pay them, coupled with an appropriate equivalent for poorer households, e.g., a stamp or coupon plan or even cash payments considered as a partial refund, rebate, or offset to the largely hidden taxes they do pay to Federal, State, and local tax jurisdictions. After all, a substantial part of their small incomes—possibly as much as 30 percent on the average—goes to pay those hidden taxes now. In periods requiring contraction, raise income tax rates only.

To sum up, I should like to re-emphasize two points. First, a "Freedom Budget" is imperatively needed, to accelerate the war on poverty and give it focus. The sooner we get it the better. Second, the "Freedom Budget" in its present form cannot yield guaranteed full employment because *guaranteed* full employment does not come as a by-product but needs in addition its own kind of envelope plan or insurance policy operating in part by way of control over aggregate purchasing power.

I would urge on the authors of the "Freedom Budget" that everything they have said about the need to assure sustained full employment is true. And more besides: in particular, it is this alone that can remove the perennial fear of a shortage of markets, and thus provide the basis for a sound U.S. international policy on trade and aid, helpful to the developing countries and others. Fortunately, guaranteed full employment can be more than a figure of speech: it can be made a reality now.

NOTES

1. Subtitled *Budgeting Our Resources, 1966–1975, to Achieve "Freedom from Want."* (New York: A. Philip Randolph Institute, October 1966), 84 pp. The "Freedom Budget" is an adaptation and up-dating of the "American Economic Performance Budget" which Dr. Keyserling and the Conference on Economic Progress have been advocating for several years.

2. The proposal summarized here is explained at length in my *Insuring Full Employment: A United States Policy for Domestic Prosperity and World Development* (New York: The Viking Press, 1964).

3. For further details on Plan B, see my *Insuring Full Employment, op. cit.*, pp. 38–39, and my "On Underwriting Consumption and Employment," op. cit. (below, pp. 124–26).

19

The Insurance Approach

I

In the past the remarkable advantages of what may broadly be called an insurance approach to the solution of major economic problems has received little general recognition. It is my hope that this book may contribute to awakening such a recognition.

With the approach to full employment described in these pages there would be no need either to trust some particular economic theory—how unemployment originates, how the business cycle works, just what economic effects a proposed law would have, etc.—or to rely overmuch on forecasts.

The conflicting views of distinguished experts about how to promote prosperity can only generate a certain agnosticism about economic theories. This lack of dedication to a theory, however, could become a comparatively harmless affliction. For example, with aggregate consumer spending insured, pegged, guaranteed, or underwritten (all these words seem appropriate, despite some recognizable objections to each), our ability to maintain the effective demand needed for full employment would not depend on commitment to a theory of oversaving, a theory of undersaving, or any other.

Thus, to select a view expressed by Simon Kuznets, that we have as a nation been saving too little—this would continue to be highly relevant to the study of the problem of growth, but the method of maintaining full employment would be quite unaffected by it. If the pegged level of consumer spending realized itself automatically from the income paid out under conditions of full employment, nothing more would need to be done about it. If it did not and fell short (business depreciation charges, etc., plus undistributed profits plus personal savings might well exceed private investment), a consumer spending booster would be applied. If consumer spending ran too high (urban rebuilding, for example, might combine with population growth and other factors to raise investment far above savings), it would be cut down. If the total employment level still needed adjusting, up or down, that would be done by changing the pace of public works.

This chapter originally constituted Chapter 7 in my *Insuring Full Employment* (New York: Viking Press, 1964).

On the technical level, this means that some of the best-known concepts in economic dynamics would also become much less relevant than before. The not easily altered relationship between consumption and income, held in some awe in the past and known as the propensity to consume, would not play a decisive part: the compensatory mechanism would simply by-pass any difficulty created by saving-spending ratios and act directly on the level of spendable income. The investment multiplier would hardly get started multiplying (by way of the induced increases in income)—nor would, for example, the export multiplier—before it would come up against the fact that the level of consumer demand, through which it must work, was now in any case under independent control.

This may possibly make the solution of the full-employment problem sound too easy. If so, a closer look will reveal a tough enough economic assignment beyond what might be considered the mechanics of operating the dual compensatory regulators. There in the background lurk the rather intractable problems involved in getting our market economy to function more satisfactorily of its own accord. In that area, it should be added, we can hardly have too much good theory and advice.

But an effective set of compensatory devices is, indeed, the very thing that would focus attention most sharply on the need to improve our basic, long-term policies with a view to having them better encourage business initiative, raise purchasing power among those who now have too little, and reverse the inroads that monopolistic practices have been making into potentially competitive areas. All those who are unsatisfied with second-best solutions—in this case heavier use of compensatory devices and larger budget deficits than would really be necessary for full employment if those long-term policies were stronger—would have the rationale of their further proposals greatly clarified. Moreover, the actual merits of their proposed measures could be more easily tested, once the optical illusions born of the business cycle itself had disappeared.

A reference was made to forecasts. One of the harrowing things about many of the economic-policy proposals since the Employment Act was first taken up for consideration has been the degree to which they have depended—or have seemed to depend—on forecasting. As the *New York Herald Tribune* said not unkindly in a recent editorial, "With the best will in the world and the greatest storehouse of statistics, Walter Heller can guess wrong. Arthur Goldberg can guess wrong. John Kenneth Galbraith can guess wrong."

Certainly this is true, as they would be the first to concede and as would be equally true of any Republicans serving in the same or other official posts. An insurance approach, however, does not rely unduly on forecasting. The present proposal looks to the use of advance estimates and judgment to arrive at suitable employment and consumer-spending levels to be guaranteed, but governmental compensatory action would be held back to await the unfolding of events. The proposal would lead not to sensing a prospective gap and filling it with a government program, but to prearranging the kind of gap-filling action to be taken only if and when a designated official index moved out of the range which Congress had decided was economically safe. (No one would be under the illusion that that designated index was perfect, either. It would simply be the most suitable index available, and as such would be treated as recording the facts relevant for operations.)

I repeat that the proposal here offered neither derives from any special brand of economic theory nor visualizes operations directly based on forecasts. The underlying economic logic is quite general. Supporting or restraining action to be taken by the government would depend on ascertained facts.

II

A set of policies capable of assuring jobs to all those able, willing, and seeking to work would manifestly solve the most formidable of the problems by which labor is beset. It turns out that such a combination of policies would necessarily also be highly beneficial to business, because, practically speaking, it would have to hinge very largely on assuring a sufficiently large market for business output in general. The benefit to farmers would be twofold: mostly they would as businessmen be helped to find markets for their food and fiber, but some would gain chiefly from the chance to find new work opportunities outside of agriculture.

As a country that needs the good will and support of other countries around the world, and one whose people in any case set unusual store by carrying out a good-neighbor policy for disinterested reasons wherever possible, the United States has vital international reasons, as well, for insuring its full employment. Not only would this demonstrate the contemporary competence of our kind of economic system, and facilitate granting the aid that the less developed countries need, but it would solve the key problem of markets in the sphere of world trade. Unsolved, that problem can raise the "overproduction" specter and frustrate our efforts to act as we would like to be able to act in the matter of exports and imports.

That our export surplus is but a small part of our GNP would not suffice to make acceptable to us the growth of our imports which the successful development of the less developed countries will progressively require, since this is a growth both in absolute terms and in relation to our exports. Such a trend can only be expected, in itself, to make the dollars available to buy American products *less* equal to the task of buying a full-employment GNP than they were before. What is clearly needed is an insurance approach that incorporates the principle of maintaining an adequate market for the output of American farms and factories regardless of the export-import relationship. By systematically offsetting any decline in the export surplus with a corresponding rise in the home market, such an approach would render a crucial service in the field of foreign relations.

Finally, there is psychological value in the insurance principle as such. When applied to the economic side of life as a whole, this principle would not only raise production sights and improve production decisions but would allow the kind of independent planning that would help Americans reach new levels of personal achievement.

It is neither possible nor in least degree desirable to adjourn the debates, great and small, on those economic-policy issues on which our different circumstances must cause disagreements to exist among us. But it would be well to conduct the debates in a propitious economic setting, likely to promote our national cause throughout the world and likely to help secure at home those things about the need for which there is very general agreement. Such a setting would be provided by insured full employment.

20

On Underwriting Consumption and Employment

The purpose of this note is to amplify one aspect of my earlier proposal for underwriting full employment in the United States[1]—the part having to do with techniques for boosting consumption when it would otherwise fall short of the target. It is probable that the subject of full employment will claim the spotlight again when and if the world situation permits major reductions in armament expenditures, and it is at least possible that a policy of assured full employment in this country, if we had such a policy now, would help to hasten that day.

The question of feasibility depends, I have argued, on whether or not aggregate consumer spending is underwritten in addition to aggregate employment as such. Without that feature, a policy of guaranteed full employment could involve the government in so large a degree of direct responsibility for the creation of jobs—such as expansion of public works, and perhaps wholesale subsidies to, and/or control over, private production—as to compromise the essentials of our private-enterprise system. Because of that risk, such a policy (as contrasted with contracyclical policy in a more limited sense) is not likely to be voted in the United States in the foreseeable future. That risk disappears if aggregate consumer spending, too, is underwritten and maintained at a proper level, one high enough to keep reliance on supplementary public works within reasonable bounds.[2] The risk of an unbalanced budget remains, but this—a corollary of the danger of oversaving itself—is not, as the other risk is, one that our system of private enterprise cannot bear.

I have elsewhere suggested a number of alternative procedures for enlarging consumers' incomes directly when personal consumption expenditures would otherwise—even at a full-employment level of income payments—fall below the underwritten level.[3] For some time I was inclined to stress tax reductions or offsets. Here I wish to bring into consideration a different method, involving the use of what might be called Consumer Sales Premiums (CSP for short). This method would provide not only

Originally published as a Communication in *The American Economic Review*, Vol. XLV, No. 4, September 1955. Reprinted by permission.

additional purchasing power but an actual inducement to spend. Where an income-tax rebate, for example, would not favor consumer spending relative to consumer saving, but rather would tend to raise the level of both, CSP would be distributed only in connection with consumer spending as such and hence would establish a direct incentive to spend more, both out of normal income and out of the premiums when cashed. Thus the target level of consumer spending would be reached at smaller cost to the government.

Certain other general characteristics of the CSP method may also be briefly noted here. It would not noticeably reduce anyone's incentive to work—a charge sometimes loosely leveled against consumer transfer payment schemes in general but actually valid in special cases only. It would be perfectly flexible as to the amount of "lift" to consumer income it could provide. And it would be reversible into a special sales tax,[4] with a minimum of difficulty or misunderstanding, in the event the problem shifted to one of avoiding an inflationary rise of consumer spending above its guaranteed ceiling.

CSP would take the form of small coupons or stamps, in convenient denominations, which would be used as follows: (1) The Treasury would distribute them to banks and designated post offices throughout the country. (2) Banks and post offices would pass them along, when authorized by the responsible agency in Washington, to "retailers"— stores, service establishments, independent professional practitioners such as doctors— in ratio to their certified current volume of consumer business.[5] (3) During periods declared to be "pay out" periods, retailers would give them to individual consumers as premiums on their purchases (value of purchase, times authorized percentage, figured to the nearest penny). (4) The individual consumer would redeem his CSP for cash at his bank or post office before the expiration date marked on the stamp's face. (5) Banks and the U.S. Post Office Department would return the CSP in bulk lots to the Treasury and would receive face value plus suitable compensation for their services as agents.

The administrative problems connected with such a scheme do not appear unduly formidable. The burden on retailers would be roughly like that of a sales tax—slightly more for bills mailed, since these upon payment would require a return receipt transmitting CSP. While there might be a number of CSP agents in a community, each retailer would normally have to choose one source of supply, and all lists of applicants would be cross-checked to prevent duplication. Each consumer would likewise normally deal with a single bank or post office selected by him. As a convenience and further precaution he probably would have a blank book issued to him, identified as his, to the pages of which his CSP would have to be affixed to be eligible for redemption in cash.

A numerical example will illustrate the effect on the economy as a whole. Assume aggregate consumer spending in year X underwritten at $300 billion, with the top limit set at $306 billion. Ignoring here the seasonal factor in sales, at least $75 billion should then be spent each quarter, or $25 billion each month. Assume that, after six weeks, the preliminary forecast for the first quarter showed only $72 billion. The responsible agency might then authorize CSP to be issued on all retail sales at a 10 percent rate during months 3, 4 and 5. If monthly rates of consumer spending rose from $24 billion in months 1 and 2 to $27.3 billion in months 3, 4 and 5 (let us suppose that the inducement of obtaining CSP raised "ordinary" spending to $25 billion; add $2.5 billion CSP converted to cash less $200 million of extra saving from this extra cash), this would bring the five-month total to $129.9 billion, as against a target minimum of $125 billion, and the responsible agency might order termination of CSP payments at that point. The premiums might have to be issued again at the same or a different percentage rate, later in the year. Or, if conditions changed markedly and total consumer spending for the year threatened to exceed the $306 billion limit, the responsible agency would bring into play the special sales tax or other agreed device for curbing a spending excess.

NOTES

1. See my "The Underwriting Approach to Full Employment: A Further Explanation," *Rev. Econ. Stat.,* Aug. 1949, XXXI, 182–92. Also my "The Underwriting of Aggregate Consumer Spending as a Pillar of Full-Employment Policy," *Am. Econ. Rev.,* Mar. 1944, XXXIV, 21–55; other papers collected in *Full Employment and Free Enterprise* (Washington, 1947); and "Employment the Key," *Christian Science Monitor*, July 23, 1949, mag. sec., pp. 2, 12.

2. See "The Underwriting Approach . . . ," *op. cit.,* pp. 184–85, for my theory of the "correct" level of aggregate consumer spending. Briefly, (1), estimated full-employment GNP, minus (2), the sum of (2a) expected government purchases of goods and services, including all public works approved "for their own sake," (2b) expected gross private domestic investment (probably, as a general rule, the anticipated cyclical-average level), and (2c) expected net foreign investment, equals (3) the level at which personal consumption expenditures should be underwritten. Thus one may advocate, as I personally do, rather generous regular appropriations for public works, but the amount included in (2a), and hence reflected in (3), depends on the will of Congress. A foreign-trade balance, plus or minus, similarly affects, and is accommodated in, (3) because it registers in (2c) and, where due to foreign aid, etc., in (2a). Actually my proposal calls for setting, not a single target figure for aggregate personal consumption, but a range between a guaranteed floor and a guaranteed ceiling, the leeway allowed being possibly of the order of 2 percent. A summary statement on how minimum and maximum levels both of aggregate consumption and of aggregate employment would be likely to be established and administered in practice, i.e., the respective roles of Congress and the Executive and the requisite amendments to the Employment Act of 1946, appears in "Employment the Key," *op. cit.;* see also *Full Employment and Free Enterprise, op. cit.,* pp. 163–70.

3. See "The Underwriting Approach . . . ," *op. cit.,* pp. 187–88. It is important to note that such measures—indeed, all *compensatory* measures under this plan, whether they be (a) such measures, taken in relation to current rates of consumer spending, to expand or contract consumer income directly, or (b) measures, taken in relation to current levels of employment, to expand or contract public works (and, incidentally, hold income payments at the full-employment level)—are viewed as *supplementing and in no sense substituting for basic or long-run policies*, a primary function of which is to make compensatory measures less necessary. The more that basic fiscal and other measures (high wages, a tax system that is progressive but encourages risk-taking, prevention of abuses of monopoly power, etc.) can do to strengthen production incentives and broaden the distribution of purchasing power, the better.

4. I am opposed to giving sales taxes, with their regressive character, any disproportionate emphasis in our tax system. However, if a special sales tax were linked with CSP in a two-way compensatory mechanism of the type here considered, the usual objection need hardly apply. The effect would be as progressive during periods when it was necessary to boost purchasing power as it would be regressive when necessary to hold purchasing power down; or more so, assuming sales tax exemptions for necessities.

5. Purchases for business account would sometimes masquerade as consumer purchases. However, "leakage" in either a real or a statistical sense (in reduced leverage value for the economy, or in excess of transactions included for CSP over transactions included in the personal consumption expenditures aggregate) should prove relatively minor.

21

Point Four, Dollar Gap, and Full Employment

When in the future some historian takes time to plot the many different roads leading to Point Four, he will undoubtedly find much to interest him in the first session of the Preparatory Committee of the United Nations Conference on Trade and Employment which took place in London in the autumn of 1946.

This meeting was in many respects extraordinary. The economies of the eighteen geographically scattered nations represented on the Committee were widely dissimilar. Their interests, therefore, and, indeed, their practical necessities illustrated most of the theoretically possible combinations. A great effort was made to harmonize these differing points of view in a constructive manner. The range of the effort was enormous. Measured by the number and importance of the general principles at stake, not to speak of the complexity of the attendant detail, it is doubtful whether there had ever been an international economic conference of comparable scope. The draft document which emerged began to suggest—bearing in mind the charters of already going concerns such as the International Monetary Fund, the International Bank for Reconstruction and Development, the Food and Agriculture Organization, the International Labor Organization, and the United Nations itself—the distinct possibility of evolving a coherent overall world economic code.

LONDON, 1946

For present purposes, the most interesting aspect of this International Trade Organization preparatory conference was the way a particular set of partly competing, partly complementary principles began to fall into place, or at least into some sort of relationship to one another. There was a kind of classic simplicity about the accommodation process at this early stage.

Reprinted by permission from *The Annals of the American Academy of Political and Social Science*, Vol. 270, July, 1950.

First, delegates from a number of economically advanced countries and others said that their governments could not bind themselves to refrain from imposing trade restrictions unless they could be assured against another depression in the United States. The economic stability of nations all over the world was dependent, they said, on what happened to employment and effective demand in the major industrial nations, especially the United States. They hammered the point that the most important issue before the conference was full employment.

At this juncture a delegate from one of the underdeveloped countries said that full employment was all very well, but that it offered no solution for the problems of his country. What was needed there was not just full employment, but productive full employment; not just elimination of unemployment, but elimination of underemployment. In short, what was needed was economic development, modern technology, industrialization.

These sentiments were thereupon echoed all around the horseshoe table. It turned out that almost all the delegates present considered that the countries they represented were underdeveloped. The draft agenda for the conference was altered forthwith to provide for separate consideration of the subject of economic development. An extra committee was set up to deal with that subject. The extra committee proceeded to draft a new chapter containing several important articles—the nucleus of what was later to become "Chapter III: Economic Development and Reconstruction" of the Havana Charter.

Thus, from its initial focus on the general need to reduce trade barriers, attention was forcibly shifted to the need to retain the contingent right to increase certain of these barriers if circumstances (for example, recession in a country like the United States) caused demand to fall off and created balance-of-payments difficulties for other countries. From the importance for the rest of the world of having full employment in the United States, the spotlight moved to the inadequacy of any underdeveloped country's own full employment unless it was productive employment—to the need for economic development, and not trade barrier reduction alone, to make that employment productive. Also, by parallel sequence, it moved from the desirability of full employment to the undesirability of maintaining it by means of a persistent export surplus—to the desirability of as much export surplus as would correspond to productive foreign investment to assist the development of the underdeveloped or the war-torn countries.

This oversimplifies, of course. There were disagreements, not always fully resolved, about interpretation of the various points here recited, not to mention disagreements on other points, such as the extent of permissible trade restrictions in the interest of economic development. But men's minds were here engaged in constructing a working relationship between full employment, Point Four (as it had not yet been called), and trade barrier reduction. Perhaps the main thing lacking in this connection was a sense of the proportions of the world trade disequilibrium—the dollar gap problem. Considered it certainly was: exceptional trade restrictions were admitted if necessary to protect a country suffering from balance-of-payments difficulties; countries were urged to maintain full employment without leaning on the crutch of a so-called "favorable" balance; and provision was made for consultation if balance-of-payments difficulties should persist. But the chronic nature and the real magnitude of the dollar gap problem were not apparent at that time.

OUR POLICIES SHOULD BE INTEGRATED

The campaign for economic development took on momentum and became a world-wide crusade. After President Truman's dramatic pronouncement in Point Four of his inaugural address in January 1949, which had the quality of a statement ushering in a new era in human affairs, it appeared that the question about economic development was no longer Should it be done? but rather How is it to be done?

Admittedly, the crusade for economic development of underdeveloped areas was so widely supported and so deeply motivated that it could not have been stopped in any case, regardless of the position taken by the United States. Moreover, deciding on the contribution the United States Government and American private capital will actually make toward action so peculiarly hard to define, or at any rate delimit, has proved to be a time-consuming process. Still, viewing the matter broadly, it seems fair to say that the Point Four goal has now been accepted here as well as abroad, and that the dominant preoccupation is with that practical question, How is it to be done?

This is harder to answer than might at first glance appear. Many of the best minds in government, business, finance, agriculture, labor, education, medicine, science, engineering, and other fields are helping to find the answer, and no one would claim that we have reached the point where good ideas about how to proceed are no longer at a premium.

Yet, with all the need to push this highly practical and immediate line of inquiry, it is permissible to ask whether another question of a somewhat different order, which seems to be getting rather less attention, is not equally vital for the United States, and equally timely. I refer to the question of how we are to establish the right *relationship* between Point Four and other major economic policies.

This second type of question, since it has to do with over-all perspective, seems to be no one's business in particular, and thus tends to be neglected. The result of such neglect is that we do not have a unified economic policy, with all the major parts organically related. Instead, we have a collection of separate policies which are forced into some kind of fit, good or bad.

Looking over the economic field, what is it that we really want? It may be assumed, for one thing, that we want to close the dollar gap. We also want to close it in such a way that exports and imports will balance at a high level, rather than at a low level. We want to help other countries to improve their lot by raising their productivity and their standards of living. We want to keep on raising our own living standards. We want our economic policies to help us hold our friends and allies abroad and win us new friends and allies if possible. We want to enhance our national security through assuring supplies of needed materials. We want to strengthen the United Nations. We want customers—a full-employment market. Without sacrificing flexibility, we want our various economic interest groups to be safeguarded in appropriate degree. On top of all this, we want to avoid excessive governmental controls.

Can such a heterogeneous lot of economic objectives be reduced to simpler terms? Well, here is a shorter list that seems at any rate to take account of all the aims just enumerated: (1) the Point Four Program for economic development; (2) a closing of the dollar gap—as far as possible by expansion of imports rather than by reduction of exports; (3) domestic full employment; (4) national security; (5) a maximum of individual freedom and initiative.

To say that successful integration of these five aims would go a long way toward solving the problems with which the United States is confronted today is not, of course, to be certain that the means of integration are at hand. It does appear, however, that much might be gained if serious attention were given to studying how to integrate three of these major elements—Point Four, the dollar gap, and full employment. The remarks that follow will be addressed to this subject, with also some incidental reference, where possible, to the other major elements in the picture.

POINT FOUR AND DOLLAR GAP

The dollar gap is financed by the American taxpayer, and involves foreign grants and loans which tend to confer a charity status on the recipient countries. Since neither of these conditions appears permanently desirable, the question of closing the gap arises. Point Four is often spoken of as one of the best ways of closing the dollar gap. Let us try to evaluate this claim.

The elements tending to support it are two, each with its own time cycle. First, while the international investments are being made—or, rather, for as long as the current flow of dollars going abroad exceeds the return flow of earnings and repayments—the dollar gap requiring official action to finance it is smaller by the amount of this net investment. Second, when the programs of economic development have reached the stage of yielding results, the countries whose production has been increased in this manner are in a position to earn more dollars through larger exports, while at the same time they and perhaps third countries as well, being less dependent on us for some of their traditional imports, are in a position to save dollars, if they will, by importing less.

These two effects, it will be noted, are quite dissimilar. What may be called the net investment effect does not narrow the export-import gap, but automatically reduces the amount of the gap that has to be filled by compensatory official financing. The increased productivity effect, on the other hand, can, if consciously directed to that end, actually help to narrow the export-import gap as such.

The increased productivity effect obviously will not become noticeable in any given case until some time after development programs are initiated. From a global point of view, of course, some of this beneficial effect is likely to overlap a still favorable net investment effect, each then reinforcing the other until further time has elapsed.

One of the big uncertainties in the picture is the question as to how long the foreign investment process can be kept up before earnings and repayments turn the net flow in the other direction, making the dollar gap problem harder to manage, rather than easier. The answer is not easy to find. Much will depend on the proportions between equity capital and loans and on the rates of amortization applied to the latter, as well as on the magnitude and time-shape of the original capital movement as a whole.

The other big uncertainty has to do with how much of the increased productivity effect will be retained to raise living standards in the countries being developed, in fulfillment of what is the major purpose of Point Four, and how much, on the other hand, will be used to improve their export-import position. It may indeed be hard to balance world trade while some countries are so unproductive that they have little to offer in exchange, but it does not necessarily follow that when those countries grow somewhat more productive, this in itself will make the attainment of world trade balance a simple matter.

On the whole, the immensity of the field waiting to be opened up by technical assistance and international investment suggests that Point Four can make solution of the dollar gap problem substantially easier, at least potentially. The fact that the net investment flow may eventually turn in the "wrong" direction is not an immediate worry. On the other hand, the size of the dollar gap at the present time, the very obvious difficulties of creating the confidence needed to get a vast amount of investment going, the delays before development programs pay off in sufficiently greater productivity to make a marked improvement in the underdeveloped countries' export-import balances possible, and the great need on the part of those countries not to think only of their export-import balances but rather to enjoy as much as possible of the benefit from that greater productivity internally—all these things warn us that Point Four, far from being the whole answer as far as the dollar gap is concerned, will prove for that collateral purpose too little and too late.

DOLLAR GAP AND U.S. FULL EMPLOYMENT

It is one of our declared national policies to make every reasonable effort to maintain conditions in which there will be afforded useful employment opportunities for all who are able, willing, and seeking to work. Aside from what the chance to work means to our own people, all the evidence shows that our success or lack of success in this endeavor is one of the crucial tests by which both the merits of our economic system and the value of our friendship will be judged abroad.

The essence of the relation between the dollar gap problem and the problem of maintaining full employment in the United States is that closing the gap will make maintaining full employment somewhat more difficult—or, to put the same thing more constructively, will make it more obviously necessary to work out a fundamental solution of the full employment problem. This follows from the fact that closing the gap will, taken by itself, tend to reduce the overall size of the market for American products.

There seems to be a fairly prevalent belief—very likely a reaction against the excessive claims of those who ask for protection against imports—that the aggregate demand for American products will be reduced only if the dollar gap is closed by reduction of exports, and not if (or to the extent that) it is closed by expansion of imports. This belief appears to be without foundation. Expansion of imports—even where the imports are commonly thought of as "noncompetitive," being high-grade raw materials for industry, or luxury goods like French lace, or "invisible" (service) items like travel abroad—will correspondingly reduce the purchasing power that might otherwise have been used to buy American goods and services. Thus American production and employment levels are bound to be affected, by way of the demand side of the equation, regardless of whether export-import balance is achieved at a low level or at a high level.

It does not follow, however, that aggregate demand for American products will be *equally* affected by increased imports on the one hand and loss of export markets on the other. On the contrary, it seems fairly clear that the adverse effect will be quantitatively less if imports are increased than if exports are reduced. For this there are several reasons.

In the first place, the direct effect, on aggregate demand for American products, of a loss of $1 billion of export markets is minus $1 billion; whereas the direct effect of an additional $1 billion of imports is almost certain to be minus *less* than $1 billion, since some part of the purchasing power used up to buy the new imports would otherwise not have been spent at all—these dollars being, so to speak, tempted away from savings.

In the second place, if we are talking about sudden, large-volume changes, the indirect or derived effects are also likely to be less unfavorable when imports are expanded than when exports are contracted. This follows from the fact that certain of our industries are so heavily dependent on exporting (machinery, iron and steel products, motor vehicles, cotton, tobacco, and apples, to name some examples) that a major reduction in export totals might create difficulties that would spread far and wide and bring about substantial secondary losses of income and purchasing power. To be sure, some of the new competition from a major rise in import totals would likewise pinpoint on particular industries and particular localities. But, on the whole, it seems likely that the impact from even a sharp rise of imports (for example, imports of rubber, oil, wool, and a wide range of manufactured products such as textiles, china, glassware, chemicals, or watches) would be more evenly distributed and have less severe secondary repercussions than would a major reduction in exports.

The points just brought out do not, of course, prejudge whether or not the Government has an obligation to assist business and labor to make such readjustments as may in fact be necessary if import competition, aided by a lowering of import barriers, forces real retrenchment in particular instances. What they do suggest is that expansion of imports is likely to complicate the problem of maintaining full employment somewhat less than it will be complicated by the loss of export outlets.

This conclusion, based on the probable over-all size of demand in terms of dollars, is reinforced by the further consideration that expansion of imports is likely to mean more production and more employment for even the *same* aggregate dollar demand, because it will result in lowered costs and keener price competition. When it is realized, in addition, that a stepped-up interchange of commodities and services could help to knit the world together, that standards of living are raised when goods move freely about the world without hindrance or subsidy in accordance with comparative efficiencies, that our national security requires that we stockpile essential raw materials and in general retard the depletion of our own natural resources, and that an expansion of imports involving a reduction of trade barriers would tend to lessen governmental controls here and abroad whereas a forced contraction of exports would necessarily tend to intensify such controls, the case for trying to make the major adjustment through larger imports is very clear.

To achieve that result will require great efforts, however. It may be truly said that the loss of export markets is no less unwelcome to those immediately affected than the loss of domestic markets which are captured by foreign competitors. Unfortunately, if barriers keep imports out, then, unless the Government holds the gap open at taxpayers' expense, inability of foreigners to buy will drag our exports down, regardless.

However, to come back to the main issue, the attainment or preservation of full employment will be somewhat complicated by closing the dollar gap, *regardless* of which way this is done. Since the gap is about $6 billion wide at the present time, the probable impact from closing it—or, let us say, the impact from closing the part not likely to be covered by foreign investment under Point Four—deserves respectful attention.

One conclusion might be that the dollar gap should not be closed at all, or even narrowed. A better conclusion would be that we need domestic policies, consistent with our various other national objectives, to assure the maintenance of sufficient aggregate demand to support prosperity and full employment. We need such policies, of course, not merely to absorb the impact from closing the dollar gap. Obviously, a shortage of markets may develop from causes quite unrelated to foreign trade. But such a shortage, then, in addition to its other disadvantages, will multiply the difficulties of dispensing with our export surplus. Clearly, if the dollar gap needs to be closed, it is essential to create conditions, through sound prosperity policies, in which the effort to close it will not be frustrated by pressures to keep imports down and exports up.

POINT FOUR AND U.S. FULL EMPLOYMENT

The argument is sometimes heard that we must aid the underdeveloped countries for the sake of our own prosperity; in a word, that full employment requires Point Four. This claim has been known to be made by representatives of underdeveloped countries, as well as by citizens of the United States. Since we have already examined the relation between Point Four and the dollar gap, and between the dollar gap and United States full employment, we should now be in a position to complete the triangle by assessing the merits of this further claim.

The first thing our previous analysis shows is that any help we obtain from Point Four in maintaining production and employment in the United States must come from the net investment effect and not from the increased productivity effect obtained in the "results" stage; that is, it must come from the temporary avoidance of the necessity to eliminate the export surplus, and not from its actual elimination. Point Four can promote better export-import balance in the world, or it can facilitate our full employment; but it cannot do both simultaneously. (Of course, it seems likely to keep our qualified technical experts pretty fully employed in any case! But what is under discussion here is our over-all employment level.) The fact that developed countries are better customers than underdeveloped countries shows that Point Four can make world trade expand, but not that it offers a magic formula to banish our "overproduction" worries. Unless the underdeveloped countries' exports increase still faster than their imports, Point Four will not, as we have seen, make any permanent contribution toward closing the gap. If it does make such a contribution, we shall be all the more thrown back on the necessity of perfecting domestic full employment policy. We cannot have it both ways.

In the net investment stage, Point Four can undoubtedly ease our internal problems more or less, depending on the size of the net investment outflow. Private savings going into foreign investment spare the budget the necessity of comparable or greater expenditures or tax reductions that would be required for maintaining the same volume of demand for American products. Heavy-goods industries geared to large export markets need not so suddenly contract. Farm surpluses need not pile up so fast. Readjustment processes are moderated or postponed. Time is gained to work out more lasting solutions. This may well mean that when exports and imports are brought into reasonable balance later on, the balance struck will be at a higher level than could be hoped for, in the face of the natural tendency for our exports to gravitate downward to the level of our imports, if the export surplus had to be squeezed out immediately. If so, this will mean that the postponement not only spreads out the impact felt by our economy, but actually lessens it somewhat in total magnitude, for reasons already discussed, and assists in gaining the other advantages of high-level two-way trade.

More than this can hardly be said. Indeed, what needs to be emphasized most is that any claim that Point Four can actually solve our full employment problem is entirely wrong. To think that Point Four is a *sufficient* condition for full employment in the United States is to cherish an illusion. For an American to think that it is a *necessary* condition is to cherish a very dangerous illusion indeed, because such ideas tend to block efforts to find real solutions of our fundamental economic problems.

A vital connection, all too often overlooked, between Point Four and United States full employment runs in the reverse direction. If we can maintain full employment, and especially if we can be sure of continuing to maintain it, that will undoubtedly help Point Four. If a business recession develops, or even, it may be, a threat that the level of demand will not keep rising so as to justify the expansion necessary to take care of increased productivity and a growing labor force, wise action will become doubly difficult. In such circumstances the pressure to economize by cutting off assistance to foreign countries, including the underdeveloped countries, will be second only to the mounting pressure to keep imports out and increasingly subsidize our exports. By contrast, the wealth and the good will flowing from a solidly based full employment will be a major factor in promoting development programs all over the world, because they will allay doubts that we can afford to give generous and continuous aid.

CONCLUSIONS

These considerations invite, I think, the following general conclusions:

Point Four will help to postpone the necessity of entirely closing the export-import gap and will facilitate, within limits and for a time, the maintenance of prosperity and full employment in the United States. A sound domestic full employment program, however, is essential to a proper perspective on Point Four, and to adequate funds for carrying it out, as well as essential to a closing of the dollar gap, especially at the desirable high export-import level.

Point Four should be supported for its own sake, and not for specious or extraneous reasons.

Sound considerations of national security are, of course, never specious or extraneous. The amount and the distribution of the aid we can render today may not correspond exactly to what would be indicated in a world in which the foundations of peace had been securely laid, a world in which all types of constructive co-operation under the general guidance of the Economic and Social Council and its affiliated agencies could move ahead with enormous strides to fulfill men's hopes. Even so, it still appears to be true that an approach dictated by a due regard for certain intrinsic functional relations between the major considerations other than defense is likely also to strengthen defense itself by winning allegiance to our cause. Such an approach, as it applies to Point Four, may be summarized here as follows:

Give profound consideration, sparing neither sympathy nor critical judgment, to the needs of the countries requesting aid for their development. Do this not merely for the sake of the people of those countries, but also for the sake of our own interest in a peaceful world in which the ideals by which we set store can be practiced, can flourish, can further evolve. Avoid a parsimonious attitude. Equally avoid any tendency to degrade Point Four by forcing its pace from ulterior motives, such as the hope of getting full employment for ourselves at bargain rates as a lucky by-product. This long-term job—the job, as President Truman put it, of "making the benefits of our scientific advances and industrial progress available for the improvement and growth of underdeveloped areas"—should be done for its own sake. It is well worth doing.

22

The Underwriting Approach to Full Employment: A Further Explanation

Benjamin Higgins' review of my *Full Employment and Free Enterprise*[1] in the May 1948 issue of this *Review* shows that the proposals I have made for assuring continuous full employment in the United States are not always understood. This has also been demonstrated from time to time by the remarks of other critics—for example, Professors Hansen[2] and Alan R. Sweezy.[3] I am frankly mystified by some of the interpretations, and welcome this opportunity to try to clear up the main misunderstandings involved. These misunderstandings, as the following discussion should show, are fundamental. Confusion is multiplied when the reader is given to understand that my thesis—which offers, I believe, a distinctively new combination of elements—is quite familiar; e.g., Higgens says that "many [economists] are ready to accept it"[4] and that these are now "old ideas,"[5] while Hansen calls the view in favor of underwriting private consumption "widely held."[6]

May I emphasize that my purpose in this article is not to argue my position but to clarify it by removing misapprenehsions about it, so that future arguments about it may be more fruitful.

First, some ideas that, with all due respect to my critics, my proposals do *not* contain: They do *not* contain the idea that full employment can be assured by underwriting or by maintaining private consumption alone. They do *not* assume that private consumption can be maintained by the mere act of underwriting it. They do *not* involve the notion that the maintenance of the "right" level of private consumption will (a) render private

Reprinted by permission from *The Review of Economics and Statistics*, Vol. XXXI, No. 3, August, 1949.

investment perfectly stable, or (b) raise private investment to the point where, averaging high and low years together, all tendency for savings to exceed investment is removed. They are *not* hostile to public works and services. These points, along with certain related issues, will be examined below in some detail.

UNDERWRITING PRIVATE CONSUMPTION ALONE NOT SUFFICIENT

Hansen's critique of underwriting private consumer expenditures is based on his thought that the proponents of this technique regard it as sufficient of itself to maintain full employment. "The view is widely held," he tells us, "that underwriting private consumption would ensure full employment . . . this misconception widely prevails. . . ."[7] "But underwriting consumption will not provide full employment. The belief that it will is based on an inadequate conception of the factors on which full employment, in all modern societies, is based."[8]

I am not sure who the numerous persons are to whom Professor Hansen attributes this view which he criticizes; they remain unidentified. I hesitate to assume, just because the footnote in which he comments on my proposals is placed in this context, that he would consign me to this abysmal ideological niche. Yet I am disturbed by what is conveyed when he says that "His [Pierson's] proposal to underwrite private consumption is . . . inadequate (as I believe he would himself admit). . . ."[9]

Of course, I have never suggested that full employment could be assured by maintaining, let alone by merely underwriting, only consumption. In the pamphlet that Hansen cites by title I strongly emphasized (pp. 158, 160, 162, 166, 168, and 169)[10] that it would also be essential to underwrite total employment as such, and that the effectuation of this further guarantee would bring into play a second balance wheel— namely, expansions and contractions of public works and services.[11] I have repeatedly stressed this point in other writings as well (pp. 19–20, 40–41, 43–44, 76, 78, 123–25, 135–36, etc., and in my earlier book, *Full Employment*).

I have gone further and warned of the consequences of any attempt to underwrite consumption alone. I will quote this warning (pp. 67–68)[12] at length: "In the first place, the underwriting of aggregate consumer spending would be hard to justify in the absence of an established policy to give jobs on public work projects to persons who might remain involuntarily idle in spite of the inducement afforded to private enterprise by the guarantee. . . . Applied by itself, if such a thing could be imagined, it could involve the government in large expense for consumption subsidies at the very time when men and women were trying in vain to find jobs. This expense would then be challenged as indefensible—with some justice, since it would clearly be better to secure a tangible product in return for the money spent—and the whole policy might under these conditions be condemned as a kind of fiscal sleight of hand." Surely, this ought to be clear.

REASON FOR UNDERWRITING PRIVATE CONSUMPTION

But, if full employment cannot be guaranteed by underwriting and maintaining private consumption alone, just what is the point of that particular proposal? My answer is: (1) The continuously assured maintenance of a suitably high level of consumer spending would certify that the total market (gross national expenditures) would be large enough to preserve full employment *with resort to supplementary public works and services kept within practicable limits*; it would thus make the guaranteeing of full employment itself politically possible. On the other hand, in the absence of such a program with respect to consumption, the volume of public works and services likely at times to be required to preserve full employment would exceed practicable limits—so clearly so that, in our economy, it would not be politically possible, under those conditions, to guarantee full employment (pp. 14, 36–39, 70, 91–93, 145–46, 158–60, 173, 176–77). (2) Underwriting consumption and employment—assuring their maintenance at stated levels *in advance*—would have a double advantage: (a) it would provide security and confidence to, and thus tend to sustain the expenditures of, producers and consumers alike (pp. 6, 22, 63, 70–71, 92, 123, 124, 146, 150, 162); and (b) it would obviate undue reliance on, and disputes over, forecasting, by placing the government's compensatory action on an if, as, and when basis dependent on current events as reflected in current operating statistics (pp. 63, 92–93, 124, 146, 162).

Could not the maintenance of consumer spending be assured by the very act of assuring the maintenance of employment itself, so that a separate underwriting of consumer spending would be superfluous? My answer to this is as follows: The guaranteeing of full employment alone would indeed give the prospect that *income* would remain at levels associated with, and in a meaningful sense derived from, full employment. But personal *consumption expenditures* would not be assured of remaining at levels favorable to the *continuation* of full employment. The larger the aggregate of business, governmental, and personal savings, the smaller, of course, the total of personal consumption expenditures. The great danger of over-saving, as I see it, would here be precisely the danger that personal consumption expenditures would be too small, even when income was initially at the full-employment level, to keep such a full-employment guarantee from breaking down by reason of the impossibility, under normal peacetime conditions, of boosting government offsets to saving *in the form of government expenditures for goods and services* sufficiently to maintain that guarantee. If, however, consumer spending were underwritten and sustained *independently*, at levels held high enough to substantially prevent or offset over-saving when it would otherwise occur, the strain leading to breakdown should be absent.

LEVEL OF PRIVATE CONSUMPTION SELECTED FOR UNDERWRITING

I have referred above to underwriting (and maintaining) a "high enough" or "suitably high" level of consumer spending. What level is "suitably high"? Although my position on this had seemed to me to be a consistent one, Professor Higgins has found this part of my thesis particularly unclear.[13] Let me therefore restate.

The objective, as I visualize it, is to underwrite the dollar volume of consumer spending at the level[14] that is expected to buy the portion of full-employment output (gross national product) that is not absorbed by (a) expected regular government expenditures for goods and services, plus (b) an estimate (explained further below) of private gross capital expenditures, plus (c) expected net foreign investment (if this is not already included in b or, it might be, in a and b). This is the substance of what I have said on numerous occasions (pp. 57–58, 70, 72, 91, 125–26, 134, 165–66, 177). The underwritten level of consumer spending would then be maintained irrespective of events. To the extent that (A) realized government expenditures for goods and services, computed *before* adjustment for any compensatory supplements or reductions, (B) realized private gross capital expenditures, and (if separate) (C) realized net foreign investment differed from (a), (b), and (c) respectively, or unforeseen price-level changes increased or reduced the purchasing power of the dollar—or, more precisely, to the extent that these various "errors" did not cancel out—unemployment or over-employment would tend to appear but would be avoided by adjusting (A) up or down, i.e., generally speaking, by supplementing or reducing public works. Next year this process would be repeated. Other things being equal, the underwritten level of consumer spending would be lifted year by year as our national productivity rose.

The only possible ambiguity I am aware of in this formulation has to do with the preferred method of estimating private gross capital expenditures; and here, although this is to some extent a subordinate point, and one on which my views are more or less implied by my whole argument, I feel that Higgins has reason to complain that I have not made very explicit statements. The issue is this: If the estimate used were to correspond simply to the best guess as to what would happen in the year immediately ahead, cyclical fluctuations in private investment would have to be offset by inducing a cyclical counter-fluctuation into the underwritten level of consumption. (This is Higgins' interpretation of my proposal when he says that occasionally I suggest that consumption "might be varied in a countercyclical manner, increasing when investment falls off and vice versa."[15]) On the other hand, if the estimate represented an unadjusted *average* of the annual amounts expected to materialize over the private cycle, and if the latter cycle continued to be rather extreme, considerable strain might be placed on the secondary employment regulator, expansions and contractions of public works.

The problem thus posed appears, however, to be quite soluble. Fluctuations in private investment would no doubt be much reduced in amplitude once *over-all* economic cycles (fluctuations in employment and economic activity as a whole) were suppressed. Moreover, when labor and other production factors were temporarily released from private construction and other lines of private capital formation, they could as a rule transfer more easily to the stepping-up of the rate of activity on regular public works, or to the initiation of emergency projects taken from the reserve shelf, than to the production of additional goods for consumption. I am, therefore, inclined to think the expected *cyclical-average* private investment figure might come to be a perfectly satisfactory basis for the determination in question. This is, indeed, a logical implication of the role reserved, in my proposals, for public works variations. Nevertheless, I should not want to preclude the possibility that, especially in the beginning, it might prove desirable to raise (lower) the underwritten consumption level slightly in years of maximum deviation of expected private gross capital expenditures below (above) their estimated cyclical average.

By way of arithmetical example, assume that, for the next year, a full-employment level of gross national expenditures was expected to be $250 billion; that regular government expenditures for goods and services were expected to come to $35 billion;

and that private gross capital expenditures (I am here including net foreign investment), estimated as an *average* over an anticipated private investment cycle, also amounted to $35 billion. The difference between $70 billion and $250 billion—or $180 billion—would then be the first approximation of the amount of consumer spending to be underwritten. At this level of consumer spending the market would in fact be cleared of a full-employment output, without any adjustment of public works, if private capital expenditures hit their estimated average level in the year in question and if everything else, including the price level, worked out as expected. If private capital expenditures seemed likely to fluctuate between annual total of $32 billion and $38 billion, then, even if they were expected to be at the bottom of their cycle in the year just ahead, it might still seem best to underwrite consumption at $180 billion, taking up all slack by expanding public works and thus raising the government component from $35 billion to $38 billion or thereabouts. ($38 billion would be the advance estimate, but unforeseen developments including price-level changes could make the dollar value of the adjustment of government programs required to maintain full employment be somewhat larger or smaller.) But if the anticipated private investment cycle ranged between annual values of $27 billion and $43 billion, with only $27 billion foreseen for the coming year, the best solution might be to underwrite consumption at, say $183 billion, instead of $180 billion, and look forward to government expenditures for goods and services aggregating in the neighborhood of $40 billion. Again, consumption might be underwritten at, say, $175 billion, and the government total trimmed to around $32 billion, if the peak load of $43 billion of private investment appeared to be due.

Turning now to Higgins' other, alternative interpretations[16] of my "objective as to consumption policy," I do *not* suggest that consumption should be "equal to (estimated disposable income at full employment) x (the average propensity to consume over some previous period)." That would be the very opposite of what I have in mind, since it would accept any over-saving as final, and hence as capable of rectification only through expansion of government expenditures for goods and services. I do *not* suggest that the aim should be the realization of a stable price level *instead of* the realization of a predetermined dollar volume of consumer spending. Of course, an estimate of what the price-level trend will be is necessarily involved in the computation of the right dollar volume of consumer spending for underwriting purposes. My point is simply that the government can itself exercise considerable control over this trend, and that a stable or slowly rising price level may prove to be the best assumption for computation purposes and, then, the best objective in following through (pp. 56, 62).[17] I do *not* mean, in proposing to maintain an amount of consumption "the confident anticipation of which would be expected to stimulate full employment, with public investment limited to items wanted for their own sake" (p. 43), that *year-by-year* stability in private investment could be expected and that, consequently, no variation in public works would be needed. While the main *"lift"* would be supplied by keeping up consumption—this part of the program eliminating any *average* or *secular* deficiency in total private spending—the public-works balance wheel would still be needed for *stabilization*. Finally, I do *not* precisely propose to "stabilize the propensity to consume," in what I take to be the most meaningful sense of that term. This last question, however, will be discussed more fully at a later point.

MAINTAINING PRIVATE CONSUMPTION AT
THE UNDERWRITTEN LEVEL

According to Professor Alan Sweezy's review of my earlier book, *Full Employment*, I have been guilty of assuming that a guarantee of consumer spending would automatically fulfill itself without requiring the government to take action (and, frequently, incur deficits) in boosting consumers' disposable income. "If it would work," he writes, "the consumption guarantee policy would obviously have great advantages. It would not only keep the government from stepping on the toes of business, but would also avoid the increase in public debt. . . ."[18] "If the government went beyond a mere guarantee and took steps to see that income actually was maintained at the desired level, the outcome would, of course, be different. But the government could maintain income only [?] by . . . the very New Deal measures Dr. Pierson was hoping to escape through his consumption guarantee plan."[19] "But there would be nothing in a mere guarantee of increased consumption to bring [increased consumption] about. It would be necessary for the government to step in and . . . [adopt] the very measures the Pierson plan is designed to avoid."[20]

This line of interpretation is quite at variance with what I have actually said.[21] On page 25 of *Full Employment*, for example, I stated that "Whenever . . . the requisite consumer money income fails to materialize through the usual channels, so that government must make a net contribution," Congress must specify how this is to be done. A great many other passages could be cited[22] in which I have clearly indicated that the government would have to stand ready (on a contingent basis) to supply a compensatory boost to disposable income in order to have the underwriting made good—as well as to reduce disposable income, or its use, when the opposite danger of too much consumer spending threatened.

To be sure, the act of underwriting should in itself *help somewhat* to bring about higher levels of private spending—although certain speculative types of investment would tend to be discouraged (p. 63). I have also suggested that the budget deficits incurred in supporting consumer spending at its underwritten level might well be less than those required to close all employment gaps—if that were possible—by additional public works and services (pp. 23, 51, 65–66, 73). Finally, various factors should help reduce the need for compensatory action to sustain full employment once a condition of full employment had lasted for a good many years. For example, the rate of saving (*ex ante*) would tend to be reduced when people commonly became able to spend their accumulated savings (dis-save) for the purposes originally intended, instead of losing them in a depression, or during inflation, as has so often occurred up to now. But these are subordinate questions.

I stress the main issue, elementary as it is, because Hansen, too, has missed my point. After stating that I am "extraordinarily vague about how in practice this established level of consumption is, in fact, to be rigorously maintained,"[23] he concludes: "The only way in which I can make his 'insurance' really mean anything would be for Congress to undertake a rigorous commitment to issue money outright to consumers in sufficient volume to maintain consumption expenditures at the desired figure. But in fact he stops short of this extreme proposal and has not, so far as I know, advocated it. The nearest he comes to that procedure is his advocacy of remission of taxes. There is in his work, I feel, a vague reliance on the belief that if the 'insurance idea' were *proclaimed* by Congress, business and consumer expenditures would automatically prove adequate. It is, I feel, never explained just how the insurance commitment is to be rigourously fulfilled. Perhaps I have failed to understand the proposal."[24]

This is, to me, astonishing. I clearly *do* advocate having Congress undertake a rigorous commitment to maintain consumption expenditures at the desired figure (or, to be exact, between desired "floor" and "ceiling" levels). I stop short of the "extreme proposal," that money be issued outright to consumers, only to the extent that I do not insist that *this particular method* must be preferred in boosting consumers' disposable income. I have suggested several procedures *besides* remission of taxes, I do *not* rely on the belief that, given the act of underwriting, business and consumer expenditures would automatically prove adequate.

In my first book and numerous subsequent papers, available to Hansen at the time he offered the foregoing critical comments, appear many statements that should have made these comments gratuitous. Page references to some of these statements have been given above. In my pamphlet, "Full Employment in Practice," which he specifically cites, I said (pp. 166–67): "A question arises regarding the ways that might be recommended for raising consumer spending to the underwritten level if—as will normally be likely to happen until real progress has been made with our basic policies—it tends to remain too low even when income payments are running at a full-employment rate. No attempt will be made here to catalogue the various methods available, but two possibilities will be mentioned by way of illustration. The President might recommend, contingent on a demonstrated need for more consumer spending, a reduced rate on the personal income tax, coupled with cash offsets or refunds, on a reasonable basis, applied to Federal, State, and local indirect taxes which largely burden those too poor to pay an income tax. Or, alternatively, he might wish to recommend, along with a reduced rate on the income tax, the distribution to low-income families of stamps enabling them to improve their nutrition and living standards by buying food and, possibly, other necessities such as clothing in the market at reduced expense. For the opposite contingency of a tendency toward an inflationary excess of total consumer spending, he might recommend, for example, a graduated spendings tax with generous exemptions at the bottom."[25] I should have thought that some attention would be paid to such statements.

The basis for Professor Hansen's feeling that I have been vague about this aspect of my proposal is, I believe, this: In order not to divert attention from the *general principle* that consumers' disposable income should be subsidized if, as, and when required in order to realize a previously guaranteed level of consumer spending—a principle which is an integral part of the policy I have suggested—I have deliberately avoided emphasizing, to the exclusion of other alternatives, any one *particular method* whereby this principle should be applied. I have, however, indicated various methods that might be used: the suspension, lowering, rebating, or offsetting of specified taxes affecting consumption (pp. 24, 46–47, 49, 72, 78, 91, 92, 93, 126–28, 134, 135, 150, 166–67, 170, 178–79); the supplementing of existing social security benefits through the general distribution of "national income security payments" (a better term might be "consumption stabilization payments") or other cash benefits to consumers (pp. 1–2, 6, 24, 47, 49,

54, 72); a "stamp plan" for low-income groups to match tax reductions for others (pp. 167, 179).[26] I have, moreover, discussed some of these methods at sufficient length to show that they should be feasible (pp. 45–47, 126–128). I am sure that ingenuity will disclose still other variant possibilities—conforming to the generally desirable criteria of adequacy of amount, broad and fair distribution, flexibility, and operating simplicity (p. 45)—and that fuller investigation of this problem can improve and refine the detail to the desired point if once the rationale underlying these measures is clearly grasped and is approved. But I have wanted to avoid side-tracking the debate. This is a case where the discussion of finished blueprints seems highly premature and unprofitable.

I do, of course, have some tentative views about specific methods. At present I am inclined to think that the best plan for raising consumer spending (when necessary to fulfill the guarantee) might involve one of the two following procedures, either of which holds some advantages over the other: (1) As mentioned first in the passage quoted above, the standard or basic income-tax rate might for the time being be lowered (an idea also favored by Hansen, and facilitated in application, as he points out, by current witholding); and meanwhile non-payers of income taxes might receive their *quid pro quo* through the payment by the Treasury to them of some uniform cash sum, allowed as a partial (though not strictly proportional) rebate or offset of other (indirect) taxes paid by them to various tax jurisdictions. (2) Income-tax payers might be treated as above, while non-payers might be enabled to make a portion of practically any of their ordinary purchases at reduced expense by buying from the government at a discount a limited quantity of multi-purpose "stamps" or coupons which retailers would be asked to accept at face value, the Treasury then reimbursing retailers for the amount of the discount.[27] I think that either of these procedures would work. However, to repeat once more, while I consider the general approach here indicated as fundamental to my proposal, I regard the precise methods of carrying it out as optional.

COMPENSATORY MEASURES; PROPENSITY TO CONSUME; DISTRIBUTION OF INCOME

It must now be obvious that I am not, as Hansen supposes, one who "minimizes the importance of a vigorous *compensatory* offsetting program."[28] On the contrary, I attach very great strategic importance to a two-sided compensatory program consisting of (a) adjustments of consumers' disposable income[28a] when necessary to fulfill a prior guarantee of consumer spending, and (b) adjustments of the volume of public works and services at times when, in spite of the direct support given to consumption, total employment still tended to fall short of (or too much exceed) *its* established mark. Incidentally, I have made a particular point (pp. 121–22, 126, 133, 149, 151–52, 161–62, 164–67, 178) of stressing the distinction between *compensatory* and *basic* measures—meaning by the latter all those measures that are adopted essentially on their own continuing merits rather than to adjust the level of income, production, or employment. This distinction appears to me to have great methodological and practical importance.

In Higgins' comment on my proposals reference is made several times to the *propensity to consume*. Higgins suggests, for example, that my criticisms of the public-investment approach to full employment might have been tempered had I taken more note of what Keynes and others have said about the need to control the propensity to consume, and he infers that what I, myself, am trying to do is stabilize the propensity to consume at some proper level.[29]

I do not think, from the context, that Higgins merely means to refer to control over the real proportions between consumption and investment[30]—a concept that, in its broadest sense, corresponds to what Hansen distinguishes as the "national consumption function."[31] In any case, on the particular questions here at issue, such a use of terms would not be very illuminating. It would seem more to the point to concentrate here on the propensity to consume viewed as a schedule of relationships between total *disposable* income of consumers and what they spend at various levels of disposable income—what Hansen means when he speaks of "the willingness of consumers to spend (consumption function)."[32] So interpreted, the propensity to consume can be controlled only by controlling the proportion between spending and saving out of a given disposable income, not by controlling disposable income itself. On the other hand, the compensatory adjustments of consumption visualized in connection with my underwriting proposal would commonly achieve their effect, not by changing the spending-saving ratio at a given level of disposable income, but rather by raising (or lowering) total disposable income itself.[33] The suggestion that disposable income be thus adjusted whenever and to the extent required to reach target levels of consumer spending has not, to my knowledge, been made by Keynes or in the White Papers or other proposals cited by Higgins. Yet this approach seems required, in the United States, in order to free full-employment policy from precarious reliance on such things as control over the propensity to consume.

A further word about this. In my proposals, the need for basic policy measures that will improve the "self-sustaining" qualities of our economy, and thus reduce the degree of reliance on deficit-creating compensatory measures, is strongly emphasized (pp. 23, 64, 72, 91–92, 106–22, 126, 133, 147–49, 151–56, 161–62, 164–65, 178). (I think it would be desirable to be able to balance the budget "over the cycle," even though I would never favor a policy of trying to balance the budget by letting full employment go. That policy would be self-defeating in any case, since, as long as over-saving was present, reduced tax revenues and enlarged relief expenditures would still bring budget deficits.) Among the basic adaptations referred to are those long-term measures favorable to consumption—measures dealing with taxes, wages, social security, etc.—which will raise the propensity to consume by making the distribution of income less unequal. Satisfactory rules for promoting competition and regulating monopoly will also have this desirable effect, not to speak of their effects in promoting investment and holding down prices.

On the other hand, when it comes to *compensatory* measures to boost the amount of disposable income in order to fulfill the suggested guarantee of consumer spending, I consider that the devices used should preferably aim at a more or less "horizontal" lifting of all incomes (pp. 45, 126–28, 167, 178–79). To introduce any strong redistributionist bias into these final-adjustment measures would be to lose sight of their true character as scientific devices for protecting everyone's common interest in the existence of an adequate over-all market. Moreover, since such an approach would invite the charge that social changes not admitted through the front door (i.e., by considered enactment of basic legislation) were now being smuggled in by the back door under the pretext of combatting depression, it would risk rejection of the whole compensatory policy. While families with low incomes undoubtedly have the highest individual propensities to consume, so that the subsidization of *their* incomes would tend to exercise the greatest leverage on consumer spending, per dollar of cost to the government, this consideration is not decisive. For its seems clear that any reasonable, broad plan for subsidizing consumers straight across the board would in fact place most of the extra buying power in the hands of those who are far from rich, and would therefore not cause any damagingly large "leakage" into additional savings.

These comments have a bearing on Hansen's view that "to underwrite private consumption *fully* . . . would divorce reward too far from production . . . would remove financial incentives to effort and efficiency."[34] That might, of course, be true if consumption subsidies were made inversely proportional to the wages, or to the total incomes, received by different persons (just as a scheme that made them *directly* proportional to wages would tend to distort the labor supply to the extent that it caused relative rewards to exaggerate differences in the marginal productivity of different kinds of work). To a compensatory program that raised incomes "horizontally," however, when consumer spending would otherwise be insufficient, these objections would not apply.

CYCLICAL VS. SECULAR DEFICIENCIES OF PRIVATE INVESTMENT

Both Sweezy[35] and Hansen[36] have argued that, inasmuch as private investment is partly of an autonomous character, it is a mistake to suppose that private investment can be stabilized by controlling consumption. Since I have never for a moment entertained this supposition, their arguments on this score do not, as the writers appear to think, apply to my proposals. What I do maintain is that the amplitude of fluctuations in private investment would be substantially reduced once the continuous maintenance of prosperity and full employment was an accomplished fact. Hansen makes the same point.[37] There is therefore no disagreement here.

Cyclical instability of investment, however, is not the whole of the matter. According to Sweezy, I have tried to show in *Full Employment* that the underwriting of consumer spending would stimulate private investment to the point where a tendency for savings (at full employment) to exceed investment would no longer be present. I take it that he has reference not merely or primarily to temporary deviations of private investment below a satisfactory average level, i.e., to instability proper, but also to a *secular* problem connected with a tendency for the average itself to be "too low."

Sweezy's misunderstanding of my position on the savings-investment issue is reflected throughout his review. "The central . . . thesis, as I understand it," he writes, recapitulating his interpretation, "is that a proper rate of increase in aggregate consumption will call forth the amount of net investment necessary to offset the saving done by the community at a high level of income and hence will keep the economy operating at a full employment rate."[38] "Now the Pierson scheme is to keep these workers employed in producing capital goods, and at the same time to provide an outlet for the profitable investment of saving . . . and the government will be freed from the necessity of spending any money itself."[39]

In thus supposing that my proposals involve the maintenance of some particular, high level of private investment, Sweezy is quite mistaken. My whole discussion of the need for the government to stand ready to take compensatory action to raise consumer spending[40] bore precisely upon the likelihood that private investment would often be too small to absorb a full-employment volume of savings; nor do I think, in addition, that there is any warrant for construing my remarks in that book as pre-judging whether the need would be purely cyclical or predominant and possibly more or less continuous.[41]

Certainly it would seem to me over-optimistic to assume that the compensatory measures needed to maintain full employment will henceforth be only contra-cyclical in the literal sense, i.e., that the amount of governmental support required in some years will be balanced by the amount of governmental restraint required in others, so that surpluses will offset deficits. Indeed I think—and I infer that Sweezy, Hansen, and Higgins do also—that there is in the United States, budget deficits aside, an inherent, average tendency toward over-saving or under-spending at full-employment levels of income. (I am not here concerned, of course, with speculations about possible aftermath conditions in the event of another war.) After we have progressed some distance with our basic policies, this tendency should become less of a problem, and may disappear entirely. Pending that outcome, the compensatory measures required will more largely take the form of deficit-creating measures to support the demand for goods and services (not that they will necessarily be thought of in those terms where defense programs are involved) than of surplus-creating measures to hold this demand in check. Finally, while policies to encourage private investment certainly should, in my opinion, form part of the basic program, I see no point in trying to force private investment above the range in which it would naturally move in a generally satisfactory economic environment (pp. 24, 42, 70, 92, 96, 160). Should such an effort succeed, moreover, it would only intensify the problem of avoiding a glut of consumption output at a later date.[42]

ATTITUDES TOWARD PUBLIC WORKS AND SERVICES

The reader of Dr. Higgins' review is likely to get the further erroneous impression that my proposals are hostile to public investment and government programs generally. The aim of fiscal policy which Higgins attributes to me "is tantamount to 'full employment without inflation, achieved with a minimum amount of government intervention other than paying subsidies and collecting taxes.' Not everyone," he adds, "considers the minimization of government activity an end in itself."[43]

I do not see how a careful reading of either of my books could possibly sustain this interpretation of what I have said. In the passage quoted by Higgins as evidence,[44] what I am alluding to is the undesirability of having to close all savings-investment gaps, whatever their tendency to persist, through emergency public activities that have not been regularly approved by the community for their own sake. I do believe that, in the United States, government programs still have to bear the burden of proof (pp. 5, 24, 42, 62, 92, 106-7, 114). On the page to which he refers, however, and on the page preceding (pp. 20-21), I have made it perfectly clear that I am personally in favor of substantial, permanent expansions of public works and services in various directions. I have time and again (pp. 12-13, 37, 71, 92, 96, 106-114, 124, 136, 142-43, 148, 164-65) advocated expanded public programs in such fields as slum clearance and housing, health and nutrition, education, conservation and development of natural resources, not to speak of an expanded social security system. (Some of these programs come under the head of public investment; some are services—as a rule, community services that enlarge real consumption.) I am perfectly open to persuasion on the merits of additional public programs that Higgins may have in mind.

At the same time, I do not think that my personal predilections, or Higgins', have much to do with the question. We are dealing with majority rule and the democratic process. As this process works out in the United States, the laws, of course, are made by Congress. The President might at some point urge a vastly expanded program of government expenditures for goods and services which, if enacted, might (though it also easily might not) suffice to maintain full employment without any additional, direct support for consumption. What I am advocating, however, is a line of policy that, if accepted in principle by Congress, would definitely maintain full employment whether or not the President put forward an all-embracing public program and whether or not, if put forward, his program was accepted in whole or in part by Congress. The President's uncertainty as to the action Congress would take with respect to his recommendations for various public program items need not, be it noted, create any difficulty, since he could submit his proposals in a form that indicated the need to *raise* the level at which consumption was underwritten if Congress decided to *cut down* his recommended public programs (p. 167).

One sometimes hears the argument that the United States should make sure of full employment by expanding foreign investment. Actually, the case bears a striking similarity, in one respect, to the case for expansion of public works and services. An export surplus and an associated positive value for net foreign investment may sometimes be highly desirable. Situations may arise in which net foreign investment is large enough to play a major part in sustaining domestic full employment. But that is not to say that full employment can safely be made contingent on shipping goods abroad (pp. 9–10, 33–34, 66–67, 73, 87–90, 130–32, 147, 163), any more than it can safely be made to hinge on approval of some particular set of plans for hospitals, schools, roads, river valley development, etc., etc. The trend in net foreign investment and the trend in government programs both follow rather complicated laws of their own. In my proposals, therefore, I have dealt with the means of maintaining full employment, not as a by-product of attaining other objectives with respect to, e.g., public programs or foreign investment, but independently of the size of these other items. In other words, I have tried to set forth the *general* case and avoid dependence on special combinations of other variables.

In conclusion, I want to plead guilty of preoccupation with finding a practical approach to *assured* full employment in a country with the particular characteristics of the *present-day United States*. This is the reader's clue. Proposals that make sense in this context may fail to do so if applied to other countries or to other times or if considered in connection with a lesser or a different objective. Conversely, proposals that are sensible if, for example, just moderating the business cycle is taken as the objective may be utterly incapable of being "stretched" into a program to assure full employment.

Hansen is opposed to too rigorous a full-employment commitment and quotes to adage that "the reed that does not bend breaks."[45] I am perfectly willing to waive certain rigorous, abstract considerations and settle for a definition of full employment in terms of a number of jobs annually fixed by Congress after studying the recommendations in the President's Economic Report (pp. 167–69, 175–76). This would provide reasonable leeway; I should say that the desirable amount of "bend" or "give" would be taken into account in the definition. But bending like a reed is no great virtue in itself. I think that we need the solid assurance that full employment, thus defined, will always be maintained.

NOTES

1. Washington, Public Affairs Press, 1947.
2. Alvin H. Hansen, *Economic Policy and Full Employment* (New York, 1947).
3. Review of my earlier book, *Full Employment* (New Haven, 1941) in *American Economic Review*, March 1944, pp. 134–37; also his Reply to Emile Benoit-Smullyan's Communication, same journal, December 1944, pp. 875–78.
4. Higgins, *op. cit.*, p. 145.
5. *Ibid.*, p. 146.
6. Hansen, *op. cit.*, p. 197. Hansen adds, however, with specific reference to my writings, "Perhaps I have failed to understand the proposal"; *ibid.*, p. 197, footnote.
7. *Ibid.*, p. 197.
8. *Ibid.*, p. 198.
9. *Ibid.*, p. 197, footnote.
10. All page numbers given in the text and in the footnotes (unless otherwise indicated) will refer to pages in my *Full Employment and Free Enterprise*, rather than in the original publications there collected. Citations will ordinarily be illustrative, not exhaustive.
11. The inclusive category is government expenditures for goods and services. A stabilizing effect will, of course, equally be achieved by variations in government purchases of items not associated with public works and services in the usual sense—e.g., military equipment, raw materials for stockpile, commodities for free distribution to consumers. (Theoretically the government might also influence certain private output decisions toward temporary expansion or contraction without varying its own expenditures.) This having been said, it will generally be convenient and sufficiently clear, in what follows, to refer simply to variations in public works or in public works and services.
12. Originally in *American Economic Review*, March 1944.
13. Higgins, *op. cit.*, p. 145.
14. I use the word "level" for the sake of simplicity; actually, some "play" is necessary, and what I advocate is a *range* between reasonably narrow lower and upper limits (pp. 52, 129, 166), the upper limit to serve as a brake on price spirals.
15. Higgins, *op. cit.*, p. 145. Incidentally, I fail to find in my book the passage that Higgins cites in justifying this interpretation. On page 44, to which he refers, I speak of inducing expansions or contractions in consumer incomes and spending, not in order to offset investment fluctuations, but rather in order to realize the consumption guarantee, which is quite a different matter.
16. *Ibid.*, pp. 145–46.
17. Also *Full Employment*, Ch. VII (see esp. p. 176).
18. Sweezy, *op. cit.*, p. 135. It is only proper to call attention to the fact that Sweezy's comments, as quoted and discussed in this article, appeared in 1944, and may not represent his present appraisal of my views.
19. *Ibid.*, pp. 136–37.
20. *Ibid.*, (Reply), p. 877.
21. I infer from certain of Sweezy's comments (esp. p. 135 and footnote) that part of his difficulty stemmed from my use of terms in criticizing the "public spending" approach to full employment. What I had in mind—the more exact terminology now current was not then in general use—was government expenditures *for goods and services*, i.e., public works and services, etc., not including transfer payments to consumers. I should have thought that the whole context made my meaning clear. Actually, of course, such compensatory governmental measures as will boost the disposable income and spending of consumers *directly* (i.e., not via public works, etc.) may involve either (a) government spending in the form of expenditures *not* for goods and services, or (b) reduced taxes, or (c) a combination of both.
22. *Full Employment*, pp. 137, 169, 170, 217, 222, 228–33, 247, 258, 271, etc. (In *Full Employment and Free Enterprise*, this point is made clear on pp. 1–2, 6–7, 23, 24, 43–47, 51–52, 54, 71, 72, 76, 78, 91–92, 93, 126–29, 134, 135, 150, 166–67, 170, 177, 178–79.)
23. Hansen, *op. cit.*, p. 197, footnote.

24. *Ibid.*

25. Presidential recommendations like these would, of course, require for their effectuation both Congressional decisions and subsequent administrative action. I followed up on the above remarks by discussing these aspects of the question (pp. 167–70).

26. Also, timed war-bond redemptions in the early postwar years (pp. 24, 45–46, 49, 72). These various methods, and other possibilities, are also touched on in the more theoretical discussion in *Full Employment*, esp. pp. 228–30. For *reducing* consumer spending (when necessary), I have mainly suggested a spendings tax (pp. 52, 55, 60, 72, 129, 134, 150, 167, 179). Other methods of taxation could be used—e.g., a special sales tax (with realized consumer spending then computed as net of the amount thus taxed), although sales taxation is ordinarily objectionable because of its regressive features (p. 52). Or the government might borrow from consumers (pp. 2, 23); this, to be really effective, would involve a forced saving program of some kind.

27. Either method assumes that families or individuals not subject to income tax would nevertheless, as a condition of eligibility, file income statements on a short form with the federal government.

28. Hansen, *op. cit.*, p. 197, footnote.

28a. See footnote 33, below, for a necessary qualification.

29. Higgins, *op cit.*, p. 145.

30. See his previously quoted reference to "(estimated *disposable* income at full employment) x (the average propensity to consume over some previous period)"; italics supplied.

31. Hansen, *op. cit.*, p. 44, footnote, and p. 161.

32. *Ibid.*, p. 40.

33. This at least is true of most of the compensatory procedures for *increasing* consumption. The available compensatory measures for adjusting consumption *downward* would vary considerably in their effects. For example, a spendings tax probably would reduce disposable income less than it would increase consumer saving.

34. Hansen, *op. cit.*, p. 199.

35. Sweezy, *op. cit.*, p. 136.

36. Hansen, *op. cit.*, pp. 198–200.

37. *Ibid.*, p. 200.

38. Sweezy, *op. cit.*, p. 875.

39. *Ibid.*, p. 877.

40. Cf. footnote 22 above.

41. See, e.g., pp. 217, 247, 258.

42. I could hardly do better at this point than quote from Dr. Smullyan's pertinent comments on Dr. Sweezy's review. "It is not Pierson's thesis that any predetermined amount of investment is necessary for full employment, or that the decision as to the amount of consumption to be guaranteed should be determined by the consideration of inducing an amount of investment adequate to offset the amount of savings that would occur in the absence of compensatory fiscal measures. Rather, it is proposed that the volume of public investment be primarily determined by what is desired for its own sake, and that the volume of private investment be allowed to adjust itself naturally to the guaranteed level of consumer spending. The latter element would be the variable. It would be set at *whatever level was believed necessary*, in conjunction with the intrinsically desirable public investment, and naturally occurring private investment, to bring about full employment." (Emile Benoit-Smullyan, "Rejoinder," *American Economic Review*, December 1944, p. 879.)

43. Higgins, *op. cit.*, p. 146. (Quotation beginning, 'full employment without inflation,' is from another author.)

44. *Ibid.*, p. 146, footnote 2.

45. Hansen, *op. cit.*, p. 197, footnote.

23

Employment the Key

Current events are stirring up the dormant interest in full employment. More and more people are beginning to say that something had better be done. What is not as commonly recognized even today is that the need to do something has been there all along. The premonitory fear of a future depression in the United States—a fear which has at no time been absent—is a potent factor for ill in both our domestic and our international relations, quite aside from the damage that results if depression actually occurs.

For instance: Large American business corporations insist on operating at low break-even points, with prices and profits high in boom times in relation to wages, because they expect to need the extra profits as a cushion against losses that will occur if markets and production later shrink—as no one at present can be sure they will not.

American labor, in turn, is always worried, and justifiably worried, about that most fundamental security problem, the job: will it last and, if it does not, will other job opportunities be available?

In this situation unions, like industry, are prone to insist on getting every possible concession for themselves here and now, and labor-management relations, in particular, suffer.

Again, other countries with which we do business—including major powers like England—have conclusively shown in recent international conferences that they will not and cannot give anything like hard-and-fast undertakings to abolish import quotas and discriminations against our trade in the absence of reasonable assurance that we on our part will maintain full employment and thus maintain the necessary high level of demand for their products. Meanwhile, the Russians say that recurring depression is inherent in the very fabric and "laws of motion" of our capitalist economy. We know how this assertion is used for propaganda purposes. We also know that it is part of the longstanding, basic Marxist text. We perhaps do not know how firmly the Kremlin now holds this belief but, above all, what we are not yet in a position to assert conclusively is that the belief is wrong. This is unfortunate because, all other difficulties aside, it is evidently a massive barrier against coming to a satisfactory understanding with Russia and laying the basis for genuine and lasting peace.

Considering such facts as these, it would seem that the answer lies in not merely taking steps to combat depression when it arrives, but in developing ways and means of assuring that prosperity and full employment will actually be maintained indefinitely.

It is often said that we can't afford the unbalanced budgets. But this puts the blame for deficits in the wrong place. The real villain of the piece, if deficit financing is required, is the too-little spending or oversaving tendency, not the full-employment policy. For, in the absence of a full-employment policy, the budget will be unbalanced anyway by shrinking tax revenues and growing relief handouts. Of course, we should develop basic long-run policies (to maintain mass markets, encourage venture capital, prevent monopoly restrictions, etc.), so that the too-little-spending tendency will be less likely to appear.

Another objection—of which a good deal has been heard lately, for obvious reasons— is that full employment means inflation. Undoubtedly too much spending must be avoided along with too little spending.

The problem of holding prices within bounds should then prove soluble on a case-by-case basis, by action against groups in intrenched positions trying to "get away with murder." Moreover, the alternative seems to be to keep always so "safely" below full employment that there is no risk at all of any prices rising—surely a counsel of despair.

The third big argument, that we cannot assure full employment unless we are prepared to have the government take over the economy, deserves careful attention. For one who may feel himself personally endangered by unbalanced budgets, a hundred will rise to the defense of individualism and the American enterprise system.

Just how the case is put depends on who is talking. Some see bureaucrats telling people how to run their business. Some visualize the government deciding where workers shall work, and on what terms. Probably the main fear, however, is of a big governmental apparatus forced by its promise of jobs to expand and expand to make up for shortages of private jobs, until private enterprise, tied right and left by miscellaneous regulations, is finally in competition with the government on such a vast scale that the traditional American system is virtually eclipsed.

Such fears have no doubt been played on and magnified for selfish ends. Some critics also have a confirmed narrow view of the fields in which public enterprise is legitimate and necessary. Nevertheless, I think it would be a grave error not to recognize that our prewar efforts to combat unemployment failed to indicate how the issue could be met squarely and the difficulty overcome. Nor have we yet an officially sponsored program that seeks to cut the Gordian knot.

If the government assures full employment, this means in the last analysis that it must be prepared to give jobs to all who cannot find them in private industry.

If there is danger that the too-little-spending tendency will become severe, and if the government has no effective way of bolstering private spending in the face of that tendency, it must either stand ready to put an enormous number of extra persons on the public payroll (or on contract work for the government) or—not assure full employment.

There are definite physical limits to the amount and rate of expansion of normal public works. Beyond those limits, the government would ultimately have to buy output for stockpiling or free distribution, organize projects of no intrinsic value, or find areas in which to take managerial decisions out of private hands. Here is the basic dilemma.

It will not arise in poor countries with small savings, in underdeveloped or war-devastated countries with a crying need for every type of capital equipment, in countries that do not dislike public competition with private enterprise. In the United States it does arise.

The Employment Act of 1946 made it the continuing policy and responsibility of the Federal Government to try to maintain "conditions under which there will be afforded useful employment opportunities, including self-employment, for those able, willing, and seeking to work."

The President, assisted by his Council of Economic Advisers, transmits to Congress at least once every year an Economic Report containing, among other things, an estimate of "the levels of employment, production, and purchasing power ... needed to carry out the policy," together with an action program. In Congress a Joint Committee on the Economic Report studies these messages and reports its findings and recommendations to the Senate and House.

I suggest that the essential amendments to the Employment Act to achieve the goal of assured full employment, in a way that avoids the aforementioned dilemma, are as follows:

1. A provision that Congress, after receiving the report of its Joint Committee on the Economic Report, should by joint resolution or otherwise specify (a) the number of jobs deemed to be required to carry out the policy declared in the act, and (b) the dollar total of consumer spending deemed sufficient to secure that level of employment without undue resort to direct creation of jobs by the government.

For example, in some year "(a)" might be 60,000,000 jobs and "(b)" might be $175,000,000,000. "(b)" would be calculated by subtracting normal private investment, regular public works and services, and the expected export surplus (if any) from the total volume of demand needed to buy a full-employment output. Hence it would be the amount that ought, if realized, to rule out oversaving and give business adequate markets for which to compete. Naturally, both the job total and the consumer spending total would tend to grow larger from year to year in line with the expansion possibilities and tendencies of our economy.

2. A provision that Congress should underwrite and agree to support the levels of employment and total consumer spending which it had thus determined to be the minimum necessary, and should also agree on a maximum level of consumer spending, as well as probably a maximum level of employment, which should not be exceeded.

Having reached its own decision on what needs to be achieved, Congress would here go on record as standing back of the carrying out of that decision.

3. A provision that Congress should lay down rules, involving contingent expenditures and contingent tax changes, and should direct the President to make periodic adjustments under those rules to raise or lower total consumer spending or total employment if, as, and when these magnitudes would otherwise tend to fall short of the minimum or exceed the maximum thus prescribed.

Under this provision, Congress would presumably direct the President to expand or contract public works and services, etc., if the designated official employment series threatened to move outside the range established by Congress. That would, of course, still happen from time to time, in spite of the steady support given to the consumer market, since moderate swings in private investment would still occur.

As for ways and means of boosting consumer spending, when necessary, Congress might (for example) prescribe as follows: that the President should—only if, as, and when the official consumer expenditure series dipped too low by comparison with the specified minimum—(a) lower the standard or basic income-tax rate, and either (b) have the Treasury transmit to nonpayers of income tax, or to all families, some uniform cash sum to be considered as a partial rebate or offset to indirect taxes paid by them to various tax jurisdictions, or (c) allow nonpayers of income tax to buy from the government at a discount a limited quantity of multipurpose "stamps" or coupons which retailers would be asked to accept at face value for all ordinary purchases (the Treasury then reimbursing retailers for the amount of the discount).

For keeping total consumer spending from going above the ceiling, Congress might (for example) enact a spendings tax or some kind of obligatory savings program, suspend its application, and direct the President to bring it into play if needed.

The approach here suggested avoids regimentation and industrial rigidity. It avoids excessive reliance on forecasts. It is fully consistent with basic policies to encourage private investment. Also with basic wage policies, social security policies, farm income measures, etc., calculated to make the distribution of income more favorable to what might be called an "automatic" maintenance of adequate consumer demand—only it would not let everything depend on those controversial policies.

Also, with the carrying out of all desirable government programs—but it would remove the major hazard that a commitment to maintain full employment might prove a commitment to expand government jobs or government controls beyond practicable or acceptable limits.

Finally, by taking the export-import balance into account as a factor in determining the needed level of domestic consumer spending, this approach would free us from any supposed necessity to send a net surplus of goods abroad in order to escape "overproduction." Our economic foreign policies would thus not reflect domestic economic worries, and could always be decided on their merits.

Events have carried the world to a point where it appears that certain conditions must soon be fulfilled if history is not to be rudely interrupted. Among those conditions—not to bring in the millennium, but to assure survival and lay the basis for further gains—would seem to be the following: new institutions, preferably through amendment of the United Nations Charter, to make resort to war virtually impossible as a matter of practical mechanics; full employment—above all, the assurance of continuing full employment in the United States; growth of a new kind of tolerance—the psychological "maturity" for which Dr. G. Brock Chisholm, now Director-General of the World Health Organization, has issued an inspiring call; economic development, particularly programs to raise living standards in the poorer countries of the world, as contemplated under "Point Four" of the President's inaugural message.

To some extent these conditions interlock. Full employment, if assured in the United

States, would be a major factor in promoting development programs to advance productivity and living conditions all over the world, because it would allay doubts that we can afford to lend generous and continuous aid. Full employment would make some contribution to psychological maturity. It offers no substitute for the international law and political machinery necessary to prevent war.

It would, however, both directly and by helping to narrow present extreme international differentials in living standards, reduce pressures that lead to political movements and events capable of breaking down the finest international peace machinery.

Assured full employment does appear to be possible—here, in the country where it matters most. We need not risk national bankruptcy or inflation in order to get it. We need not overturn our individualistic habits and institutions. We can solve this particular problem any time we like, without international negotiations. We would derive from assured full employment new freedom and power to deal with our other problems in a confident, firm, and generous manner.

24

Full Employment in Practice

In discussing "Full Employment in Practice," I propose to observe two limitations. First, I am not going to speak about how full employment might be practiced in any country other than the United States. It may be that the practice of full employment in Great Britain, for example, or in Australia, would be largely like our practice here; or, on the other hand, perhaps it would be quite different. That is an interesting question and an important question, but it is also a question on which I do not care to speculate here. If what I have to say can contribute to the understanding of the ways and means that are open to us in the United States, I shall be fully satisfied.

The second limitation that seems essential is this: the phrase, *full employment in practice*, does not, I take it, refer to how things might look at that happy but possibly rare moment between painful recovery and tragic collapse—that moment when the man of affairs and the business cycle theorist can clasp hands and say: "Boy! This is it!" On the contrary, when we speak of full employment in practice, we undoubtedly mean the way of operating our economy whereby full employment would be *permanent, continuing, and assured.* That, at any rate, is how I interpret my assignment, and I ask you to bear this carefully in mind as we go from step to step.

The point where innumerable discussions of full employment go off the track is the point where one party begins to talk about things to do to moderate our depressions. This brings scientific exchange of ideas on how to maintain full employment to an abrupt close. The practice of full employment is not the practice of moderating our depressions and our unemployment; it is the practice of not having any depressions, or any unemployment beyond the inevitable amount consistent with full employment.

What is full employment? Although I mean to come back to that again later, certainly something should be said at once to make it clear that this distinction between

---

This paper was presented on December 19, 1945, as an address before a special seminar on "Full Employment in a Free Economy" conducted by the Institute on Postwar Reconstruction at New York University. It was subsequently published by the Institute in pamphlet form.

maintaining full employment and moderating unemployment is not just a play on words.

Of course full employment allows some slack in the system—some between-jobs or frictional unemployment—no one has ever denied it so far as I am aware. But please take note of these two points about genuine full employment. In the first place, employment does not fall below, or unemployment does not rise above, some quantity agreed upon in advance. In other words, performance is checked against and governed by a standard. In the second place, the standard adopted is intended to produce a situation in which there will really be work opportunity for all who are able to work and desire to do so, and, from time to time, the operation of this administrative standard is reviewed to see if this standard needs revision to make it correspond to the essential idea of universal employment opportunity.

There in a nutshell is why maintaining full employment is not the same thing as seeking to moderate unemployment or, as some propose, seeking to avoid mass unemployment. Whether or not it is the same thing as maintaining *high* employment would seem to depend on how high a level of employment is meant.

If full employment in practice means a state of affairs in which employment is not allowed to fall below a certain mark set ahead of time (or one in which unemployment is not allowed to rise above a certain mark set ahead of time), how in practice is full employment to be maintained?

Surely there can be no doubt about one part of an answer. There cannot be the assurance that continuing full employment will be maintained unless in the last analysis the Federal Government stands ready to hire extra workers if necessary, directly or through private contractors or agents. Let us call this rather obvious conclusion point number one.

Point number one is enough to give a great many people the shudders. Certainly a point number two is badly needed to take the weight off point number one by showing that the necessity to rely on extra government jobs can be minimized. We are not prepared in this country to look with any pleasure at the possibility of an unlimited expansion of public works or public employment in general. There are limits to public construction in the ordinary sense, and if other public jobs are expanded too far the twin dangers arise of useless "leaf-raking" projects and unfair competition that will discourage business.

Fortunately, analysis shows that there is a point number two ready at hand in the form of certain measures that should minimize reliance on public works, etc., our measure of last resort.

When production falls below the level required to provide full employment, this means that, in relation to existing costs and existing profit requirements—neither of which can be forgotten in this connection—the total volume of demand for goods and services is too small. The total volume of demand for goods and services consists, let us say for convenience, of three components: consumer demand, business demand or capital formation (including here any surplus of exports over imports), and the demand of Federal, State, and local government.

Theoretically, when these three components add up to a total that is too small, the Federal Government can provide the needed extra jobs by sufficiently increasing its own expenditures for goods and services. That is the method described under point number one. Unfortunately we have no assurance that business demand plus consumer demand will automatically be large enough to keep the need for this extra government employment within manageable limits, *even if our economy is running at full employment initially.* The income earned and for the most part paid out at full-employment levels of operation of our economy may not return in the form of consumption and investment sufficiently completely to prevent a wide gap from opening up. It would, of course, be rash to assert that such a deflationary tendency must always be present. But it would be equally rash to trust that such a tendency will *not* appear when the special wartime factors of accumulated savings and deferred demands at home and abroad have spent their main force. In fact, the analysis of habits and trends in consumption, saving, and investing as exhibited over a lengthy period before the war indicates that, once the special factors no longer dominate the situation, the emergence of a strong tendency of this kind is the likeliest thing in the world.

I ask you to join with the average business man in considering again the impracticality of trusting to public employment to meet this situation—the impracticality of closing this gap (which might be a very wide gap, year after year) solely or primarily with extra public employment, over and above the employment already being provided on regularly budgeted public works and public services. As I have said, I find it impossible to believe that this method would yield continuing full employment in practice.

Let me therefore suggest the answer that seems to grow out of the logic of the case. If it is not feasible for government to maintain full employment by expanding *its own* demand in the market whenever private demand tends to fall short, the government can instead so regulate its revenues and expenditures that, by and large, *private* demand is prevented from falling short. In the main, this involves expansion when necessary—and also contraction when and if necessary—of *consumer* demand, brought about through government action affecting *directly* the level of purchasing power. Thus the government does not go into competition with business but instead supports the general market for the normal products of business.

This is, I believe, the way continuing full employment will be practiced if we are going to practice it in the United States. One other main element needs to be added, however. Since business is a forward-looking process, and investment in particular is based on calculations of probable consumer demand for years ahead, the effectiveness of a policy that continuously maintains a high but not too-high level of consumer demand will be strengthened by having the government adopt the practice of underwriting from year to year the volume of consumer demand considered to be adequate.

*   *   *

Before I proceed to particulars I want to spend a few minutes calling attention to some of the general implications of this approach to the employment problem. I shall here mention, in turn: (1) how it would affect the proportions among private consumption, private investment, and government expenditures for goods and services; (2) its relation to balancing the Federal budget; (3) the way it would integrate our compensatory policies with what may be called our basic policies; (4) its relation to forecasting; and (5) its significance for policy on foreign trade and investment.

1. In the matter of proportions, the main point about this approach is that it emphasizes expanded consumption. It does this by making the production and sale of consumer goods and services take up most of the slack that is likely to occur in the system. No obstacle whatever is put in the way of private investment or worthwhile

government expenditures for goods and services. I believe that everyone wants to encourage private investment, and parenthetically I may say that personally I am a believer also in very substantially expanded public expenditures for health, education, slum clearance and low-cost housing, conservation, and development. Suppose, however, that businessmen are already making all the private investments that they will naturally make under conditions of continuing prosperity. The voters' representatives will meanwhile have brought public works and services to the level that they regard as necessary and proper. The approach I am proposing assumes that it is more logical to have the rest of our labor force producing for consumption than to be forced to make additional expansions of public works and services merely to create jobs. At the same time this approach does recognize that expansion of public investment and public services is the proper way to adjust for a contraction of private investment where the latter is not the manifestation of a long-run trend but rather occurs temporarily in spite of steady support given to consumption.

2. One of the most controversial questions in the debate over full employment is this: Will not a full employment program involve a continuous and disastrous series of deficits in the Federal budget? Some opponents of full employment not only say that it will and must involve continuing deficits, but also say that we cannot stand these unbalanced budgets and therefore cannot afford full employment. Some advocates of full employment, not satisfied with pointing out that deficits are inevitable if we run into unemployment and depression, go on to argue further that full employment will bring a balanced budget because it will create a large taxable income.

The approach we are considering here takes neither of these extreme positions. Rather it assumes two things: first, that, if the objective of full employment and the objective of a balanced budget come into conflict, it is the balanced budget that must for the time give way; and second, that firm and intelligent action must be taken to rectify more and more those things that so unbalance our economy as to make full employment and a balanced budget likely to be incompatible. As you can see, this second point presupposes the view that full employment will not, in the first instance, normally bring a balanced budget— that it will not tend to do so until we, ourselves, do something about such things as excessive inequality of income, monopolistic restrictions, and several other very troublesome problems. I may say that, in my opinion, we would overlook this obligation at our peril.

3. This question may be clarified further by emphasizing a distinction between basic policies on the one hand and compensatory fiscal policies on the other. The role of basic policies, in the approach under discussion, is to minimize reliance on compensatory policies that will usually occasion budget deficits to prevent deflation and unemployment or else may involve last-minute, emergency action against a threatened inflation. The role of compensatory fiscal policies is to provide further support and flexibility as needed, to the end that assurance can be given that full employment will be maintained without inflation, irrespective of how sufficient or insufficient the basic policies currently in operation may be for that purpose.

A commitment is therefore given that compensatory policies will be used if necessary to prevent over-all deflation, or to prevent over-all inflation. But at the same time basic policies are pressed vigorously—i.e. policies, of whatever kind, that will minimize long-run deflationary tendencies—not forgetting measures to prevent speculation and localized inflation from getting started and thus setting the stage for a violent tendency toward deflationary reaction at a later period. In this context, obviously, the question asked about any basic measure that may be proposed is not "How much additional employment, if any, will result if basic policy X is adopted?" but rather, "Will the deficit or other difficulty associated with maintenance of full employment become smaller if basic policy X is adopted?"

4. I have mentioned that the insurance idea is an essential part of the approach under consideration. The first advantage of insurance is that it provides security and confidence—in this case, both to consumers, who will be able to look ahead to steady jobs and steady incomes, and to business. Business under this approach will be assured not only that the total national market will be maintained, but also that the final market for normal products of business will be maintained at a high enough level to preclude a threat of competition from bigger and bigger government operations.

This, however, is not the only point to be noticed about the insurance approach. Another feature of equal importance is its relation to forecasting. One way of trying to maintain full employment is to have the government estimate in advance what deficiencies in expenditure and employment are likely to result in the absence of government action to create additional expenditure and employment, and then set forth policies and programs designed to keep these prospective deficiencies from materializing. Unquestionably it is difficult for the government to make such estimates with a high degree of precision a considerable period ahead. It is also doubly difficult for the government to secure general acceptance among private experts of the accuracy of the forecasts made.

The approach we are considering here is therefore based on a different principle. The thing to be settled by the government is not the prospective deficiency, if any, but rather the levels of expenditure and employment regarded as necessary and the means to be employed *if* (but only if and so long as) those levels do in fact fail to be maintained automatically. Thus the speculative factor disappears. The need for compensatory government action, if there is a need, is proved by events.

At this point it may be well to recapitulate what has been said thus far about the nature of the government policy visualized in this discussion. The main elements may be set forth briefly in four general "rules."

A. *Federal budget rule*: Incur deficits if necessary for full employment, but develop basic policies to make deficits unnecessary.

B. *Public works rule*: Be ready to increase expenditures for public works and services as a last resort to maintain full employment, but, in general, use revenue and outlay measures that will maintain private expenditures for goods and services in preference to increasing such public expenditures beyond the recognized need for the works and services themselves.

C. *Insurance rule*: Underwrite total employment at the level regarded as corresponding to full employment, and underwrite total consumer expenditure at the level likely to maintain full employment in a manner consistent with rule B; i.e., without excessive reliance on extra public works and services.

D. *Anti-inflation rule*: Avoid basic policies likely to create undue inflationary pressure; in underwriting total employment and total consumer expenditure, set ceilings as well as floors; and be ready to hold these ceilings should that prove necessary.

5. The final point before I go on to questions of Executive recommendation, Congressional policy determination, administration, and statistics has to do with policy on foreign trade and investment. We are all aware, I take it, of the great advantages in the form of strengthened international security and higher living standards to be gained from an expansion of world trade along liberal lines permitting countries to specialize and exchange in accordance with comparative efficiencies of production. We are also aware of the economic and political advantages of expanded foreign investment that will help to repair the ravages of war and also help to develop and raise up those countries and areas where methods of production are primitive and standards of living low. Finally, we know that the market outlets created by such foreign investment on the part of the United States will be a boon in the immediate future to our own heavy-goods industries which so greatly developed their productive capacity during the war.

All this, however, does not alter the fact that any compulsion to find additional foreign markets as the only way of preserving full employment in this country could lead in time to the most unfortunate consequences both abroad and at home. Instead of being in the position to make foreign trade serve us by promoting the cause of welfare and peace, we would then become slaves to the dangerous necessity of an export surplus.

Such a predicament, it should be noted, need not arise under the methods contemplated here. If total consumer spending is underwritten, the level at which it is underwritten will take account not only of normal government expenditure for goods and services but also of total private capital formation *including* the export surplus, if any. In other words, domestic consumption will be held at a slightly lower level if exports exceed imports than if imports equal or exceed exports, but no question of a failure of demand as a whole is admitted regardless of how the foreign trade balance may happen to stand.

*   *   *

We come now to operating problems. Please keep in mind the general principles already discussed. If these are applied, I think you will find that the problems of recommendation, legislation, administration, and statistical information present no insuperable difficulties.

1. *Executive recommendations.* It is clear that, in making recommendations to Congress in connection with the maintenance of full employment, the President and his advisers—I assume that he will have the benefit of the advice of various nongovernmental groups as well as of his Executive Office and Cabinet—will need to deal with the basic economic policies on which the ability of the economy to operate at high levels without compensatory adjustments largely depends. He will also have to deal with the compensatory adjustments to be made if the current performance of the economy actually proves not satisfactory. Moreover, some kind of quantitative evaluation of the problem in the form of a full-employment national budget will be indispensable.

Great importance attaches to the first requirement—the basic policies required to set our economy on a course where excessive dependence on compensatory action and Federal deficits will not be needed. These in general are long-run policies, not dependent on the situation of the moment or the situation believed to be immediately ahead but rather dedicated to the continually valid propositions that private enterprise and competition need to be encouraged through removal of deterrents and restrictions, that purchasing power needs to be broadly distributed and sustained, and that welfare needs to be promoted by direct government action in areas where it cannot be otherwise made secure.

A full-length exploration of these basic policy fields is neither possible nor necessary here. Obviously one very crucial field is that of taxation, where we face the twin problems of eliminating regressive influences in our tax system in order to protect mass-purchasing power, and of finding ways, over and above the maintenance of mass markets, of preserving and improving the incentives for venture capital. Another field is that of competition and monopoly, involving such considerations as special aids to new and small business, antitrust policy, patents, international cartels, and regulations to prevent the raising of prices and the restricting of output and employment by those economic units that in the nature of the case must inevitably be in a position to exercise a substantial degree of monopolistic control. A third field is that of wage policy, where the general frame of reference is given by the desirability of achieving the highest feasible wage-price ratios. Another relates to the special problems of agriculture. Still another, the field of social insurance, involves not only such questions as adequacy of benefits and coverage, but also pay-as-you-go financing versus reserve accumulation, and, again, the problem of the best distribution of the taxes to support the benefits.

A fifth broad field, or series of fields, covers policy with respect to government's own direct contributions toward welfare through its expenditures for health, education, housing, conservation of natural resources, regional development, social services, scientific research, etc. The substantial capital investment connected with some of these welfare programs, not to mention other standard forms of public works, creates a further question of possible recommendations for budgeting capital items separately and carrying only the interest and amortization on the current budget. The basic policies of importance also include those affecting the ability of our system of public employment exchanges to do a good, nation-wide job of helping to bring available workers and available jobs together.

So much for this part of the President's recommendations. No one could tell, in most cases, exactly how much compensatory action could be spared if a given policy change of the basic type were proposed and adopted by Congress. Nevertheless, it seems clear that substantial results of this kind can be expected from appropriate action in some of the areas mentioned. The problem is, therefore, one of moving with as little delay as possible in all sectors where the potential gains seem large, and then reviewing at least once a year the scope and effectiveness of the existing basic legislation to see what further modifications or additions should be proposed.

The President's compensatory recommendations are quite another matter. Here quantitative guides will be necessary. Following out the line of thought developed earlier in this discussion, I think that the really essential quantities are these three:

A. The estimated volume of employment (including the self-employed in industry and agriculture) corresponding to full employment in the year ahead, taking into account the estimated size of the labor force and allowing for necessary frictional unemployment.

B. The estimated aggregate volume of expenditure for goods and services by private enterprises, consumers, State and local governments, and the Federal Government, required to purchase, at the expected level of prices, a gross national product of such volume as would be created at full employment.

C. The estimated aggregate volume of expenditure by *consumers* required to purchase, at the expected level of prices, such portion of a full-employment gross national product *as will not be purchased* by private enterprises, State and local governments, and the Federal Government under what may be considered as optimum conditions—these conditions being: (1) a level of capital expenditures by private enterprises based on the confident anticipation of continuing full employment and continuing high-level consumer demand, and (2) no extra government expenditures for goods and services required in order to combat unemployment. (The private capital expenditures item, of course, as previously noted, includes the export balance.)

For example—to use some purely illustrative figures that are not intended as a prediction—in a given year full employment (item A) might be estimated as equivalent to an average of 56.5 million civilian jobs, with 2.5 million others in the armed forces; at the expected level of prices aggregate expenditures for goods and services amounting to about $185 billion might be estimated (item B) as needed for full employment; and it might be estimated that private gross capital expenditures and government expenditures for goods and services would each, under the stated conditions, be likely to reach about $25 billion. In that case, the necessary volume of consumer expenditure (item C) would be $185 billion minus $50 billion, i.e., $135 billion.

Having had this kind of computation made, the President will be in a position to add to his basic recommendations the compensatory recommendations needed to round out his report. Essentially the latter recommendations fall into two categories, those relating to maintenance of consumer demand and those relating to public works.

Under maintenance of consumer demand will be a recommendation that total consumer spending be underwritten at a certain level (say $135 billion); recommendations in regard to preferred policies for raising consumers' incomes if observation shows that their spending is falling below the rate underwritten; and recommendations in regard to preferred policies for preventing, if necessary, a rate of consumer spending yielding more than a slightly larger amount such as, for example, $138 billion.

Under public works what will be presented is a diversified and geographically distributed reserves shelf, including also nonconstruction or service projects and including feasible expansions or accelerations of regularly budgeted items, with a request for authority to initiate or expand operations based on this shelf if necessary, i.e., if support of consumer demand at the specified high level, together with all other measures taken, proves insufficient to maintain full employment at an average level of, say, 56.5 million civilian jobs. Authority will also be asked to close down the operation of projects from the reserve shelf if employment rises appreciably—perhaps half a million or so—above the level designated as full employment. Further authority will be asked to slow down certain items included in the *normal* budget if employment threatens to rise too high, as it may do if the original estimate of private capital expenditures proves too low.

A question arises regarding the ways that might be recommended for raising consumer spending to the underwritten level if—as will normally be likely to happen until real progress has been made with our basic policies—it tends to remain too low even when income payments are running at a full-employment rate. No attempt will be made here to catalogue the various methods available, but two possibilities will be mentioned by way of illustration. The President might recommend, contingent on a demonstrated need for more consumer spending, a reduced rate on the personal income tax, coupled with cash offsets or refunds, on a reasonable basis, applied to Federal, State, and local indirect taxes which largely burden those too poor to pay an income tax. Or, alternatively, he might wish to recommend, along with a reduced rate on the income tax, the distribution to low-income families of stamps enabling them to improve their nutrition and living standards by buying food and, possibly, other necessities such as clothing in the market at reduced expense. For the opposite contingency of a tendency toward an inflationary excess of total consumer spending, he might recommend, for example, a graduated spendings tax with generous exemptions at the bottom.

Before leaving the subject of Executive recommendations, it should be made clear that the recommendation on underwriting consumer spending can be kept as flexible as desired. For example, the President might consider that, in the light of experience, $25 billion was the probable aggregate of regularly budgeted Federal, State, and local government expenditures for goods and services, but at the same time he might feel that Federal expenditures for such things as education, health, conservation, etc., should be substantially increased, bringing the total to $28 billion. A good method of handling this situation would be for the President to recommend that Congress underwrite consumer spending at $132 billion if it went along fully with his new programs on education, health, conservation, etc., that it underwrite consumer spending at $135 billion if it rejected these new programs, and that it set an intermediate figure for consumer spending if it accepted these programs in part.

2. *Legislation.* Under our Constitution our national policies are established by Congress. If the first operational step in maintaining full employment is the preparation of Presidential recommendations, the decisive step is the enactment of legislation. Let us therefore try to visualize the general nature of Congressional action under conditions corresponding to those established as the subject for this discussion—namely, full employment in practice.

Speaking broadly, the type of action required of Congress in these circumstances involves the final establishment of goals and the commitment to attain them; the enactment of basic legislation tending to promote the spontaneous occurrence of high-level production and employment; the approval of tax reductions to be made or contingent funds to be expended if and when these goals are not being reached spontaneously; and the determination of rules, governing such tax reductions or supplementary expenditures, to guide the President in maintaining the operating levels called for by Congress.

In the light of what has been said already, much of this requires no further comment. The first point that concerns us here is this: unless Congress will decide what it means by full employment by setting a floor below which it will not allow employment to fall, there can be no assurance, and probably no likelihood, of continuing full employment.

Congress, of course, need not accept the President's recommended definition. It may set the goal somewhere lower. But if it sets the employment goal so low that operation at the indicated level would not in fact provide everyone with the opportunity to work, then "full employment" becomes a misnomer. Presumably the pressure of public opinion on Congress can prevent this from happening, once it is recognized that, with private consumer spending underwritten at a suitable level, full employment will not require the expansion of government operations at the expense of private enterprise.

To be sure, the question of the proper relation between the level of consumer spending and the level of employment will require careful consideration. If Congress sets too low a level of consumer spending—or if, perhaps, it underwrites employment without making any separate decision about consumer spending—what can normally be expected to happen is that the spending and saving habits of the public will make it necessary in maintaining total employment to expand government employment unduly. To take the opposite extreme, in theory at least, Congress might underwrite consumer spending at a high level, and employment at a low level or not at all. This, however, would be likely to create an undesirable situation in which the government was subsidizing consumers while many job seekers were out of work. In short, the problem confronting Congress, as well as the President, is partly one of absolute levels and partly one of balance.

For this and other reasons it seems clear that, in an economy that provides continuing full employment, Congress will have some kind of joint committee of both houses to which the President's report with its national-budget estimates will be referred for study. This committee will then make its own report to Congress as a whole, and Congress, finally, will decide what it wants to accomplish and how it wants to accomplish it.

According to the analysis set forth herein, this means, as noted, that Congress will: (1) set minimum and maximum limits for employment and for consumer spending during the ensuing year; (2) designate specific methods to be used by the President if necessary to keep employment and consumer spending from falling below the minimum limits or exceeding the maximum limits; and (3) appropriate as contingent appropriations such sums for supplementary public works and for supplements to consumer incomes as may possibly have to be used, according to the methods prescribed, to achieve the results demanded. In addition, Congress can be expected (4) to legislate on general measures tending to reduce the relative importance of the program of compensatory adjustments.

3. *Administration.* Without embarking on a lengthy discussion of problems of administration connected with full employment—a field in which, in any case, our knowledge will largely have to be developed as we go along—I should like to call attention to the general nature of the administrative apparatus required if the foregoing conclusions on policy are valid.

Consistent with the distinction between maintaining employment as such and maintaining consumer spending as a means of supporting private employment, the problem divides itself into two main parts. One agency or set of agencies must watch employment, set in motion the expansion of public employment when that is needed, and bring about the contraction of public employment when that in turn is the action indicated. Another agency or set of agencies must watch the flow of consumer expenditure, provide for expansion of consumer disposable income, under the rules established by Congress, when consumer expenditure would otherwise be too small, and if necessary also provide for the application of temporary restraints on consumer expenditure.

Each of the two administrative centers, incidentally, has its own indexes to watch, irrespective of the operations of the other. This follows from the fact that, while employment naturally tends to create consumer spending and consumer spending naturally tends to create employment, neither one when maintained at the level at which it is underwritten can be counted on to maintain the other at *its* underwritten level.

As far as employment aggregates are concerned, there is obviously needed a Federal agency in the labor field which will keep an up-to-date count of the labor force, employment, and unemployment, together with the distribution and composition of each and such information as can be obtained on trends and outlook. When total employment is about to dip below its established floor, this agency must be in a position to advise the agency responsible for Federal action on public works concerning the type and location of reserve-shelf projects that need to be called into action or are likely to be required soon.

Similarly, when private employers are increasing their demands for labor to an extent calculated to raise total employment above its ceiling, the agency keeping track of employment must advise the public works agency to stand by to terminate certain of its operations. Finally, appropriate standards must be applied in the field to make sure that placement, vocational guidance, retraining, and relocation operations are coordinated with each other and with unemployment compensation in an efficient and equitable manner.

On the side of consumer spending, much depends on the specific legislation enacted. In any case, however, what is required first of all is an agency such as the Department of Commerce to keep track of the actual rate at which consumer expenditures are flowing. The facts can presumably be reported at any given time with a lag of no more than a month or six weeks, and if, after due allowance for normal seasonal variation, consumer spending proves to be too low or too high, the proper agency or agencies can be notified and can act in accordance with Congressional instructions to rectify the situation.

For example, if it proves too low, and if Congress has decided that such deficiencies should be handled exclusively through specified tax adjustments at quarterly intervals, fiscal experts must calculate the additional consumer spending likely to result per dollar of tax relief or rebate granted, and consequently the size of the adjustments needed to restore consumer spending to within the acceptable range. It should, however, be recognized that the subsidization of purchasing power, whether handled through tax adjustments or otherwise, will in all probability require the maintenance of files showing the income status of all families and single individuals, rather than merely the records now kept by the Bureau of Internal Revenue for income-tax payers.

4. *Necessary statistical information.* It is sometimes thought that an enormous mass of statistical information is required for the practice of full employment. Yet perhaps this view of the matter exaggerates somewhat the difficulty of the operating problem.

The first thing needed—primarily because it sets the main goal and secondarily because it is one of the elements upon which our estimates of the requisite aggregate of expenditures for current output must be based—is information about the prospective size of the labor force in the coming year. From this the President and Congress can determine, after making allowance for the fact that a small volume of turnover unemployment is necessitated by dynamic growth and movement in our economy, what they consider the volume of employment to be that best expresses for administrative purposes the true meaning of the concept of full opportunity to work.

Current series of this kind are now compiled by the Bureau of Labor Statistics, the Bureau of the Census, and the Bureau of Agricultural Economics. While by no means perfect, they are certainly usable for the purpose of setting a goal and checking performance. A decision must, of course, be made regarding the best method of handling seasonal variation, but this raises no very serious problems. During the present transition period a considerable degree of caution is required in predicting the size of the labor force, swelled as it has been during the war by millions of abnormal entrants into the labor market, some of whom will leave while others elect to stay. In this period caution is needed also in determining the volume of frictional unemployment required by industrial and geographical shifts. Ordinarily, however, trends are steady enough to make the probable range of miscalculation of the over-all labor magnitudes rather small.

According to the procedures described in a previous section, the expenditure estimates required in drawing up a national budget are not very numerous or hard to obtain. Essentially what is called for is, first, an approximate magnitude for a full-employment aggregate of gross national expenditures for the next year, and second, a magnitude for representing the probable sum of (a) normal government expenditures for goods and services and (b) business expenditures under continuing full employment and full consumption. From this and the aggregate expenditures magnitude is derived by subtraction the magnitude actually used for operating purposes—namely, the volume of consumer expenditure to be underwritten.

Inasmuch as offsetting errors in calculating the total and the other components tend to cancel out in arriving at this consumer expenditure goal, and inasmuch as the purpose of the consumer expenditure commitment itself is only to keep ordinary private markets large enough to make extra public works more or less unnecessary, a high degree of precision is hardly essential. It is not the case, under this formula, that everything hinges on the accuracy of the estimates. When the volume of private capital formation fluctuates, or if cost and price levels move a little out of the expected line, some adjustment in the volume of publicly created employment will be necessary in any case to make the final adjustment. The estimates of dollar magnitudes therefore serve in the last analysis as a scaffolding with the help of which a frame of policy can be erected to maintain full employment and yet minimize reliance on those public works that are not valuable enough to be approved on their own merits. A scaffolding need not be set up as carefully as the house it helps to build.

This is not to say, of course, that the wealth of detail on various subcomponents of business, government, and consumer expenditures now being accumulated is not extremely valuable. Undoubtedly it is valuable, and undoubtedly it also needs to be improved—especially, perhaps, in the field of prospective business capital expenditures. For immediate purposes, however, the essential point is that the work already done by fiscal experts in the Bureau of the Budget and elsewhere appears to be sufficiently advanced to permit the preparation of usable national budgets along lines here described.

Two further kinds of statistical requirement remain to be mentioned—the compilation of current figures on consumer spending, to see whether or not adjustments are necessary to keep consumer spending from falling below or rising above the limits established by Congress, and the more or less detailed continuing analysis of employment and unemployment, to see among other things whether the administrative definition of full employment under which the economy is operating is a satisfactory definition.

Since the former requirement has been mentioned already in connection with administration, no special comment is necessary here. The Department of Commerce, along with its other national income series, keeps records of consumer spending which will readily develop into the official guide for the purposes of this part of full-employment administration.

As far as the labor-force data are concerned, however, stress should be placed on the need for both quantitative and qualitative research with the aim of steadily improving our ability to register through our administrative definitions and devices the essential meaning of the concept of jobs for all. Unemployment should be analyzed by type, by location, by duration, and by group affected. Part-time employment should be studied to see where it is involuntary and where it is preferred. If concealed unemployment exists in agriculture or elsewhere, because of absence of other opportunities, this should be made known. The number of unfilled vacancies offering reasonable wages should be compared with the number of employable job applicants. Out of such investigations as these can be expected to come valuable suggestions for improvement in the services rendered by our employment offices and allied agencies, as well as knowledge that may lead to significant changes in the level at which, or possibly the terms or form in which, full employment will be administratively defined. In short, such studies can promote the growth of human opportunity.

*   *   *

In conclusion, let me point out that this attempt to picture how I believe that full employment in practice is likely to operate in the United States neither depends on any special theory of how unemployment originates, nor implies that we can forecast the future accurately, nor seeks to define how far the government should go in expanding its own works and services.

This approach does not imply acceptance of the stagnation hypothesis or of any particular brand of business-cycle theory. It does assert that few if any know the measure the over-all inflationary pressure in coming months, or exactly when deflationary strain will develop, or how great this strain will be, and it challenges the contention that we can be sure of maintaining full employment without taking out some form of insurance on our economy.

Regarding the form of this insurance, some may feel confident that needed and ready programs of public works and services will always be able to offset any tendency toward deflation and unemployment. I imagine, however, that not very many who have fully considered the technical and the legislative problems have confidence in this special solution.

The procedure whereby the assurance of continuing full employment is facilitated by the underwriting of aggregate consumer expenditure presents, by contrast, a general and not a special solution. It does not attempt to prejudge or predict the things that cannot be prejudged or predicted. Essentially all that it requires is that, as a nation, we decide how much employment we consider desirable, and about how much public employment, and agree to see that we get what we want, in the proportions we have chosen.

25

Guaranteeing Employment Opportunity

On all sides we hear talk of the desirability of postwar full employment, but the real issue that is shaping up is whether or not employment opportunity should be *guaranteed*. If it is to be guaranteed, it must be done by the Federal Government. Obviously, no one else can do it—no one business, no one community, no one trade union. Well, then, shall the Federal Government guarantee to maintain conditions in which everybody will have—and nobody will be denied—the chance to work?

Personally, I think the answer should be yes. If we do not guarantee full employment—which, of course, by definition allows of a small, agreed-upon amount of frictional or turnover unemployment—but merely agree to *try* for as much employment as possible, then that is nothing at all new, costs nothing, and may be entirely inadequate.

I don't want in the least to belittle the efforts of business men and groups like the C.E.D. It must be true that hard work, hard thinking, enthusiasm and a sense of public responsibility are resulting in plans for business ventures—and hence for employment—that might otherwise be overlooked. But as much employment as is possible without invoking the powers of the Federal Government is not enough. Nor is there any reason to believe that it is easier to maintain a level of employment three or four million less than full employment than it is to maintain full employment.

If you have no arrangements for holding a flag at the masthead, is it any easier to hold it at some point lower down on the staff?

Some people are sincerely distrustful of specific employment goals and commitments.

In slightly different form this paper was originally given as an address on "Postwar Employment Policy" at a University of Michigan Extension Service meeting in Detroit on June 22, 1945, and was printed in the *Congressional Record* of July 27, 1945, in the extension of remarks of Senator Lister Hill of Alabama. The revised version here presented was published in the August, 1945 issue of the *American Federationist*, under the title, "A Full Employment Program."

They view the idea of setting such goals with alarm. If told that specific goals were necessary, they would regard them as a necessary evil. I think that their view of the matter is entitled to respect. But I also think it can be said to such people that, however good the reasons for their point of view may be, they at least overlook one tremendously important fact—the fact that the right kind of goals and guarantees can in themselves have a great lifting power and make the solution of the employment problem much easier.

To get down to cases, here, in brief, is my suggestion. I hope that my sketchiness will be forgiven—it is a huge subject and my space is limited. Also let the reader be warned against thinking that my suggestion or any other could prevent reconversion unemployment during the transition. I don't want to leave the impression that there may be some formula by which our economy can swing back to peacetime production overnight or without causing a large number of people to go through short periods of unemployment. Undoubtedly we are going to have to lean heavily on our unemployment compensation systems at this stage of affairs, and undoubtedly also, as the President has said, these systems will have to be strengthened.

Now let me come back to full employment program in the broader sense, as dintinguished from demobilization program. Three things seem to me to be needed. First, an insurance approach to the problem. Second, a number of basic national policies, including but certainly not limited to government expenditure and tax policies. And third, a balancing mechanism to make sure that we actually deliver on the employment commitment even before we have succeeded through our basic policies in bringing our economy into a natural balance. Let me take these three points up one at a time.

First is the insurance approach. This means the giving of commitments in advance. In other words, it involves government underwriting. There are, I think, two essential things involved—first, a guarantee of full employment itself, and, second, a guarantee of the total national consumer market at a high level. I want to emphasize that this refers to *aggregate* employment opportunity and *aggregate* consumer demand, and is not a proposal to guarantee any individual jobs or the market for any individual products.

A guarantee of full employment itself would obviously assure us of a high national income. This would provide security to the worker, would stimulate confidence, and would prevent the kind of hoarding of money that grows out of fear of future depression. To carry it out, a national budgeting approach is needed, as recommended by the sponsors of the full employment bill, with additional public jobs available as a last resort if other employment falls short.

But it surely is not a good idea to put exclusive or even primary emphasis on government jobs. We want all jobs—public and private—to result in worthwhile products and we don't want to have business exposed to the risk that an unlimited number of jobs may have to be artificially created. Therefore, in addition to a guarantee of full employment as such, I think we need a further guarantee that total consumer spending will not fall below a specified high level. This would in particular provide confidence for private business because the consumer spending target would show that business itself could profitably provide the bulk of the number of jobs guaranteed, so that public works would not have to be expanded unduly.

This kind of guarantee would meet the over-saving problem head-on. The income paid out by full employment production does not necessarily yield an ample market for business because too much of this income may be saved and too little may be spent. The consumer market guarantee, on the other hand, would give to business the assurance that this unfortunate thing would not happen.

I want to stop for a moment to give additional emphasis to the importance of this insurance approach, as I see it, because it is a rather new idea and seems to have tremendous possibilities for cutting the Gordian knot in which our economy was tied for a number of years before the war. Its possibilities are such, for both labor and management, that the exploration of these possibilities would seem to offer a very promising new field for cooperative action. Of course, without the support of management and labor, no approach to these problems is likely to get very far.

The first advantage of the insurance approach is that it provides security and confidence. Let me give an analogy. Now that bank deposits are insured, people are not very likely to start runs on banks. Similarly, if employment and markets were insured, business men would not be so likely to take their money and energies out of the economic game.

But this is not the only advantage. Besides promoting confidence, the insurance approach would greatly reduce the government's need to rely upon forecasts for the determination of what it should do. It would therefore very much reduce the disputes about the necessity for government action—disputes that are bound to arise when people disagree about the accuracy of the forecasts the government is making.

Let me clarify this point. If employment and expenditure goals are set for the economy and then, because of deferred demand, accumulated war savings or any other factor, these goals are met automatically by the unaided operation of the system, then in that case the government, which is acting as underwriter, need not and should not take any additional action in behalf of expenditure and employment. But if, on the other hand, the goals as finally determined by Congress are not being met out of the unaided operation of the system, then clearly government action will be called for, and it is hard to see how any dispute could arise over that.

Parenthetically, most of the calculations made by the economists who have thoroughly studied this subject show that there is every likelihood that shortages of expenditures and employment will tend to develop after the war—at least when temporary demands have been satisfied—if nothing is done to prevent it.

There is, therefore, a strong probability that the government, acting as underwriter, would have some gaps to fill.

But the point is that, if we adopt the insurance approach, we don't need to waste an undue amount of time wrangling over just what we see in the future as each of us looks into his favorite crystal ball.

Notice further than a guaranteed total consumer market, by taking pressure off the public works device, would make guaranteed full employment entirely favorable from the standpoint of business, instead of partly favorable and partly a threat of competition from bigger and bigger government operations. Also it would be a sure way of promoting high consumption—and nothing could be better than that for standards of living throughout the country. Hence, it would relieve us of the necessity of expanding investment, for the sake of employment, more than was really needed by any other test.

In fact, it would really free us from the piece-by-piece approach to full employment. If the various other pieces failed to add up to full employment, this would simply mean that general purchasing power would be expanded instead.

Thus, in the last analysis, this approach would relieve the haunting fear that we have become too productive in this country—that we are unable to consume as much as we are able to produce—a haunting fear that tends to drive us into a search for larger and larger export markets even if this finally goes beyond the bounds of common sense and of mutual advantage to ourselves and other nations.

So much for insurance. Let us turn now to the next idea. The second thing we need is a series of basic governmental and private policies designed to make our economy balance as well as possible, so that the guarantees would be as nearly self-enforcing as possible without further government action. Of course, these basic policies deserve the fullest discussion. But this is out of the question here, and therefore, in the limited space at my command, I shall merely try to review a few of the main ones for the reader's further consideration. I hope this will not be interpreted as an underestimation of their importance.

First of all, there is the desirability from the economic point of view of having wages as high as productivity will allow. This is important, and hence collective bargaining is important, if for no other reason than that the wage stream largely goes into spending and adds very little to the oversaving problem.

Next, there is the need for a low-price, high-output policy on the part of business. Such a policy should also be enforced through government antitrust action when necessary, and through sound patent legislation, regulation of cartels and monopolies, aids to new and small businesses, etc.—all such measures being aimed at promoting competition and checking the restrictive practices of monopoly. This line needs to be taken in order to encourage new investment, dampen down over-saving and make sure that an adequate market for goods and services really gets translated back into full production and full employment.

Thirdly, it seems essential that we do everything possible to eliminate substandard incomes in agriculture and in whole regions, such as the South. Quite aside from other considerations, this will help greatly to maintain the markets we need.

Fourthly, we need a permanently strong, efficient and properly recognized nationally coordinated employment service, to help bring available workers and available jobs together.

Coming to those basic policies which are financial or fiscal in character, we have the whole question of taxes and government expenditures. As to government expenditures, the Labor Committee on National Policy of the National Planning Association recently sponsored a report which, in a preliminary way, goes into our national needs in the fields of housing, health, education, conservation and development of natural resources.

In these fields alone, and without including other important matters, such as recreation, cultural programs, social services, research, rural electrification, etc., where the sums involved are much smaller, it was estimated that additional amounts of nearly ten billion dollars a year would need to be spent by Federal, State and local governments to attain adequate minimum standards of living and opportunity for the whole population. This amount does not allow for the possibility of national medical care insurance. Of course, there is little doubt that our social security system should be broadened in various ways and the benefits expanded. I believe it would also be helpful to the solution of our employment problem were these benefits financed in a less deflationary manner than at present by adoption of the pay-as-you-go method and by contribution to the funds from general taxation.

Turning to taxation as a whole, the important thing here is to give fullest application to the principle of ability to pay while at the same time not discouraging genuine initiative and investment. Taxes should fall more heavily on those with large incomes than on those with small incomes because this is fair and because it will help to sustain mass buying power. This means that excises ought to be largely eliminated, gift and estate taxes strengthened, and heavy reliance placed on the individual income tax—but with higher exemptions to take the burden off subsistence incomes.

In the complicated matter of corporate income taxation, my personal opinion is that the best solution might be to set the rates where they will strike a level about halfway between wartime and prewar corporate tax revenues. In this connection, everything that will help to remove discrimination against risk capital, as compared with passive loan capital, certainly ought to be done.

Now I want to get my third main point—the need for a balancing mechanism. Let me repeat that the basic policies I have so lightly touched on are of the utmost importance. If they are given the attention they deserve, this will very much reduce the necessity for running a Federal budget deficit in connection with maintaining full employment. It will also mean that we are going after fundamental problems, like monopolistic restrictions and the distribution of income. Nevertheless, we also need a balancing mechanism operating by means of fiscal policy, because it is totally unrealistic to act as though we had solved all the basic problems and got rid of over-saving any time before these things actually had been accomplished.

Following the lines of the guarantees mentioned earlier, there are two parts to a well-rounded and practical balancing mechanism. The first is a public works reserve—an ample, diversified and geographically distributed reserve shelf of construction and service projects. Construction should be carried out through private contractors unless for special reasons that proves impossible in a given case. I think it is important that jobs on the public works reserve should pay prevailing rates of wages. The reserve, after all, would not in this setting be a relief proposition, but rather a part of the provision made to assure everyone the opportunity to have a real job. These supplementary public employment projects, unlike the regularly budgeted items for schools, hospitals and so forth, which cannot afford to be postponed, would be shut down when private employers again had more jobs available. But the readiness of government to shut them down as private employment opportunities expanded—this, and not substandard rates of pay—should be the safeguard against anyone's staying on the public payroll too long.

The one thing that is always emphasized in connection with the public works reserve may as well be said here again, because it cannot be stressed too much or too often. This is the need for *advance planning*. I wish it were possible to feel that the Federal Government and the States and local communities were ready at this time to meet the demands for extra public works that the are likely to encounter in the transition period.

The second part of the needed balancing mechanism lies at the point in our economy where money is spent for consumer goods and services. The government keeps current records of the total rate of consumer spending. Having guaranteed a certain minimum rate, it would have to match the actual rate against this commitment. If the actual rate was falling short, the government would have to promote additional consumer spending by some device that left or put more money in consumers' hands. One way of doing this would be to refund, suspend or offset certain taxes that affect consumption. But it would be important, for the sake of avoiding a leakage into further excess savings, to offset the hidden or indirect taxes that affect the poor man and not merely reduce the witholding rate on the income tax which is paid by those who are better off.

A crucial point to note is that any such offset to taxes would be allowed only if and as long as current consumer spending tended to remain below the guaranteed rate. Hence, the proposal is not in the least inflationary. In fact, on the contrary, I am sure that the commitment ought to set a ceiling over consumer spending as well as a floor underneath it. Many people with real justification are afraid that full employment may lead to price inflation. One of the best ways of ruling that out is to set a maximum as well as a minimum limit to total consumer spending. If, then, in some period—for instance, in the immediate transition period—consumer spending should threaten to go through this ceiling, a special tax or some other restraint would be brought into play temporarily. Possibly the best device for this particular contingency would be a graduated spendings tax. This could have generous exemptions at the bottom and would avoid the unjust and undesirable features of the sales tax, which has little to be said in its favor.

To sum up in as few words as possible the things that I think might be accomplished by the kind of full employment program I have tried to present in this brief sketch, here are some of the main possibilities:

First, insurance of our economy against depression. *Second,* a contribution to the safeguards we need against inflation. *Third,* a spotlight on the importance of getting ahead rapidly with our basic policies, while at the same time we do not postpone full employment until all the basic policy issues have been settled. *Fourth,* development of a sound relation between domestic and foreign markets, meaning by this the promotion of beneficial foreign trade and investment without the pressure to go to dangerous extremes in our dependence upon them. *Fifth,* creation of confidence based on job security and high markets—a state of confidence free of those conflicting emotions which might develop in the business community if it seemed that full employment could only be maintained through a forced expansion of the government's own operations. And, *finally,* conditions in which opportunity in the broadest sense of the word could become real for everybody, regardless of race, sex or any other consideration.

26

Exports, Imports, and Jobs

How many American jobs will be in fields connected with the great business of exporting and importing if we can succeed in expanding our postwar foreign trade as we hope to do? That is a good question. Another good question is this: aside from what full employment will contribute to expansion of foreign trade, how much can we expect foreign trade to contribute to the maintenance of domestic full employment?

The trouble is, these two questions about actual jobs *in* foreign trade and the net number of jobs *dependent* on foreign trade keep getting mixed up, and arguments run in circles. Perhaps it is presumptuous to assume that these questions can be untangled. Nevertheless I want to raise my voice on behalf of those who think it is most important to try to keep these two questions separate, judging each one on its own merits.

Of course they really are separate, because we might have the same total number of jobs at two quite different levels of foreign trade; the jobs would simply be distributed somewhat differently. Let me take an analogy from another field. At the present time nearly 1,700,000 men and women are at work in the manufacturing of aircraft and parts. Two years after the war the number may be in the neighborhood of 200,000. Does anyone think that total national employment must be a million and a half smaller after the war on that account? I hope not, because we are going to need a number of million *more* civilian jobs after the war than we have right now, and yet aircraft production certainly is going to decline, not to mention the ordinance industry, shipbuilding, and others.

Now, question number one—how many jobs will be in fields connected with exporting and importing if we can succeed in expanding our foreign trade?—is obviously of the greatest interest to a large number of people. For instance, it is of the

An address presented at a meeting of the Institute of World Economics on March 29, 1945, and subsequently printed in the October-December, 1945, issue of *World Economics*. The original title was "Exports, Imports, and Full Employment Policy."

greatest interest to businessmen's associations where the importing or exporting of primary products or manufactures bulks large so far as the industry in question is concerned. That point does not need any special elaboration.

I do not have much to contribute toward answering this question. So far as past experience is concerned, the Department of Commerce has made an estimate of the number of persons engaged in the production and distribution of goods for export in 1929, 1933, 1935, and 1937. Preliminary estimates made by a unit in the Bureau of Labor Statistics of the non-agricultural employment attributable to exports in the year 1939 seem to tie in pretty well with the 1937 Commerce figures. Of course, whenever such estimates are constructed, certain simplifying assumptions necessarily have to be made, and it may not be possible to keep these assumptions 100 percent realistic. I would suggest that the B.L.S. inter-industry relations method of estimating—sometimes referred to as the "input-output" method—may be capable of yielding the most refined results, relatively speaking, because this method makes it possible to trace the indirect effects and also makes it possible to state with a good deal of precision exactly what is being estimated.

All such computations as these essentially rest on ratios of dollar value of exports to dollar value of an industry's total output. It is assumed that employment ratios will be about the same as dollar value ratios, except where we have definite evidence to the contrary. Hence you can take your pick of the various guesses now in circulation as to the probable or possible dollar value of our total postwar trade, the size of our gross national product, and the total number who will be employed, and make your own rough estimate of jobs connected with foreign trade. The trade volume estimates vary rather widely at the present time. Take a guess near the upper end of the range—say $14 billions of exports and $8 billions of imports. If 60 million were employed altogether, and the total gross national product stood at $200 billion, we might say that 7 percent (14 divided by 200) of our jobs, or about 4.2 million jobs, could be considered to be tied up in some manner with exporting, with a substantial number of other workers engaged in the handling and processing of imports.

This is only for purposes of illustration. As to what the actual size of our exports and imports may prove to be, I can only say I trust that this will be determined on the basis of mutual advantage to ourselves and other nations, and that the role of our national policy in helping to determine the outcome will be based on the broadest conceptions of our common welfare, in the light of all the relevant economic and political considerations.

This brings us back to question number two—how much can we expect our foreign trade to contribute to the maintenance of full employment in this country? If trade expands, it certainly should make for greater world security and higher standards of living—in other words, increasingly *productive* jobs. But what about the *number* of jobs?

We are now no longer trying to count up the jobs in particular industries in which we may personally happen to be especially interested, but rather we are thinking of the national situation as a whole and trying to assess the net difference, if any, between the total number of American jobs if foreign trade is suitably expanded. This is not simply a question of adding or subtracting certain specific jobs, because—as in the case I mentioned of wartime aircraft production—the possibility of substitution, or different proportions, comes in. The fact that at a given time 5 million, say, are holding jobs connected with exports or imports is no indication that, if we had no foreign trade, these five million persons would necessarily be unemployed.

I don't know how many people will be shocked by this, but my own view of the net contribution of foreign trade to U.S. jobs is that foreign trade will significantly raise U.S. employment only as long as we have an export surplus, resting on foreign investment, and that it will have practically no effect as soon as imports come to equal exports, *no matter how large they both become.* I am going to qualify this a little in a moment, but not very much.

Let me first say a word about the situation in which the dollar volume of imports—I mean services or "invisibles" paid for, as well as commodities—equals the dollar volume of exports—merchandise plus services. (Incidentally I am inclined to suspect that some persons who find it hard to see why, with large imports and large exports, the net gain in our employment should be zero, just because these two magnitudes happen to be equal, are not really thinking in terms of imports equal to exports. They may believe in the abstract that trade is a two-way affair in which the two movements of goods and services must balance out in the long run; but, when they turn to employment, what they actually have in mind is a particular export industry, or perhaps a so-called favorable balance of trade in which exports are larger than imports.)

Why should the net effect of foreign trade on our employment be practically nil if our exports and imports balance? The shortest answer to this is, I think, that the money we spend on imports subtracts from our markets, our production, and our employment just about as much as the money foreigners spend for our exports adds to our markets, our production, and our employment.

A slightly more elaborate answer would run somewhat as follows: First, the *marginal* employment per dollar of exports is probably somewhat smaller than the *average* employment per dollar of output in the export industries as a whole. I mean by this, for example, that a typical industry that exported 10 percent of its product would probably not fire 10 percent of its workers if its output fell off 10 percent as a result of losing its foreign market. In manufacturing that might happen. But certainly it seems doubtful that agricultural employment—in cotton, for instance—has fallen off proportionately, if at all, when farm exports have declined in the past. In other words, if all our exports were to disappear completely, it is questionable whether the number of people who soon afterwards would have to change their jobs would be as large as the number who appear to be dependent on exporting if you merely use average ratios of workers to dollars' worth of output. In the second place, the aforementioned factor of *substitution* comes into play. If we lost an equal dollar volume of exports and imports—keeping, say, our really critical or strategic imports but giving up the rest—the reduced payments to foreigners would leave us with additional purchasing power to expend at home, and this would create about as many new jobs as were lost through elimination of exports. Some of these added jobs probably would be in the same industries as before, although most of them no doubt would be new jobs in different lines of activity.

Now certain qualifications are necessary, as I said before. For instance, as long as we continue to be subject to business cycles, with their alternating periods of boom and depression, a severe shock to a series of important industries could easily start or intensify a down-spin. This seems to me to be the reason why the free trade doctrine of the Classical School of economists looked so unrealistic to so many practical people. The theory said that substitution of one use of labor and capital for another—for instance, when protective tariffs were removed—would take place *automatically*. Skeptics replied that a bird in hand was worth two in the bush. In other words, we should hold on to the *particular* industries we already had, and not count too heavily on developing others if we lost those. And this argument never could be settled in the absence of a fundamental policy to eliminate business cycles by insuring continuous full employment.

Moreoever, quite aside from the phenomena of the cycle as such, no one would claim that we could calmly face the loss of major exports and imports all of a sudden and expect a quick and painless reshuffling of workers into new jobs. Men and women are not like statistical tables—subject to immediate revision. Their geographic and functional mobility, as economists would say, is not perfect. In short, they get attached to a particular job in a particular community. So does capital. Neither labor nor capital can be uprooted and transplanted without hardship.

But I think it can fairly be said, without seeming thereby to belittle the seriousness of such shifts for the individuals affected, that difficulties of the kinds just mentioned are not the central issue. They do not destroy the presumption that the additional purchasing power made available domestically by a decline in payments for imports is likely after a while to stimulate new production and employment to an extent capable of offsetting the effects of a comparably large decline in exports. Still less do they suggest that a balanced *increase* in both exports and imports will be likely to add materially to the total volume of demand for domestic products.

A more fundamental argument is sometimes made, however. It is sometimes said that imports, far from subtracting jobs, actually are neutral or even add jobs to the total. It is pointed out by those who take this position that some of our imports consist of luxuries and specialties not produced in the United States, together with "invisible" imports in the form of expenditures for travel abroad and remittances to relatives abroad. Why should these things adversely affect employment in this country? Moreover, American jobs are created in the shipping, unloading, processing, transporting, and distributing of our merchandise imports, so that a substantial fraction of the consumer's dollar paid out for imported articles or articles using imported raw materials never goes abroad at all but stays in this country to help furnish jobs to Americans.

This kind of argument has a practical sound, but I am reasonably sure that it is not practical at all, because it concentrates so closely on the factors in the foreground that it completely overlooks the offsetting factors in the background. If American consumers spend money on foreign travel, foreign remittances, or imported specialty articles, that *does* detract from domestic industry because it uses up dollars that would otherwise have been available to purchase the products of American industry. You cannot have your cake and eat it too. Moreover, the jobs created in the shipping, unloading, processing, transporting, and distributing of imported commodities would equally well have been created in handling alternative goods produced at home to meet additional domestic demand.

It all comes back in the end to the question of the *motivation* for productive activity. What *causes* production to take place? The answer to this question cannot be disregarded without losing touch with reality. Hence the answer is worth giving here, obvious though it may seem. In the Soviet Union, production takes place almost entirely as the result of the forming of a national production plan. On the other hand, in the

United States production takes place for the most part in response to the pull of the market: no market, no production. Hence, if imports use up the same number of dollars that exports bring in, employment tends to remain unaffected.

At this point certain further qualifications will be conceded, these being true qualifications in the long-run sense and not merely temporary or cyclical factors, like those previously mentioned. (1) First and perhaps most important is the fact that an expansion of both exports and imports, if this is brought about by reduction of trade barriers, will probably cause some net addition to production even without any increase in the dollar demand for products, because it will lower prices and increase competition. This is the same effect that would follow elimination of monopolistic restrictions of a purely domestic character. (2) Production may be stimulated, without any net increase in total demand, if we ourselves have something of a monopoly position in acquiring our imported raw materials. By getting these raw materials for less than they would bring in a truly competitive market, we may cut our costs of production and sell more at a lower price. (3) If we are importing luxury goods, spending money on foreign travel, and so forth, this may come in part out of money that would otherwise have been saved but not invested, instead of entirely out of money that would otherwise have been spent for domestic products.

In addition, the amount of labor used in export industries may be higher per dollar of output than it would be in other lines that might take the place of the exports achievable by an expanded foreign trade program. This of course depends on circumstances. The fact that our exports so largely come from mechanized, mass-production industries, and from agriculture in which employment is relatively insensitive to markets, suggests that it might well work the other way round.

These seem to be the main considerations, although there are doubtless others. The essential point about them, however, is that they appear to be only relatively minor qualifications to the proposition that employment is *not* increased by expanded exports and imports if the additional exports and imports are equal in volume. The exceptions should not be confused with the general rule. The desirability of a balanced expansion of exports and imports does not rest on increased domestic employment, but rather on the likelihood of improved standards of living and greater world security. If we want to talk about how foreign trade can expand U.S. jobs, we must talk about an export surplus.

The same line of reasoning, by which it can be seen that jobs are not markedly increased by foreign trade if imports equal exports, shows that U.S. jobs probably *will* be increased if our exports exceed our imports. Our exports will exceed our imports if we put the necessary additional dollars into the hands of foreigners who want to buy our products. We can do this, if we like, by lending them the money. In other words, we can develop an export surplus and increase our employment by means of a foreign investment program. Is that, perhaps, the answer to our employment problem? I get the impression that many people think it is.

I should like to emphasize as strongly as I possibly can my own belief that the idea that foreign investment can for any considerable length of time solve our employment problem for us is a dangerous illusion.

It can be readily conceded that various foreign countries—Latin American countries, Russia, China, parts of Africa, India, and others—will need help in the form of long-term investment for development purposes, quite apart from relief and rehabilitation needs resulting from the war, and that the United States will be uniquely qualified to lend a helping hand. I believe we should be generous in extending such assistance to other countries to enable them to raise their standards of living, even if this results in some temporary abstention from the maximum of consumption we might be enjoying here at home. From a long-run point of view it can be seen that this will be in our own interest, since it will promote world security. The Bretton Woods proposals show how some of this might be accomplished. Our liberality, incidentally, should not only appear in the amounts we are willing to lend abroad, but should also extend to the terms on which we make these funds available. Interest rates should be as low as possible.

Not only will such capital exports be desirable from the standpoint of international relations, but they will also provide a considerable number of jobs here in the United States. What is particularly important is that they will provide jobs in our heavy goods industries, the very industries that have expanded most phenomenally during the war and face the greatest cut-backs when the war is over. In order to industrialize, foreign countries will need to place orders with our metal products industries in particular, especially orders for industrial machinery and transportation equipment. This dovetails nicely with our own capacity to produce, and can therefore materially assist us in reducing the severity of industrial dislocations and frictional unemployment in the early postwar years.

These are the obvious advantages of foreign investment. But to say that foreign investment can solve our employment problem is quite another matter. Let me briefly mention three reasons why I have called that conception a dangerous illusion.

First may be considered the sheer magnitude of the employment problem to be solved. No one can tell at this moment how wide the so-called deflationary gap is likely to be when the sustained effects of deferred demands by domestic consumers and producers begin to wear off. There are still too many unpredictables. But suffice it to say that many careful estimators think they discern a very wide gap indeed, so much so that an appraisal could reasonably be defended in which the export *surplus* might have to be in the neighborhood of $15 billion a year to keep this gap closed. Foreign investment on such a scale as this, year after year, looks quite impossible. Cultures widely different from our own would probably not be willing and able to adopt our machine technology overnight even as a free gift, but in any case the practical question narrows down to the considerably smaller amounts they will take at the lowest rates of interest and on the most favorable terms of repayment we are willing to accept.

In the second place, if we exert too much pressure to expand our foreign investment, the favorable international effects obtainable from a more moderate policy are likely to turn into just the opposite. Any sense of *compulsion* on our part to have a big export surplus year after year certainly could lead to actions at variance with our desire to maintain the best of political and economic relations both with the borrowing countries and with, let us say, Great Britain, whose need to expand her exports is more obvious than our own. I need not labor this point. Surely anyone familiar with the history of foreign investments to date will recognize that, in spite of their advantages, and in spite of the improved chances for avoiding frictions which the new international approach to foreign investment appears to offer, there are limits to this whole process which can be trancended only at the risk of dangerously straining the friendly relations among nations and among peoples.

The third and perhaps most serious objection of all to trying to solve our employment problem through exports supported by foreign investment is the risk that this policy might stand in the way of the development of a fundamental full-employment program in this country. Thus, after stimulating our production temporarily, it might actually contribute to economic collapse when the export surplus tapers off. Our experience growing out of our foreign loans in the twenties should warn us that to place heavy emphasis on an export surplus as a basis for domestic prosperity is a short-sighted policy. Yet by relieving for a few years the symptoms of a deep-seated lack of economic balance, a big export boom would in all likelihood make it more difficult to face up to the necessity for a genuine cure. Then would come the relapse—at a time when, both psychologically and in terms of the size of adjustments needed, a cure would be much harder to bring about than immediately after the war.

It is clear enough that the real reason why so much effort is devoted to trying to prove that expanded foreign trade is good for domestic employment is the fact that many people do not think full employment can be achieved at all without tremendous export markets. Any attempted solution—even on a piecemeal and highly precarious basis— seems better than nothing. On all sides we hear it said that the United States has become so productive that it cannot possibly consume its whole product, but must export a part of it to other lands. Where is foreign purchasing power coming from to pay for this? Well, never mind, we'll loan them the money. When it comes to building up purchasing power, distance apparently lends enchantment.

In the more specialized language used by economists, it is said that we need a volume of investment, and other non-consumption offsets to saving, equal in magnitude to the volume of savings forthcoming at a full-employment level of national income; that we are not likely to come anywhere near attaining such a volume of investment, etc., through the unaided operation of natural forces; and that foreign investment is a peculiarly strategic kind of investment for purposes of closing the gap.

This poses two basic questions—aside from the precise relative advantages of foreign investment as against domestic investment. The first is the question whether we really are faced with a big savings-investment gap (or deflationary gap, or under-spending problem—call it what you will) assuming that matters are simply allowed to take their natural course. To this question I personally am ready to answer "yes," reserving judgment only on the subordinate question "how soon?" which is particularly difficult to judge since deferred demand backed up by accumulated savings, and other special factors including a possible export boom, may obscure the real structure of the problem for a few years. As a matter of fact, the issue of "how soon?" does not really matter so far as my own views on solving the problem are concerned, since my proposals are based on the insurance principle, as will be made clear in a moment. The only thing that is essential for my point—and here I don't see how there could be any controversy at all, for could anyone be found to deny it?—is the proposition that we have absolutely no assurance that a wide gap will *not* develop.

The second basic question is whether the gap, if and when it develops, must be filled by additional investment and other non-consumption offsets to saving. And here I personally will answer "no." In fact, it seems to me to be necessary to go farther than that and say that only a policy that expressly assures that *consumption* will be expanded so that additional investment can be held to a minimum will have the character of a practical full-employment policy for the United States.

As I see it, the basic factors in employment policy in this country are these:

(1) For the unparalleled benefits this will confer both domestically and internationally, employment opportunity must be assured in this country after the war. This involves setting up an administrative definition of full employment in terms of existing labor market statistics and having the Government underwrite full employment as thus defined.

(2) In achieving full employment, maximum stress must be placed on incentives to private business to expand its volume of production and employment. The key to this— and the suggestion I am making is comparatively a new idea—is the underwriting of total consumer spending at a level high enough to provide a market for a full-employment volume of output minus the output to be covered by normal business capital expenditures and normal government expenditures. For example, if $185 billion appeared to be required to buy a full-employment output in a particular year, and if expected private capital formation including foreign investment, plus government expenditures excluding any that might be made for the sake of employment, added up to an estimated $50 billion, consumer spending would be underwritten at $135 billion. Among the companion measures should be an active antitrust policy to foster competition, and effective forms of regulation to prevent price profiteering and output restriction where monopoly is unavoidable.

(3) Public investment and public services should be planned first of all on their own merits without reference to current employment considerations. The confidence generated in business by the assurance of continuously high private consumption—a confidence affecting private investment as well as the production of consumer goods— will very much reduce the need for supplementary public works. In spite of this, however, an ample reserve shelf of construction and non-construction projects should always be kept in readiness, and, when full employment requires it, supplementary public jobs should be provided by accelerating regularly budgeted programs or taking new programs off the reserve shelf.

(4) The condition of full employment thus brought about (either with or without supplementary public works) will produce a full flow of income, and consequently as high a rate of consumer spending as existing taxes and existing savings habits will permit. Where consumer spending is still below the level underwritten, however, government must provide additional purchasing power in some manner—for example, by suspending, refunding, or offsetting direct and indirect taxes in whole or in part while the tendency toward deficiency persists. Of course, great emphasis should be placed on getting rid of the root causes for this tendency toward deficiency—notably the following causes: excessive inequality in the distribution of income, caused by low wages and other factors; exercise of monopolistic powers to restrict production; needlessly large institutional saving; and financial insecurity in the face of the various contingencies confronting individuals and families. Any supplementary tax adjustment or similar measures to bring consumer spending up to the guaranteed level is to be regarded merely as a balancing device at the margin which is necessitated because we have not yet dealt satisfactorily with the underlying maladjustments. Incidentally, since we want to guard

against the possibility of inflation as well as against the more generally prevalent likelihood of deflation, it will also be necessary to provide for reducing total consumer spending by taxation or otherwise in the event that it threatens to rise spontaneously above the guaranteed level by more than a reasonable margin, this margin to be specified in advance.

That is a very brief outline of a subject that might be elaborated at almost any length. Actually the principles involved in this combination of factors are simple. The heart of this approach to full employment lies in its use of the insurance principle for the broad national purpose of establishing a sustained feeling of security and confidence on the part of employers, as well as on the part of the general buying public. Useful public investment is not in any sense restricted. My own personal feeling is that we ought to devote far larger public expenditures than ever before to facilities and services that will assist in attaining high standards for the whole population in fields basic to the general welfare, such as education, health, housing, social security, and the conservation and development of our natural resources. But—be the duly accepted public functions large or moderate—the suggested procedure should prevent those paralyzing situations from arising wherein legislators feel forced to choose between their interest in maintaining full employment and their interest in avoiding govenment expenditures that appear to them to be either wasteful or unduly competitive with business.

In terms of savings and investment, the proposal runs directly counter to the often repeated dictum that investment must be expanded to equal savings. What is suggested instead is that, except as investment is judged to be intrinsically necessary by business or by the voters and their representatives, the expansion should take place in consumption and in free consumer choice. This involves a reduction of real saving down to the level of investment, but need not in any way interfere with the individual right to save. Savers may do as before, or as they would do under conditions of expanded investment.

Government fiscal action to maintain employment is by this procedure limited to offsetting deficiencies as they actually materialize, whether in private consumer spending (as indicated by comparison of current spending rates with the rates found necessary and underwritten) or in total employment (as indicated by comparison of current employment figures with full employment as administratively defined). Employment on public works is expanded only when that is clearly necessary as a device to back up all other measures. When consumers' incomes are increased directly, by tax offsets or otherwise, that is in no sense a substitute for wages that might have been earned by doing useful work, but only an additional measure necessitated by a tendency for too little money to be spent for goods and services even when everyone willing and able to work already has a job. In short, subsidies to consumption that may be called for under this policy are not given for nothing, but rather are given to maintain the level of demand that business requires—which might be put slightly differently by saying that they are given to avoid having to have public enterprise instead of private enterprise in places where there is no evidence that public enterprise is preferred.

How does expanded foreign trade fit into this picture I have tried to sketch? To that question I would give a threefold answer.

In the first place, expanded foreign trade does not need to be justified as a means of increasing domestic employment. It is fully justified and required on other grounds.

Assuming it is brought about in a situation in which trade barriers and discriminations are at a reasonable minimum, so that advantage can be taken of regional specialization in accordance with comparative efficiencies of production, expanded foreign trade should make a striking contribution to international harmony and security and to higher standards of living here and abroad.

In the second place, expanded foreign trade may make some slight net addition to our employment even with exports and imports in balance. This is particularly likely if trade barriers are low, because competition will then tend to be keen and prices reasonable. Moreover, trade will definitely make a net addition to our employment as long as we have an export surplus, such as can be created with the help of a foreign investment program. Practically speaking, however, the employment-creating effects of foreign investment are not sufficiently great or sufficiently permanent to constitute anything like a solution to our employment problem. Pursued in a liberal spirit, foreign investment can be another agent making for a better world of tomorrow, but any attempt to treat foreign investment as a domestic full-employment program would create serious dangers on both the domestic and the international fronts.

Turning the relationship around, a sound domestic program for full employment is the best guarantor of expanded foreign trade. The high national income and production associated with full employment in the United States will tend to contribute more than anything else we could do to the expansion of our imports and of our purchase of other world-trade commodities upon which the prosperity of other nations depends. This in turn will expand the markets for our exports, and will minimize the reluctance of other nations to abandon practices that restrict trade—a reluctance that is quite understandable in the absence of a reasonably assured market for their products in this country. Finally, a sound domestic program for full employment, founded on internal measures and not dependent on export surpluses, will create among American business men, workers, and farmers the conditions and the psychology on which broad American support for liberal trading practice must ultimately rest.

27

A Program to Sustain
Our Economic System

The basic employment issue was not created by the war. Nor was lack of security for industry, the farmer, and the worker. Business cycles with their depressions, ruin, and misery have existed since the beginning of the industrial era. The war has, nonetheless, shown us what our economy can do in providing what we once considered incredible expansion, prosperity, and economic security for industry, farmer, and worker—the security and high national income resting upon full employment which in turn rests upon an ample market.

The plan to be outlined was developed with the following goals in mind: (a) full employment, (b) consequent elimination of the business cycle, (c) absence of regimentation, (d) establishment of an ample and expanding market for business to compete for, (e) insured security for industry, farmer, and worker. Briefly, it is suggested that these goals could be reached by underwriting the national consumer income (actually, the total consumer expenditure for goods and services) with much the same results on confidence as are achieved in preventing runs on banks by insuring depositors' accounts.

Thus the proposal looks to having private enterprise itself provide the needed jobs. This probably is the alternative that most Americans would prefer, but it presents difficulties when the stimuli of war or of transient speculative booms are absent. Any attempt to deny these difficulties, or to go further and suggest that laissez faire is what is needed, must be set down as pure politics.

A word about full employment. In the society of the future the right to a job will rank with the right of free speech and other precious rights we consider fundamental to the

---

This paper was awarded one of the $1,000 prizes in an essay contest sponsored by the Pabst Brewing Company in 1944. It was published, under the title "A Program to Underwrite Full Employment," in *The Winning Plans in the Pabst Postwar Employment Awards*, 1944.

preservation of human dignity. The right to a job is more than getting an income; it is the right to perform a useful function and to preserve a respected social status. Psychologists, sociologists, and economists agree that long-continued unemployment distorts and destroys human personality.

The right to a job cannot be assured unless we resolve as a national policy to maintain full employment. This goal does not require that people have jobs who do not want them, or that unemployables be given jobs, or that all others without exception must be employed at a given time. But it does mean that, except for a small, defined quantity of normal frictional or between-jobs unemployment, there are real jobs—jobs that serve a useful purpose and meet prevailing standards as to wage rates, hours, and working conditions—for all persons able and wanting to work.

It is generally recognized that production and employment depend, with us, on the volume of effective demand for output. Strictly speaking, they depend—temporary shortages of equipment and materials aside—on the relation between: effective demand (current and anticipated); production cost (wages, taxes, interest, depreciation, etc.); and the degree of monopolistic restrictionism (or tendency to limit output to increase price and profit). In addition they may be affected by business optimism or pessimism. But chief stress belongs on current and expected demand, because this is the factor that society can most promptly adjust up or down; moreover business expansion and contraction, and new business ventures, seem particularly responsive to the revenue side of the equation.

Savings do not create demand until they are invested. Thus the savings-investment relation is central. Furthermore, there now appears to be a general tendency for the savings that accrue at full employment to exceed the available profitable investment opportunities. Hence total demand—for consumer goods plus capital goods—tends to fall below the level required to secure or maintain full production. The solution frequently proposed is that, pending adjustments toward a better natural balance, we high-pressure private investment and fill the remaining gap with public investment.

However, conceding that we are not yet investment-saturated, neither are we investment-starved. Also, although our capital-goods industries are now expanded, we are not immobilized for all time in particular industries and localities. Most important, we are not likely to create enough jobs through public investment, because of the dilemma of "boondoggling" on the one hand and "government competition" on the other, and because the private-interprise sector tends to become pessimistic when this policy is pushed to its logical conclusion.

It is therefore suggested here that government instead maintain aggregate consumer spending at the level needed to give jobs in the consumer-goods industries to all who are not employed by "naturally occurring" private investment or "preferred" public investment, and that government *underwrite* this aggregate in advance so as to open the draft on the fires of business enterprise, including capital formation.

Federal, state, and local government would still carry on all public investment considered desirable for its own (rather than employment's) sake. For example, housing, health, education, and conservation of natural resources are so important that public investment should be expanded to any extent required to secure universally high standards in these fields. To the degree that private enterprise cannot be encouraged by low interest rates, incentive taxation, or other legitimate inducements to satisfy requirements, or where it is entirely excluded by the nature of the situation, public investment and, where necessary, public operation should be extended.

Moreover, government would also originate employment projects, drawn from a well-stocked, diversified shelf of useful, planned undertakings, whenever a temporary lag in private construction or some other circumstance (such as incomplete reconversion) made this necessary for full employment in spite of the assurance of customers for private enterprise in general. The underwriting would thus apply to employment as well as to consumer spending. Indeed, the only purpose of underwriting consumer spending at all would be to have a larger share of the full employment in normal enterprise, leaving less to be supplied by fill-in projects.

Then, finally, supposing the consumer money income flowing from full-employment production (from wages and salaries, rents, interest, profits, and also social security benefits, etc.) brought about less than or more than the guaranteed consumer spending, which could happen as the result of either too much or too little saving, government would subsidize or tax consumption directly to prevent spending from falling below the guarantee or rising more than a stipulated amount above it.

This constitutes the core of the proposal for maintenance of effective demand, and the distinguishing feature of the proposal as a whole. Its detailed application is a matter in which there are numerous options. What requires particular emphasis, however, is not the detail but the way the main principles—on (a) government underwriting of total consumer spending, (b) private and normal public investment, (c) fill-in public works, (d) financing of public expenditures, and (e) control of monopoly prices—are linked together.

Excessive prices restrict production and employment in spite of the demand, besides limiting progress and fostering concentrations of wealth. Fiscal measures would therefore be greatly aided by an active campaign to enforce competition and control monopoly prices—presumably with stress on the former wherever that alternative was available. In this connection we need prompt settlement of subcontractors' claims, wise war plant and surplus disposal policies, patent reform, better capital and credit facilities for small business, grade labeling, vigorous antitrust action. The further growth of cooperatives would also assist. For monopolies that are here to stay, prices should be fixed by commissions, or controlled indirectly if methods can be devised to give management incentives for expansion.

With respect to the public-works regulator, the first requirement is a decision on normal frictional unemployment—some fixed amount (for example, 2 million) or a seasonally varying figure. Experience with "loose" and "tight" labor markets should suggest the range within which a compromise fair to both workers and employers can be struck. The Employment Service—which must be greatly strengthened against demobilization—can then know when to signal the agency responsible for starting and stopping public work projects.

To avoid inflationary and deflationary gaps, the agency estimating for the consumer spending guarantee would calculate trends in productivity, deduct for private investment and output purchased by government, and adjust for expected changes in wage rates, business taxes, other production costs, and profits. This technique offers an additional instrument, operating through publicity, for combating the wage-price spiral feared in connection with full-employment situations. In calculating, the guarantee would be raised when the export balance was declining and vice versa, so that reliance would not have to be placed on exports to sustain the over-all level of domestic employment.

For ability to adjust total consumer income in either direction, as required by deviations of currently recorded consumer spending rates from guaranteed rates, administrative discretion would be necessary, based on policies established by Congress. The law would perhaps call for application of a spendings tax, for example, against excessive spending; the demobilization period might bring this into play, especially if rationing controls were lifted immediately.

A number of factors including minimum-wage, social security, and progressive tax laws, highly desirable in themselves, can eventually be expected to minimize the underspending tendency. In the near future, however, the underwriting would usually require consumption subsidies. It is suggested that, after exploring the practical limits of timing the redemption of war bonds and rebating selected taxes, the government bridge any remaining gap with outright "national income security payments," distributing these (through the post office or otherwise) on some share-alike basis to all families and single persons. This would be equitable and would result in the spending of a high percentage of the total subsidy. And the subsidization under these circumstances could hardly be impugned as an inferior substitute for payments for useful work, being actually required to neutralize oversaving in a situation with everyone already at work.

The financing of this program—consumption subsidies and work projects as needed—would be self-defeating if it involved taxes that reduced purchasing power, increased business costs, or penalized genuine enterprise. Uninvested (hoarded) savings, however, could be tapped without detriment to production or infringement of legitimate rights, thus using the existing money supply to the full and avoiding needless creation of new money. A penalty tax on "excess" demand deposit balances and currency, but with option to the holder of buying special low- or zero-interest government securities, would stimulate private investment and spending, and to that extent obviate subsidies and projects, as well as bring money into the Treasury. Additional amounts needed to sustain production could perhaps most readily be borrowed at low rates from the banking system.

Any other full-employment program would encounter similar financing problems. The underwriting plan would probably be less expensive than the public investment approach. To begin with, the extra cost of the latter due to larger volume of projects— increased by the discouraging effect on business of the public investment approach itself—might well be greater than the cost of consumption subsidies required to neutralize underspending of full-employment income. Moreover, the underwriting procedure would throw the spotlight on monopolistic restrictionism and over-saving as causes for necessary expense, and should therefore hasten the removal of those causes.

A full-employment program must be essentially "shockproof" in relation to foreign trade. As noted, the underwriting procedure would free our economy of dependence on a "favorable" trade balance. A further requirement is that exchange rates be not held rigid. In addition, the greater the predictability of our foreign trade, the better, so that our industry and agriculture may avoid needless dislocations and frictional unemployment.

For our part, we should take fullest advantage of opportunities to raise the American standard of living and promote world security through beneficial foreign investments and relaxation of trade restrictions. Receding prosperity, however, develops an enormous pressure for tariffs and export subsidies—for all measures that restrict, preempt, and exclude. Only if we are secure in our ability to maintain full employment will we, in fact, avoid the rise of policies that deny the spirit of international cooperation and undermine the hope of lasting peace.

28

Underwriting Aggregate Consumer Spending

The solid establishment of full employment after the war is a matter of profound importance.[1] Full employment creates its own problems for society.[2] However, if serious unemployment is allowed to develop, the following results may be confidently expected: widespread individual misery and frustration; a tendency for wage rates and working conditions to deteriorate because of excessively keen competition for the scarce existing jobs; bitter conflicts and animosities between Negroes and whites, women and men, ex-servicemen and civilians, older and younger workers, farmers and industrial workers, skilled and unskilled, native and foreign born—tensions from which will come pressure groups endangering democracy itself; a weakening of the production base which constitutes the foundation for the structure of social security and all similar institutions; and the ascendency of aggressive economic foreign policies that violate the spirit of cooperation and undermine the hope of lasting peace.

1. It is frequently asserted (1) that no one knows what full employment means, and (2) that full employment is a "counsel of perfection" and cannot be wholly achieved. The second of these allegations requires some analysis.[3] But the suggestion that full employment cannot be defined or identified carries little weight and may be disposed of in preliminary fashion by answering that full employment means a real job at all times for every able-bodied person who wants to work. That is to say, it means as many real jobs as there are employables wanting to work, *less* a number corresponding to normal frictional unemployment. A job is "real" if it serves a useful purpose and meets currently prevailing standards as to wage rates, hours,[4] and working conditions. Anyone is "employable" who is capable of meeting certain minimum physical and mental requirements. Anyone who "wants" to work can so signify to the Employment Service. "Normal frictional unemployment"—required because the system needs some slack for

This article appeared in the March, 1944, issue of the *American Economic Review,* under the title, "The Underwriting of Aggregate Consumer Spending as a Pillar of Full-Employment Policy."

reasons of turnover, et cetera—is a statistical magnitude representing the amount by which it is agreed that labor force (employables wanting to work) can exceed employment without impairing full employment in the technical sense. The problems of concept and measurement concealed by this explanation are real, but they are not such that practical men cannot know what full employment means and when it exists.

It is, of course, very important to know what full employment means, in the operating sense. Uncertainty on this score would paralyze action with respect to the public work projects yielding smaller benefits than might have been derived from *a different*

THE PUBLIC INVESTMENT APPROACH

2. The best-known proposal for securing full employment in our peacetime economy encounters such serious difficulties as to raise grave doubt whether it could ever provide a fundamental solution for the problem in hand. This is the proposal, advanced by Hansen[5] and other distinguished economists, that public investment be used to compensate for deficiencies in the private sector of the economy.

This idea has made an indelible impression on the thinking of the past decade. It has an imposing theoretical base—the most famous exposition of which was given by Keynes[6]—in the consideration that, in a modern high-income economy operating at capacity or near-capacity levels, voluntary saving tends to exceed the available (profitable) private investment outlets, so that resources threaten to go unused altogether. Empirically it derives support from the fact that the capital goods industries, whose activity corresponds to real investment, contract and expand more violently in the course of the business cycle than do the consumer goods industries.

But there are serious objections when it comes to drawing from these premises the conclusion that public investment should be used to offset secular as well as temporary deficits in private investment. In the first place, such a policy ultimately risks offending against the canon of efficiency or economy, since it may involve public investment projects yielding smaller benefits than might have been derived from *a different* allocation of labor and other resources. The inference is by no means to be drawn that this is characteristically the case with public investment. Indeed, there are certain kinds of public investment hitherto not developed to any significant extent that are probably at least as badly needed as anything else we could produce. Nevertheless there is clearly no reason to believe that any public investment project undertaken to fill an employment gap must automatically be desirable from the standpoint of relative usefulness, unless we are justified in assuming that alternative employment opportunities and products simply could not be created in other ways. This assumption seems of doubtful validity. There may well be ways of getting just as much employment along alternative lines yielding products that are wanted more than the end results of the public investment projects.[7]

In the second place, public investment applied as a compensatory technique—fill-in investment—does not squarely meet the over-saving problem. It palliates the difficulty by absorbing the excess savings. But it fails to assure a level of consumption adequate to maintain full employment with public investment limited to items regarded by the general public as worthwhile for their own sake. (Hence, this is really a special aspect of the previously stated objection on grounds of efficiency.) On this point there is little help to be got from the argument that public investment puts out purchasing power and thus indirectly takes care of the consumption level. Public investment does indeed increase consumer income. If pushed to the point of full employment, it will enable us to achieve what may be referred to as a full-employment-*caused* level of national income and of consumer income.[8] But it cannot be counted on to give us a full-employment-*causing* level of consumer *spending*—meaning by this a total adequate to induce full employment without public investment fill-in programs. For the independent decisions to save out of income, or to dis-save, have still to be reckoned with. In the immediate demobilization period, *particularly* if public investment can be used to secure full employment, the cashing of war savings may well lift consumer spending above the cost value of the maximum output of consumer goods deliverable at that time. Thereafter, if or when the over-saving tendency reasserts itself, the volume of income payments flowing from full-employment operations will not in itself suffice to assure an adequate return flow of consumer spending in the sense indicated above.

The third objection relates directly to the question of feasibility rather than to economic principle, and must be weighed accordingly. Practically speaking the fundamental consideration, so far as concerns the possibility of maintaining full employment, is that a public investment program, *used as the main weapon against unemployment and expanded to whatever extent might be necessary to prevent unemployment*, would probably seriously discourage private enterprise. Our experience with a limited volume of public works in the thirties, which did not bring about full employment, provides no conclusive test of this statement one way or the other. Many types of public investment are noncompetitive at least in the sense that they do not compete with private enterprise in the market for products. Furthermore, public projects often provide an obvious stimulus to business—notably to contractors and to suppliers of building materials and equipment. Even "noncompetitive" public invest-ment does, however, compete in the labor and capital (and land) markets and, ultimately, in the market where philosophies or systems of production are selected. This is especially obvious if public ownership and operation are involved, but it remains true even if the government merely assumes *responsibility* and the workers are on private payrolls. Systematically applied on a grand and, in principle, indefinitely expansible scale, public investment would probably discourage private enterprise by throwing private enterprise into partial eclipse. Naturally, this is a situation in which business will not readily allow itself to be placed.

The above difficulties with the public investment approach as a solution for the unemployment problem may be reformulated, from the standpoint of its political prospects, along the following lines: (1) The cry of "boondoggling" will be raised to discredit this program; worse than that, examples of relatively useless public investment projects will be cited to support the allegation that full employment itself necessarily means an inefficient or uneconomical allocation of resources. (2) Incidentally, although this touches on the theoretical premises for the program rather than on the program itself, members of the public investment school will be accused of "selling America short" when they argue that public investment is necessitated by a widening secular gap between saving and private investment opportunity. (3) In the end, these arguments plus straightforward opposition to government competition will to a considerable extent prevail, especially since the concept of investment (as contrasted with the concept of consumption) is somewhat lacking in broad popular appeal. The opposition will not prevent large-scale public investment projects from being undertaken, but almost certainly will prevent full employment from being maintained by this method—which is the question that concerns us here.

At this point it may also be well to emphasize that some of the theoretical apparatus most commonly associated with the case for a public investment solution does not prove that public investment is the answer to the problem. The multiplier principle indicates than an increment of aggregate investment will produce a more than equivalent increase in national income, since it will also raise consumption. It does not tell us that an expansion of *public* investment will yield a corresponding increment (or, for that matter, *any* increment) of *aggregate* investment; this prior question cannot be resolved unless we know the reactions of private enterprise to the public investment program, and these reactions may well depend on the point to which the later is pushed, as suggested above.

Similarly, the principle of relative constancy of the consumption-income ratio, or consumption function, or propensity to consume does not tell us that a tendency for saving to exceed investment at full-employment levels must be corrected by expanding investment. For it does not settle the question whether public policy might not equally well or better expand consumers' incomes or their disposable cash directly, and in this way increase consumption instead.[9]

ELEMENTS OF AN ALTERNATIVE PROGRAM

3. While the "mature economy" or "secular stagnation" thesis—the suggestion that the passing of the frontier and the slowing of population growth are narrowing private investment opportunities—is under fairly heavy fire,[10] the familiar conclusion from this premise seems to be taken at face value. It appears to be pretty generally believed that *if there is* a deficiency of private investment, relative to the tendency to save at full-employment levels of income, the gap must be closed by expanding aggregate investment. The other alternative would be an increase in consumption, which would involve a reduction of aggregate real saving. Before this alternative is examined directly, consideration will be given to the elements that a program would have to contain to meet the objections raised above against the public investment approach.

The objection on the grounds that public investment invites an uneconomical allocation of resources would be met if it were possible to have a full employment program in which public investment was limited to permanent priority items and fill-in items according to the following criteria: (1) The permanent priority items would be only those which the majority of persons would prefer as against the alternative of individual consumption out of individual incomes, supposing that existing incomes could be adjusted to the necessary level under a politically feasible program of direct support to individual consumption. (2) The fill-in projects, which would be drawn from a well-planned shelf of public works or work projects, would be operated only when needed to offset short-term deficiencies in employment opportunity that might develop in spite of maintenance of consumption at levels regarded *a priori* as adequate to secure full employment.[11] These residual deficiencies would still occur from time to time, particularly as a result of changes in the rate of introduction of new inventions, fluctuations in the rate of replacement of fixed equipment, and, perhaps, fluctuations in inventories. The items on the regular list would be in place of alternative output, but would represent a better allocation of resources so far as it is humanly possible to judge such matters. The only alternative to the fill-in projects, when these were required, would be no output at all. To put it differently, the development of an employment gap in spite of measures taken to provide business with sufficient customers would raise the marginal value of public investment as a whole and require the inauguration of the projects highest on the waiting list. To be sure, there are bound to be sharp differences of opinion about some of the items that might be included on the regular program. But the democratic process resolves these differences into some kind of answer at any given moment and should be able to express the state of public opinion with fair accuracy as time goes by.

The element required to meet the second objection against the public investment approach—that it does not squarely meet the over-saving problem—would be direct control over total consumer spending. If it were possible to exercise such control, consumption could be held at a level adequate to maintain full employment—i.e., full employment with private investment taking its natural course and public investment operating according to the principles enunciated above. Thus, any over-saving or under-spending tendency would be corrected instead of covered up, as under a policy of equating investment to saving.

If it were possible to control total consumer spending, then it should also be possible to underwrite this total. To do so would seem desirable from the standpoint of giving solid encouragement to private enterprise while restraining speculative excesses. In short, consumer spending might be (1) controlled, (2) held at levels permitting public investment to represent on the whole a deliberate social choice of products for their own sake rather than in large part a bowing to the supposed necessity of filling an investment gap, and (3) *underwritten to allow the prospective demand to exert its full stimulating force upon all enterprises producing goods or services for market.* If all this could be done, it would appear that the third objection, the discouragement to private enterprise inherent in an all-out compensatory public investment program, might also be avoided.

4. What has been suggested may be summed up as the principle of burden of proof for investment, the principle of underwriting or insuring the economy as a whole, and a combination of these principles through application of the underwriting to aggregate individual consumption.

The principle of burden of proof for investment implies that the criterion for the appropriate volume of private investment should be its natural response (in terms of expansion and replacement) to changes in tastes and techniques, and to levels of and changes in rates of interest; that the volume of public investment should be decided by judging the end products on their merits as against alternatives that might result from higher levels of individual consumer spending; and that the balance of our resources should be employed producing goods and services to be bought by individual consumers in the proportions they think best. In other words, this principle rests on the premise that "over-saving" really means over-saving (under-spending) and not under-investment.

Public investment may from this standpoint be considered as including all public spending for goods and services, and hence extends not only to the purchase of munitions by the army but also to all collective consumption in the sense of community expenditure for general public use (as opposed to consumption represented by individual consumer spending). Thus, it covers public expenditure for free medical service as well as for construction of hospitals and clinics; for teaching and free school lunches and library service as well as for construction of schools and libraries; for the maintenance as well as the laying out of parks and playgrounds. The principle of burden of proof for investment therefore implies that community consumption, like public investment in producer goods, should stand on its own merits—which are often quite sufficient—and should yield to individual consumption wherever the superiority of the former over the latter has not been established. Expansion of community consumption merely to compensate for absence of other demand would fail to satisfy requirements, since the principle in question rests on the assumed desirability of individual consumer sovereignty as well as on the supposition that production should be carried on for the sake of consumption.

The principle of underwriting the economy rests on the inference that underwriting the effort of private enterprise is better than continually meddling with it here and there, so long as private enterprise is supposed to be held in esteem. Of course, it does not preclude government ownership and operation or government regulation where necessary or desirable. Nor does it imply that new rigidities should be introduced through a guaranteeing of markets to individual producers or individual industries. But it does postulate the desirability of assuring an adequate effective demand in the over-all sense—the desirability of seeing that the "game of hazard," as Keynes calls it, played by business men should not be one in which, to continue his phrase, "the players *as a whole* will lose if they have the energy and hope to deal all the cards."[12]

The application of the underwriting to aggregate individual consumption (as well as to employment as a whole) appears desirable if the two underlying principles are valid. A guarantee to fill all employment gaps with public investment, without a simultaneous guarantee of adequate overall consumer market, would prevent (if it could be made good) a decline in consumer income but would still expose the economy to over-saving—concealed by a corresponding degree of over-investment.[13] A nonspecific guarantee to offset saving one way or the other—either by expanding public investment or by supplementing consumers' spending by way of their incomes—might or might not eliminate over-saving, depending on which of the two courses the government elected to follow. But in any case it would create needless uncertainties and broaden the opportunities for arbitrary government action.

5. We may now formulate a preliminary outline of how a policy of underwriting aggregate consumer spending would operate—always assuming that the practical means could be found for executing the steps required. After that the question of ways and means will be explored.

It is clear that the steps to be taken by the government would be three in number. (1) The government would first have to calculate the "right" dollar amount of aggregate individual consumer spending (say for the next year)—this being the amount the confident anticipation of which would be expected to stimulate full employment, with public investment limited to items wanted for their own sake. The government would announce this amount and would guarantee that consumers' incomes would be adjusted if necessary so that the designated amount of spending would actually be forthcoming. (2) It would next have to fill the employment gap, if one occurred in spite of the inducement to private enterprise afforded by the guarantee of consumer spending, by starting or expanding appropriate projects from the public work shelf. (3) Finally, it would have to expand or reduce total consumer spending via consumer cash incomes,[14] if and as this proved necessary, in spite of the existence of full employment and a full-employment-caused volume of income payments, in order to prevent under- or over-fulfillment of the guarantee.[15]

Consideration shows that numerous combinations or sequences of events would be possible—six altogether. The underwriting of consumer spending might or might not altogether obviate the need for a fill-in program of public work projects. Full employment, whether achieved with or without fill-in employment, might result in aggregate consumer spending equal to the amount guaranteed, might require an addition to consumer incomes to increase their spending in order to realize the guarantee, or might require a deduction from consumer spending to prevent over-fulfillment.

THE UNDERWRITING AND CONTROL OF AGGREGATE CONSUMER SPENDING

6. As a practical matter, how could aggregate consumer spending be guaranteed? How could any guarantee be made good? First and foremost, how could consumer spending be raised when it threatened to fall short?

The general answer to this half of the problem,[16] as already suggested, is that consumer spending would be raised by giving consumers additional spending power. This could be handled in a variety of ways. Congress would, however, presumably want to consider the following principles in ruling how this should be done. (1) *Adequacy of amount*: the formula selected would have to permit payments to be made to consumers up to a total sufficient to take care of any under-spending likely to arise in a full-employment situation. (2) *Broad and fair distribution*: (a) payments should in general go to the broad ranks of Americans throughout the country, which means in effect that a large part of the total would go to low-income groups. This is necessary for reasons of equity, and it is necessary also in order to keep down the cost to the government, since the low-income groups would spend a larger fraction of these payments and save less. (b) The purpose of maintaining the over-all market should not, however, be subordinated, or normal competitive incentives undermined, by treating the underwriting program as essentially a vehicle for redistribution of income. (c) The distribution should not favor special interest groups. In general, wherever particular groups have a legitimate claim to preferential treatment, such treatment should be accorded by special legislative enactment and not by introducing biases into the program for maintaining the over-all spending level. Any balancing payments required under the latter program should be made available to the general public with a minimum of distinctions between persons. (3) *Flexibility*: the formula would have to contain within itself, as part of the policy laid down by Congress, features enabling the payments to be started, stopped, expanded, or contracted on short notice (say, each quarter) so as to adapt to changes in the ratio of consumers' spending out of their regular incomes. (4) *Operating simplicity*: the program should not be unduly complicated in administration, and as far as possible it should use agencies and mechanisms already in operation.

It is not the purpose of this paper to suggest what formula would best meet these and any other necessary specifications. That is the kind of general policy decision that can only be made by the American people acting through their elected representatives. Some typical alternatives, which by no means exhaust the possibilities, may, however, be mentioned to show that the problem is soluble.

One possibility of considerable interest is that of timing the repayment of war bonds according to the need of the post-war economy for restricted or expanded consumer expenditure. The practical importance of this alternative is no doubt related to the question whether or not the United States shortly adopts a program of forced saving to raise revenue and combat wartime inflation. By the end of 1944 some 50 billion dollars' worth of war savings bonds might be outstanding, of which 20 billion, possibly, might have been subscribed under a forced savings plan involving rebatable income or Victory taxes and rebatable sales taxes. In enacting such legislation, Congress might retain for the government the right to pay back these savings by redeeming the bonds any time within, say, five years after the end of the war. A similar stipulation might be attached, in conjunction with tax exemption privileges, high interest rates, or some other special inducement to future issues of war bonds subscribed voluntarily or exchanged for present holdings of demand bonds. At the right time after the war the government might, furthermore, encourage redemption of bonds not callable at government option by offering full value on accrual bonds if turned in promptly and correspondingly favorable terms on other issues. Conceivably the government might also, by appropriate concessions in the form of higher interest rates, acquire substantial control over the timing of interest payments.

It appears unlikely, however, that any combination of such devices could secure to the government the disposition or timing of payments in excess of, say, 30 billion dollars altogether, on the basis of war bonds subscribed by the end of 1944. Moreover, a large fraction of such payments would undoubtedly be reinvested or held in bank accounts rather than spent; even assuming a large forced savings program heavily weighted to build up the bond holdings of the low-income groups, the increment of consumer spending would hardly exceed 50 percent of interest and principal payments on the bonds. It therefore appears that the total expansive effect to be gained in this manner is limited—although less limited the longer the war and the period of bond accumulation. It also seems self-evident that bond redemption does not in itself provide an instrument of fine precision for adjusting aggregate consumer spending to guaranteed levels. On the other hand this mechanism, if skillfully handled, could be useful for securing rough first approximations, or at any rate movements in the desired directions, in the early post-war years.

Another possible formula for raising consumer spending in order to achieve guaranteed levels involves the rebating of taxes paid by individuals—i.e., the payment of rebates over and above those which may have been provided for in advance in connection with wartime forced savings programs. Such payments might be made on the principle that it is sound policy to give individuals back their own money to spend when enterprise requires larger markets in order to prosper. The rebates might be applied to the previous year's income taxes and payroll taxes, with provision in the latter case that the government would reimburse the social security accounts for any sums drawn out for this purpose, to prevent impairment of the funds available for benefits. Any spendings taxes or sales taxes enacted could likewise be rebated; as a simpler though cruder alternative to requiring the presentation of sales tax receipts, payments might be made based on standard assumptions regarding the sum of all indirect taxes borne by the average family or individual. The total of the taxes levied on individuals in any one year—which, including payroll taxes, would perhaps have a general order of magnitude around 10 billion dollars—provides a measure of the maximum amount that could be rebated.

Of course, if suspension or forgiveness of current taxes were added to the rebating of taxes for the previous year, the effect would be doubled temporarily, but with the result that in the following year the principle could not be applied except on the pretext that the taxes paid several years before were now being returned. The tax rebate device, therefore, like the timing of bond redemptions, has definite quantitative limits. Nevertheless it might have merit as a control mechanism within a limited range of operation, particularly if applied to taxes levied on low-income groups, such as payroll taxes,[17] the refunding of which would increase consumers' spending considerably more in proportion than would the refunding of even a broadly based income tax with low exemptions.

A third possibility would be a system of "national income security payments" on the basis of residual equity claims assigned to the general public. All families and single persons throughout the country might be treated as though they were the holders of stock in a business enterprise. Assuming 30 million families and 10 million single persons, the payment of $100 (tax free) to each family and $50 to each single person, for example, would increase total disposable income by 3.5 billion dollars. Making the conservative assumption that 80 cents out of every dollar thus distributed would be spent by the recipient for consumers' goods or services (which probably underestimates the marginal ratio of spending to saving in this case), consumer *spending* would thereby rise to the extent of 2.8 billion dollars. A doubling of the dividends would almost double the effect upon spending. The rates actually applied would depend on how much expansion was required, so that this kind of formula, coupled with quarterly distribution, and used either alone or with the other devices when they were insufficient, would permit of complete flexibility over an unlimited range.

7. Because of the relative unfamiliarity of some of the available devices for expanding consumption directly, a discussion of them may have a tendency to obscure two points that it is essential to bear in mind. The first is that the subsidization of consumption here contemplated is merely such subsidization as may be needed (but at other times will not be needed) to prevent under-spending[18] from occurring *in conditions of full employment*—the full employment having been secured either with or without fill-in programs of public works. The second is that the costs and difficulties of this procedure for maintaining full employment must be weighed against the costs and difficulties inherent in other methods.

To make this clear and specific, two parallel columns of figures have been set up in Table 28.1 showing a hypothetical post-war total and breakdown of the national product and the uses made of distributed income. The first column depicts a condition of full employment secured by underwriting aggregate consumer spending and subsidizing it to offset over-saving; the second column depicts a condition of full employment secured in the same over-saving situation through compensatory public investment. Interpreted in prices that prevailed in the first half of 1943, the gross national product of 170 billion and

Table 28.1 Hypothetical National Output, Income, Savings, Consumption, Etc., for Full Employment in 1946, Assuming End of War in December 1944 (in prices of January – June 1943)

Item	Full Employment via Underwriting Approach, with Consumption Subsidy	Full Employment via Public Investment Approach
	(in $ billions)	
1. Gross national product (2+3)	$170	$170
2. Government expenditures for goods and services:		
a. unadjusted	24	24
b. adjusted for $8 billion public investment fill-in		32
3. Goods and services available for private use (4+5)	146	138
4. Private gross capital expenditures	22	22
5. Value of consumption output	124	116
6. National income	140	140
7. Business savings (corporate business)	4	4
8. Distributed income (total shares transferred) by business enterprises) (6−7)	136	136
9. Income payments (8, adjusted for social security and other transfers):		
a. unadjusted for subsidy	134	134
b. adjusted for $10 billion subsidy to consumers[a]	144[a]	
10. Direct personal taxes	8	8
11. Disposable income (9−10):		
a. unadjusted	126	126
b. adjusted for $10 billion subsidy to consumers[a]	136[a]	
12. Net individual savings:		
a. tendency to save from current income 15		
b. tendency to spend war savings 5		
c. unadjusted savings (a−b)	10	10
d. savings adjusted for 20% of $10 billion subsidy	12	
13. Consumer spending:		
a. unadjusted (11a−12c)	116	116
b. adjusted for 80% of $10 billion subsidy	124	

[a] Subsidization of consumption may or may not increase income payments and disposable income (as thse terms are ordinarily used), depending on the method of subsidization followed. For example, repayment of war bonds may be conceived of as raising consumer spending without affecting disposable income or income payments; tax reductions and tax rebates may be regarded as increasing disposable income as well as consumer spending, but not income payments; and special "national income security payments" will evidently expand income payments as well as disposable income and consumer spending.

the other magnitudes involved might be those of 1946, assuming the war had closed at the end of 1944. The quantities shown are, however, only illustrative and do not represent forecasts.

In the first column it has been assumed that government expenditures for goods and services, including construction, defense, salaries, interest on the public debt, and other expenditures (not forgetting essential public expenditures along these lines in connection with expanded programs of education, health, slum clearance, and conservation), amount to 24 billion altogether.[19] This means, if full employment requires or will yield a gross national product of 170 billion, that the private sector of the economy must utilize 146 billion dollars' worth to achieve full employment. Assuming that private gross capital expenditures, including a large housing program, amount to 22 billion,[20] the full-employment level of consumption output is 124 billion.

A gross national product of 170 billion might involve a national income of 140 billion, with business taxes, depreciation, and other charges making up the difference. If corporate savings amount to 4 billion, this leaves 136 billion to be distributed by business enterprises.

If employer and employee contributions to social security funds, et cetera, exceed the transfer payment from the government consisting largely of the benefits paid out from such funds—as may occur on a fairly large scale under programs at present contemplated—income payments coming into the hands of consumers at full-employment levels of production may amount to only, say, 134 billion. If the government takes 8 billion in direct personal taxes, that leaves a disposable income or purchasing power of 126 billion. At this level of current disposable income, consumers may have a "normal" tendency to save 15 billion. But, quite independent of current income, they will also still have large accumulations of war savings, which they may decide to cash and spend to the extent of 5 billion, thereby lowering net individual savings for consumers in the aggregate to 10 billion, and leaving 116 billion to be spent for goods and services.

Consumer expenditures of 116 billion cannot buy consumption output worth 124 billion without serious losses to the producers of that output. (Of course, this larger output may conceivably be produced and the unsold portion added to inventories—a form of capital formation—but that will discourage production in the ensuing year.) Under a program of underwriting aggregate consumer spending, private enterprise, given a guarantee of a consumer market of 124 billion, would have a reasonable incentive to produce that amount. If it does so, this will secure full employment, i.e., the 170-billion gross national product shown in the table, without the need for fill-in public works,[21] since 46 billion dollars' worth of output is being produced for other buyers—24 billion for government agencies and 22 billion for private purchasers of capital goods. To make good on this guarantee, however, government will have to subsidize consumer spending power, by one of the methods discussed above or some other method, sufficiently to raise actual consumer spending from 116 billion to 124 billion. Assuming a marginal propensity to consume—speaking in terms of dollars available for consumer spending—of 0.8, the subsidy required to expand consumer spending by 8 billion is 10 billion. This balances the picture, enabling business as a whole to sell its product without loss. Incidentally, it also somewhat increases consumers' dollar savings.

At this point, comparison should be made with the figures in column two. According to the public investment approach, the picture is balanced in another way. Instead of lifting consumer spending from 116 to 124 billion, a consumption output of 116 billion is assumed to be the most obtainable, and 8 billion dollars' worth of additional public investment is undertaken to close the gap between 162 billion of private plus normal public production, on the one hand, and the 170 billion required for full employment, on the other.

It will be observed that, with the figures used in this illustration, the compensatory spending required by the public investment approach amounts to only 8 billion dollars, whereas it comes to 10 billion (or at any rate some figure higher than 8 billion, the exact amount depending on the marginal propensity to consume) according to the underwriting approach. There are, however, certain dynamic considerations, to be noted later, which seem likely to make the underwriting approach an instrument of budget economy if applied over a period of years.[22] Moreover, even in the immediate situation it should be recognized that the 8-billion figure rests on certain assumptions, extremely favorable to the public investment approach, which are by no means certain to be realized in practice.

In the first place, consumption goods are perhaps rather unlikely to be produced in the amount indicated unless the government definitely pledges itself to support income payments (if not consumer spending) by closing all unemployment gaps with public investment. That is, while they might as a result of speculative activity be produced even in *excess* of the volume indicated, the real basis for a consumption output of 116 billion is less solid in this case than is the basis for a consumption output of 124 billion under the alternative program unless the government specifically guarantees full employment— without which consumer spending will not reach 116 billion. In the second place, the production of capital goods as well as the production of consumption goods requires a reasonable amount of encouragement. If 22 billion of private capital formation is the quantity to be expected with consumer spending underwritten at high levels for the current year and for succeeding years as well, a question may be raised whether the same quantity is likely to be forthcoming in the absence of such assurances. Finally, it is not certain that private production—in particular, private capital formation—may not be rendered somewhat cautious and pessimistic as a result of the additional government participation in or responsibility for production represented by the public investment fill-in. If it so happens, for example, that as the result of these various considerations private consumption output amounts to only 114 billion, and private gross capital expenditures to 18 billion, the necessary investment fill-in will cost the government 14 billion instead of only 8.

8. A program of underwriting aggregate consumer spending involves the idea that spending will be held down to the guaranteed level as well as that it will be kept from falling below this level. This two-way operation is one of the advantages of such a program, since it makes it possible to link anti-inflationary measures, when they are needed, with the promise that anti-deflationary steps will be taken later on.

The criteria by which any formula for contracting consumer spending should be judged are essentially the same as the criteria applicable to programs for expanding this spending—namely, adequacy of amount, broad and fair distribution (in this case, distribution of the *deductions* from spending power), flexibility, and operating simplicity. With regard to broad and fair distribution, the plan definitely must restrict the spending of the average man, but, on the other hand, it should be so framed as to avoid regressive features such as are found in the ordinary sales tax. The spendings tax, which in one form or another seems capable of satisfying these requirements remarkably well, provides an example here. It can restrict spending to any desired extent, both by reducing disposable income and also by causing some people to save more of their disposable income and spend less. It can permit exemptions according to family status, and employ the principle of progression in accordance with ability to pay. It can be collected along with the income tax, thus simplifying the administrative problem. Like the income tax, it can in large part be withheld at the source on a current or short-interval basis, thus allowing the brakes to be applied to consumer spending, and again released, without any loss of time.

A point requiring further analysis, and perhaps some experimentation, is the width of the margin that should be allowed between minimum and maximum levels of aggregate consumer spending. The guarantee should not be so inflexible as to create administrative problems out of all proportion to the gain to be hoped for from elimination of a fractionally small upward pressure on prices. On the other hand, the controlling agency could probably operate quite comfortably with the top limit standing only a very slight percentage above the guaranteed minimum. For example, experience might show that a 2 percent margin was sufficient. In that case, under the conditions illustrated in Table 28.1, an underwriting of consumer spending at a level of 124 billion dollars would mean that the government would not allow the total to fall below 124 billion or rise above 126.5 billion.

PROBLEMS OF ADMINISTRATION CONNECTED WITH
AN UNDERWRITING PROGRAM

9. There would be two main problems of administration involved in carrying out a program of underwriting aggregate consumer spending. First, there would be a problem of *adjusting aggregate employment* to prevent the development of unemployment, which might well necessitate public work projects in spite of the inducement to private production afforded by the guaranteed support of consumer markets, although hardly on anything like the scale required in the absence of this guarantee. Second, there would be a problem of *adjusting aggregate consumer spending* to guaranteed levels, which might well be necessary in spite of full employment, although usually not to the extent that would be required in the absence of full-employment-caused levels of consumer income. Both problems call for flexible administrative control, applied in accordance with policies established by Congress. The administrative agencies in question should presumably be required to submit reports to Congress at regular intervals.

To maintain full employment, the U.S. Employment Service would require current information on the size of the labor force and the number of persons employed, together with an official definition of the number of persons constituting "normal frictional unemployment." This might be a fixed number (such a 2.25 million) or it might be a number fluctuating seasonally (between 2 and 2.5 million, for example), depending on the rule worked out by experts and approved by Congress. The absolute size of this normal slack in the system would necessarily depend, in part, on the amount of technological development and other change, requiring disemployment and re-employment, going on throughout the country. In part it would depend on decisions previously made as to the amount of effort and money that should be devoted to improving the nation's training and placement services. And, finally, it would depend on how "tight" a labor market was considered workable and desirable. On the last two points the major parties at interest, employers and organized labor, would presumably want to have a voice before action was taken leading to official designation of the number of persons, on record as wanting to work, who could be jobless without creating excess unemployment—i.e., an unemployment situation in the technical or operational sense.

Whenever the Employment Service anticipated the development of unemployment in excess of normal frictional unemployment, it would notify the Federal Works Agency to be ready to start public work projects of some appropriate type in the regions where the unemployment problem was expected to center. This presupposes that an ample shelf of useful public work projects would be in readiness. The shelf should place at least as much emphasis on small as on large projects, to facilitate termination when private employment opportunities again expanded. It should include nonconstruction projects (in the fields of public health, education, research, recreation, conservation, and general public welfare) as well as heavy and light construction items, so as to provide fair opportunities for women and others who cannot or should not be asked to enter the construction industry. It should exclude all such projects as do the community no good and offend the worker's self-respect.

When employment in private production and regular public activites fell short of the total labor force by more than normal frictional unemployment, appropriate public work projects should be started—preferably by state and local units if they were ready to start them. Employment on such projects should be on a par with other local employment so far as concerns wage rates for similar types of work and working conditions. It should also be on a par with other employment in the matter of the number of hours worked per week and per month. An incentive to return to private employment as soon as possible would remain, for many persons, because of the manifest impossibility of using individual skills and meeting individual job preferences on public works even as well as this is ordinarily accomplished elsewhere, and, more generally, because of the uncertainty of job tenure on the fill-in program.

This particular uncertainty should be deliberately fostered, through establishment of the principle of priority for private construction and private work in general. When private employers were ready again to expand employment at locally prevailing rates of pay, et cetera, they should be assisted to do so by being assigned prior claims to locally available labor (and equipment and materials), as well as to labor available on a voluntary basis through interregional clearance. In other words, the Employment Service should be kept informed by private employers of their prospective needs for labor, and at the proper time this agency should give notice to the Federal Works Agency to reduce or terminate its fill-in operations as rapidly as possible consistent with preserving the value of the work already done.

10. The other major administrative problem connected with an underwriting program would involve the Treasury Department, Office of Economic Stabilization, or some

other agency set up to administer fiscal policy in the interests of full-employment stability. The agency in question would be charged by Congress with the continuing duty of expanding or contracting aggregate consumer spending power, in accordance with the law, to the extent that might prove necessary to make actual consumer spending correspond to the guarantees previously given. In short, power would have to be delegated to this agency to make distributions of money, and to suspend, increase, or even impose certain taxes under conditions prescribed by Congress.[23] Congress would determine what formulas should be used for expansion and for contraction. The agency in the executive branch would exercise discretion as to the rates of subsidy or tax required to effectuate the policy.

As the basis for action, the executive agency would compare the current rate of consumer spending, as shown by the series prepared by the Department of Commerce on "consumer expenditures for goods and services" (if that were designated the official series) with the "right" rate, derived by applying appropriate seasonal factors to the guaranteed total for the year. The quarter might be the most convenient unit of time for administrative purposes. A guarantee of 124 billion dollars of consumer spending for the year might mean a norm of 29 billion for the comparatively slack first quarter. If, in fact, consumers were spending at a rate of only 27 billion, the agency would proceed to increase consumer spending power, as prescribed by law, by an amount believed to be at least large enough to make up the 2-billion deficit in spending (i.e., by at least 2.5 billion, if the form of subsidization prescribed appeared to involve an 0.8 marginal propensity to consume). If, on the other hand, consumers were spending at a rate of 31 billion, the agency would order the application of a spendings tax formula, or other formula prescribed for contraction, at rates which in its opinion would effect about a 2-billion reduction. Proceeding thus on a quarterly basis and making due allowance for time-lags, the agency should be able to bring the year's total of consumer spending, as indicated by the best statistics available, up to the minimum required to satisfy the guarantee and yet not above the maximum allowed.

The points just discussed emphasize the kinds of delegation of authority by Congress without which it is difficult to conceive of maintaining stabilized conditions of full employment. In some respects these delegations of authority to the executive branch seem large, as compared with present practice. They appear to be necessary and legitimate means, however, for effectuating policy as laid down by Congress, and the actions of the agencies administering these laws would be circumscribed in kind and limited in extent to the mandatory fulfillment of requirements clearly stated in the laws themselves.

11. Determination of the proper amount of consumer spending in connection with an underwriting program would be a technical matter, presumably left to the executive branch but under policy directions from Congress, involving a number of considerations into some of which this paper will briefly digress but cannot enter in any detail. These considerations have to do with choices between alternative price-level policies, with prospective cost levels, with prospective levels of private capital formation, and with prospective levels of demand on the part of foreigners and the government itself.

A large part of the statistical information suitable for preliminary estimates is provided in the various national income series and related series prepared in the

Department of Commerce. In general it may be said that the various statistical estimates that would be required in connection with an underwriting program will have to be made in any case, whatever policies are adopted. It also may be said that the statistical tools available to the government are constantly being improved, but that some over-all framework (such as would be provided by the program under discussion) is indispensable to clarify what statistics are really needed and to bring these series into harmony with each other.

As the over-all productivity of the economy rises with the passage of time, output available for individual consumption also is likely to rise, and thus an increase in aggregate consumer spending is required if the consumer-goods price level is to be free from downward pressure. If consumer spending rises more rapidly than consumption output, prices will tend to go up. If consumer spending falls, remains constant or rises less rapidly than consumption output, prices will tend to fall. Thus, selection of the right trend in the guaranteed rate or amount of consumer spending—the particular trend that would be calculated to effectuate the preferred price-level policy—would require appraisals of trends in man-hour productivity, hours of work, size of the labor force as determined by population changes and other factors, and ratio of individual consumption output to gross product. Selection of the best price-level policy is a matter of some importance although probably not, inside reasonable limits, a major consideration. Inasmuch as the gains associated with price competition do not require a falling price level (since they depend on the relationships among prices and not on the way the average trend is moving), and inasmuch as a stable price level makes for justice between debtors and creditors, tends to discourage speculation, obviates the need to change publicly administered or regulated prices repeatedly to keep them in line with other prices, and simplifies reckoning generally, price-level stability is likely to appear on the whole the best policy, at least in principle. It might, however, be decided on grounds of expediency (which will be examined below) to allow a gradual rise in the price level, notwithstanding the fact that this might tend to require some form of compensatory action to preserve normal relations in foreign trade. But in any event, so far as the underwriting of consumer spending is concerned, the relations may be indicated by saying that, if the volume of consumption output purchased by individual consumers were expected to rise, say, 2 percent each year, and if it were desired to hold the price level steady, the guaranteed aggregate of consumer spending should also rise 2 percent annually.

Naturally, the costs of doing business affect the amount of employment that can be induced by any given dollar demand for end-products. Hence spontaneous rises in costs (as opposed to rises "imputed" back to the factors of production after a prior advance in business revenues) would, if they could not be prevented, create the practical necessity for a year-by-year increase in the guaranteed amount of consumer spending sufficient to permit prices to rise without restriction of the volume of production and employment. The question of increases in money rates of wages, which would be of particularly obvious and direct importance in this connection, will be taken up shortly. Similar considerations apply to levels of business taxes; also, perhaps in lesser degree, to interest charges and rent payments; also to financial practices with respect to the allowances for depreciation, obsolescence, and insurance of various kinds which are treated as costs before profit is calculated. Finally, great significance attaches to the degree of unregulated monopoly power exercised by producers, since this affects the amount of production and employment that can be expected in association with a given total amount of net profit—or, stated differently, in association with a given combination of aggregate consumer demand and aggregate business cost. For example, if 124 billion dollars of consumer demand were sufficient to induce full employment with the given degree of monopolistic restrictionism in the economy as a whole, this same total of consumer demand would be insufficient for full employment in a situation containing a greater amount of monopolistic restrictionism, and more than sufficient for one characterized by a larger element of free competition.

Turning to the demand side of the picture, it is clear that the size of the aggregate individual consumer spending guarantee requisite to induce full employment at a given price level would be fundamentally affected by the volume of output not sold to individual consumers—i.e., by the volume of output marketed domestically but paid for by business or the government,[24] and by the volume of output paid for by foreigners. In addition, if spending were defined as including only transfers of cash, allowance would have to be made for expansions and contractions of consumer credit, which equally affect the marketing of, and hence the inducement to produce, consumption output, notably in the important industries producing consumer durables. As a practical matter, this last question is taken care of by the technical characteristics of the series on consumer expenditures for goods and services issued by the Department of Commerce, which measures the full value of output purchased on open credit and installment accounts rather than the current payments of cash on account of such items.[25]

Like private domestic capital expenditures, the government's expenditures for goods and services, whether for war or for peace, obviate the need for a corresponding volume of individual consumer expenditure. Payments by foreigners for American goods have a similar effect, this effect presumably corresponding rather closely to the magnitude of the item, net export of goods and services (or net change in foreign claims), as included in statistics of private gross capital formation. If experience should show that these quantities were peculiarly hard to estimate in advance, it would be possible to ease the difficulty, without sacrifice of the essential principle involved in the guarantee, by making the amount of the guarantee contingent upon the realization of specified magnitudes of government purchases or net exports or both, the final total of individual consumer spending, however, to be subject to changes that would offset unexpected changes in these specified magnitudes. This safeguard would probably be unnecessary although in the case of government expenditures for goods and services there might be an ulterior advantage in such an arrangement, since it would provide a technical loophole in case the agency charged with adjusting aggregate consumer spending miscalculated the propensity to consume to such an extent that it failed to bring aggregate consumer spending within the prescribed limits by the end of the year.[26]

12. In the immediate demobilization period we face the twin dangers of unemployment on the one hand and price inflation on the other. In this situation the government should do everything possible to expand civilian production, which will raise income payments, and at the same time do everything possible to hold consumer spending down to the level of the available consumption output. An underwriting program would help solve both parts of this problem.

At the production end, the ultimate limits to what can be done all at once will be the limits imposed by stubborn physical facts—the time required to re-tool plants, re-assemble materials and skilled labor, re-schedule production, re-build distributive organizations, and so forth. In spite of voluntary withdrawals from the labor force, the chances are certainly all against our escaping unemployment in the early months after the war, except on the basis of a sizeable program of public work projects. In this particular period, in the face of rapid military and industrial demobilization, fill-in public employment will be needed because of the sheer impossibility of bringing private industry into full-scale operation immediately, even if the effective demand for products appears to be virtually limitless. At the same time, if sound plans are made in advance, this necessity can be converted into a real opportunity to start clearing away our slums and filling accumulated deficits in construction items and services of various kinds.

As a matter of fact, however, what is likely to happen, in the absence of definite assurance that a slump in national income and buying power is not going to follow a year or two later, is that private enterprise will look to the storm beyond the horizon and refrain from placing orders with the capital goods department of the economy. Even the current production of consumers' goods may suffer some jolts, if the general public, with its current income reduced[27] and further trouble apparently looming ahead, spends more cautiously than had been expected. If these situations should be permitted to develop, then obviously the attainment of full employment would require a far larger volume of public works than would be called for by the irreducible strains, lags, and frictions connected with transferring the economy from a war to a peace basis. What might be hoped for from an underwriting program would be a limitation of public works to the necessary minimum, as a result of the assurance given to private enterprise and consumers alike that buying power would remain ample and firm indefinitely.

For purposes of illustration, we might assume that the rate of output possible under full employment six months after the war, measured in average prices for the first half of 1943, would be 160 billion (see Table 28.2).[28] Under an underwriting program, this gross national product might be built up as follows: normal government expenditures for goods and services, 31 billion, including armaments not yet fully tapered off and programs of housing, health, education, and conservation not yet fully expanded to their peacetime levels, and including a sizeable lend-lease program of exports for relief and rehabilitation; supplementary public program, 10 billion; private gross capital expenditures, including some replenishing of inventories, 19 billion; and consumption output, 100 billion. If income payments, including any special termination allowances to servicemen and war workers, were running at this time at a rate of 128 billion figured on an annual basis, and ordinary direct personal taxes at a rate of 10 billion,[29] current operations would be making disposable income available at a rate of 118 billion. Assured of future incomes, consumers might cash and spend their war savings at a rate of 10 billion a year, which would reduce their net rate of saving to perhaps 4 billion,[30] leaving the unadjusted rate of consumer spending at 114 billion—14 billion in excess of the consumption output made available by the incompletely converted production system. In this situation, a special spendings tax designed to raise 12 billion dollars a year, imposed by the fiscal agency designated by Congress, would immediately bring the actual rate of consumer spending below the established maximum, assuming a 2 percent margin between minimum and maximum limits.[31]

Table 28.2   Hypothetical Post-War Output and Consumer Income, Saving, and Spending Totals under Conditions of Full Employment via Underwriting Approach, Assuming End of War in December 1944 (in prices of January–June 1943)

Item	Mid-1945 (annual rate) (in $ billions)	1950
Gross national product	$160	$184
public investment fill-in	10	— a
Value of consumption output	100	137
Income payments	128	150
Disposable income	118	144
Net individual savings: unadjusted	4	12
adjusted	4b	13.25c
Consumer spending: unadjusted	114	132
adjusted	102b	137c

a Assumed not needed; cf. discussion in connection with Table 28.1, column 1.
b Assumes a 12-billion supplementary tax on consumers, with savings unaffected.
c Assumes a consumption subsidy of 6.25 billion, 4/5 of this being spent and 1/5 saved.

To illustrate certain other points mentioned in the foregoing discussion, hypothetical figures may be considered for the year 1950, treated as the sixth year after the end of hostilities. At prices prevailing in the first half of 1943, a full-employment gross national product might amount to 184 billion, assuming a 2 percent increase in over-all productivity (due partly to growth in labor force and partly to greater output per worker) compounded year by year from 1946. Government expenditures for goods and services might be 27 billion. For the sake of the argument we might assume that a negative trade balance had begun to develop, holding private gross capital expenditures down to 20 billion, and that the value of consumption output, reflecting this shift away from production for foreign markets, would stand at 137 billion. Income payments, assuming a reduced rate of accumulation of undistributed corporate profits and a balance restored between income distributed by production and income received by consumers, might amount to 150 billion. With direct personal taxes at 6 billion and net individual savings—no longer reduced by the cashing of war savings but lowered considerably as the result of elimination of the cyclical pattern which in the past has brought unusually high profit incomes and hence high savings at times of relatively full employment—at 12 billion, unadjusted consumer spending would be 132 billion. In these circumstances, as shown in Table 28.2, direct subsidization of consumption costing the government somewhat in excess of 5 billion would restore the balance between consumer spending and the value of consumption output.

13. The inference that an effective program for limiting as well as supporting aggregate consumer spending would prevent priçe inflation is subject to this critical comment, that influences from the supply side might send prices up even with demand held at predetermined levels. Indeed, the very fact that under the underwriting program aggregate consumer spending would not be allowed to fall below the guaranteed minimum would in itself tend to support and necessitate rising prices if private production for market were unexpectedly curtailed in the face of the guarantee. This might happen, for example, as the result of business combinations in restraint of trade. It might also happen as the result of strong upward pressure on money wage rates, if the rates rose far enough to reduce profits below prevailing competitive levels.

The underlying problem is, of course, the danger of an upward wage-price spiral, which *would not be caused by the underwriting program* since the same danger is present in *any* situation in which full employment is attained or even approached. If wage rates rise, income payments and consumer spending will also tend to rise if the government has a full-employment policy and absorbs any displaced workers into an expanded public work program. Under close inspection, therefore, it appears that any inflationary pressure associated with the underwriting program would probably be *less* than what would be experienced in the absence of an enforced top limit on aggregate consumer spending, although it would be greater than what would be experienced if the top limit were arbitrarily lowered as private consumption output fell off.

This consideration immediately suggests that the guaranteed amount might be made contingent upon realization of at least the expected volume of consumption output—which reintroduces a question raised above when the possibility of changes in the proportions between government-purchased output and ordinary consumption output was approached from the standpoint of unforeseen spontaneous changes in the government component. At the moment, this modification would hardly seem to the writer to be necessary, or even desirable if it would have to be presented in a way that appeared to weaken the guarantee. A safeguard against such contingencies might perhaps better be sought along the lines of having the government sell some of its own additional output direct to consumers—for example, by charging for various services— or sell them certain surplus stocks accumulated during the war, and thereby restore the supply of goods and services sold to consumers rather than cut down the consumer spending.

The danger of the wage-price or price-wage spiral has to be faced resolutely and realistically in any case, unless full employment itself is deliberately avoided. A program of underwriting consumer spending should prove a positive asset in this connection, since by judicious management it could be made to yield to the upward pressure just enough to enable it to resist and prevent really serious dislocations. The known existence of a top limit on consumer spending would have publicity value in connection with deliberations concerning the advisability of increases in particular production costs, including collective bargaining conferences to adjust particular money rates of wages. Where increases in such costs appeared in advance to be desirable or inevitable, this would be taken into account in deciding upon the dollar amount of spending to be guaranteed for the ensuing year. In other words, a slight increase in spending and prices could be allowed.

ADVANTAGES OF THE UNDERWRITING APPROACH

14. A number of the advantages that government underwriting of aggregate consumer spending might have, as an instrument to help effectuate full-employment policy, may be briefly reviewed at this point.

In the first place, such an approach would emphasize individual consumer choice and sovereignty, which is another way of saying that it would let consumers buy all the goods and services that our economy could produce for them, after taking care of genuine investment needs, and would let them decide by their own preferences what kinds of goods and services ought to be produced in greater quantities. Practically everyone agrees that consumption should be expanded (relatively as well as absolutely) if possible; and although it is definitely arguable that there may be numerous cases in which community consumption paid for out of tax money has social advantages over individualized consumption, at the moment the burden of proof is still on community consumption. It is a noteworthy fact that economists who advocate the public investment approach are themselves for the most part agreed that a greater emphasis on consumption would be desirable if it could only be brought about. But since they do not feel that this could be done, short of fundamental institutional changes over a long period of time, their analysis and recommendations have a somewhat pessimistic tone.

In the second place, the approach by way of guaranteed consumer spending would hold definite advantages for the business man and the farmer. The potential stimulus to the retailer and producer of consumer goods is particularly obvious. But the effect would not end there; the producer of capital goods should also derive some benefit. For example, a manufacturer considering whether or not to buy new equipment would be aware that the market in which the products from that equipment would be sold would not be subject to periodic collapse for reasons of general underspending. Hence he would tend to go ahead, if other circumstances were favorable, and place his order with the maker of the equipment. It may be a debatable question whether in the past the speculative risks introduced by the business cycle have not given us more capital formation in the long run rather than less. On the other hand, elimination of the business cycle on the basis of establishment of continuing full production and employment should stimulate private capital formation, not attributable to this particular form of speculation, up to the level required by the economy. It should render a further benefit by reducing the amplitude of fluctuations in the industries concerned.

A third advantage of the underwriting technique, applied to the over-all consumer market, would be that it would maintain the conditions in which competition would have all the scope possible under modern conditions of mass production. Unlike the proposals sometimes advanced for establishing and underwriting quotas for particular industries or particular producers, it would refrain from guaranteeing anything to any particular industry or producer but instead would assure private enterprise that full-employment levels of production would return a fair profit when averaged over the whole. Thus it would encourage flexibility rather than promote industry-by-industry stratification.

A fourth major consideration is that the underwriting of aggregate consumer spending would, on the one hand, not require unnecessary government actions and, on the other hand, not conflict with other beneficial programs. It seems unwise to count on accumulated war savings to create adequate consumer spending for any protracted period after the war, *but if in fact they do so, then the underwriting would not require any government spending to make it good.* As far as reforms are concerned, no valuable change would be impeded. Selective revision of tax laws to make them more encouraging to enterprise would still be highly desirable; if accomplished, the incidental effect on the underwriting program would be to reduce somewhat the size of the necessary consumption guarantee.[32] Small business would still stand in need of better capital and credit facilities, and sound legislation along these lines might again, to some slight extent, reduce the guarantee requirements. Adequate investment programs in the fields of slum clearance and housing, health, education, and conservation of natural resources, and in any other fields, including areas of community consumption, in which such programs can really stand on their merits, would still have all their original value. If put into effect, they would reduce the volume of ordinary consumption output, and thus again would limit the size of the guarantee necessary and possible for aggregate individual consumption. Adequate social security benefits and elimination of regressive taxes would also still be matters of the greatest importance. As progress was made along these lines, probably raising income payments and certainly reducing net individual savings, subsidization of consumption out of the public treasury to fulfill the guarantee of consumer spending would tend to become less necessary.

Thus, the relation between the underwriting approach and all the progressive programs that command substantial followings is not primarily one of substitution but rather one of mutual assistance. Underwriting would provide immediately such support for consumption as is required to permit the economy to operate at full-employment levels without fundamentally changing its production characteristics. In other words, it would secure immediate adjustability pending fundamental long-run adjustments that, when finally made, might largely eliminate the need for the underwriting apparatus. The long-run adjustments in question are those increases in personal security and modifications in the distribution of income, and those changes in public and private practice with respect to accumulation of insurance reserves, and in corporate practice with respect to retention of earnings, that are necessary before a "natural" balance, as between savings and investment at the full-employment level, can be struck.

15. Fifth, an underwriting program might well have advantages over alternative approaches to full employment strictly from the standpoint of fiscal economy. In a previous section it was shown that, if full employment were to be achieved in an over-saving situation by a program of compensatory public investment, the cost to the government could be slightly lower under optimum conditions than the cost of consumption subsidy associated with an underwriting program, but that in practice it might well be higher rather than lower.[33] To the extent that underwriting eliminated the need for public investment fill-in that would otherwise be required—including what might be required as additional offset to any curtailment of private investment attributable to use of the public investment approach—underwriting would save the government money. To the extent that over-saving out of full-employment levels of income—including any additional saving out of the consumption subsidy itself—required the payment of money to consumers that would not be paid under the public

investment program, underwriting would add to the cost of government. A careful weighing of these pros and cons would probably not establish underwriting as likely to be the more expensive approach from the outset.

But the case need not be allowed to rest there. Quite aside from the tendency that continuous full employment would have, by whatever method it might have been achieved, to promote greater equality of incomes and hence smaller total savings, the underwriting approach would appear to have certain characteristics peculiarly likely to reduce the strain on the budget over the course of time. Since it would sharply separate the two halves of the problem—first, the reaction of private-employment levels to an environment judged to be adequate to support full employment; second, the ratio between saving and spending out of full-employment-caused income—it would tend to throw the spotlight of publicity on the causes for government expense with an accuracy not ordinarily obtainable. This should broaden and strengthen the campaigns to eliminate these causes, whether they were monopolistic restrictions on production and incentive-destroying business taxes on the one hand, or regressive consumer taxes and needless institutional saving on the other. Undoubtedly, cost reductions could thereby be brought about. At least equally important is the other consideration that, once the underwriting program was in force, it would thus tend to harness the drive for budgetary economy to the realization of a better general balance—and not merely a better financial balance—than our economic system now possesses. In other words, underwriting would not only not conflict with other beneficial changes, and not only effect essential adjustments quickly before it became possible to make these other changes, but would also in an indirect way tend to assist in getting these changes made.

16. A sixth advantage of a full-employment program involving the underwriting of aggregate consumer spending is that it would provide a sound basis for a liberal foreign economic policy. The ability to maintain full employment by domestic adjustments, regardless of the state of the foreign trade balance, is the first prerequisite for securing a continuously ample volume of a country's foreign trade in general and, in particular, the relaxation of trade restrictions, with resulting enhancement of world security and benefit to the domestic standard of living through encouragement to worthwhile international specialization. A nation liable to depressions is sooner or later bound to adopt illiberal foreign policies such as high tariffs, export subsidies, harsh immigration laws, exploitation (if the nation is powerful) of low-cost foreign sources of raw materials, and aggressive currency devaluation, since these expedients promise to secure additional markets and additional employment opportunity for the domestic population.

Among various alternative domestic full-employment programs, one utilizing the underwriting technique would evidently have a natural affinity for liberalism in international trade. Perhaps it may be said that it would be at least as favorable as any other domestic program to the kind of international arrangements contemplated in Article VII of the Mutual Aid agreements, since it would have no tendency to strengthen vested interests in any particular industries. As to the matter of mechanics, it would, as previously noted, preserve the over-all size of the market for the products of domestic enterprise by providing for automatic expansion of aggregate domestic consumer spending when the net export balance declined (or the net import balance increased) and for automatic contraction of aggregate domestic consumer spending when the net export balance increased (or the net import balance declined).[34] Thus, it would sensitively adjust to any state of the trade balance, including a negative balance such as would be associated with the repayment of foreign loans. Incidentally, since the consumer spending total would be somewhat smaller when exports exceeded imports than when exports equalled imports, and since it would be at its largest when imports exceeded exports, the public would have a graphic demonstration of the fact that imports rather than exports are what raise the standard of living.

17. A seventh major advantage of the underwriting technique is its reversibility; as noted, it would guard against inflationary excesses of consumer spending as well as against too little consumer spending. With this is closely linked its special applicability in the immediate demobilization period. The inflationary possibilities inherent in a situation in which current income payments may be supplemented on a large scale by the cashing of savings accumulated during the war, while support for rationing and price controls becomes doubtful and the flow of output has not yet achieved its full dimensions, are generally appreciated. What the underwriting technique would permit is a matching of aggregate consumer spending with the aggregate value of consumption output all along the line—90 billion against 90 billion, 100 against 100, 110 against 110, and so on up.

This introduces a final consideration that might well be of immediate interest today. An advance decision to underwrite consumer spending after the war as a continuing policy would be an indication to the American people that their government not only was interested in eliminating an inflationary gap during the war and for as long after the war as might prove to be necessary, but that it was equally interested in eliminating a deflationary gap thereafter. The term "deflationary gap" deserves a moment's thought. It might refer to a deficiency of consumer spending as against whatever happened to be the current volume of consumption output. The deflationary gap provided against by an underwriting program, however, would be a deficiency of consumer spending measured against the *largest volume of consumption output deliverable at the time, under full-employment conditions.* Emphasis on this central feature of a post-war underwriting program would establish more firmly in the public mind the rational basis of wartime fiscal policies, since it would indicate that the government was concerned at all times with having the public spend up to the limit of whatever goods and services could be made available to it but not any greater amount. This might appeal to the public as a rather sensible idea. In short, it is not altogether improbable that a decision to apply an underwriting program after the war would make it easier to combat inflation during the war.

THE PROBLEM AS A WHOLE

18. Lest criticism fasten on minor details and neglect the basic difficulties connected with the program herein discussed, full emphasis should now be placed upon those difficulties. In the first place, the underwriting of aggregate consumer spending would be hard to justify in the absence of an established policy to give jobs on public work projects to persons who might remain involuntarily idle in spite of the inducement afforded to private enterprise by the guarantee. The underwriting could serve as a pillar of full-employment policy, but in itself it could never take the place of the determination to prevent unemployment. Applied by itself, if such a thing could be imagined, it could involve the government in large expense for consumption subsidies at the very time when men and women were trying in vain to find jobs. This expense would then be

challenged as indefensible—with some justice, since it would clearly be better to secure a tangible product in return for the money spent—and the whole policy might under these conditions be condemned as a kind of fiscal sleight of hand.

In the second place, the benefits from underwriting could be rendered rather trivial if restrictions of all kinds on production were allowed to multiply unopposed. A rapid increase in monopolistic restrictions, keeping output down and prices up, could drive the guarantee to great heights and still prevent the attainment of full employment without a heavy fill-in program of public works. Successful application of the underwriting would therefore require an active campaign to enforce competition and control monopoly prices—presumably with stress on the former wherever that alternative was available.

These difficulties should provide sobering food for thought, if such be needed. But it is worth recalling also that the approach to full employment by way of the underwriting of consumer spending would tend to confine government intervention, in the sense of competition, mainly to the capital or money market, where government intervention or competition absolutely cannot be avoided if men and resources are not to be allowed to go out of use. This means that, while it would invite the opposition and other risks that any full-employment program of necessity must encounter, it would escape the further conflicts inherent in programs that raise uncertainty as to who is to be responsible for production. With total consumer spending underwritten at a reasonable level, responsibility for production would be clearly assigned.

NOTES

1. I am indebted to Dr. Theodore F. Marburg for assistance in exploring portions of this field, and to Marvin Hoffenberg for statistical assistance; also to Dr. Emile Benoit-Smullyan, M. Elizabeth Fite, Dr. Emory Q. Hawk, Leonora L. Jensen, Edgar E. Poulton, and Betty E. Stern for valuable suggestions made during the preparation of this article.

2. It tends at first, for example, to create or strengthen inflationary pressures. This will be considered in section 13.

3. In this article, discussion will be limited to an economy operating on the general philosophy of free enterprise or individualistic production for market, since this condition is usually assumed in these allegations, and since in any case there is little need to debate the possibility of maintaining full employment in a system of planned production such as that of the U.S.S.R.

4. Prevailing hourly standards may be unsatisfactory, as a result of spread-the-work programs, in the absence of policies that maintain full employment by maintaining effective demand. In discussing policies of this positive type, however, it can be assumed that the prevailing work-week will be about as long as most people want it to be.

5. A. H. Hansen, *Fiscal Policy and Business Cycles* (New York: Norton, 1941), and other writings.

6. J. M. Keynes, *The General Theory of Employment, Interest, and Money* (London: Macmillan, 1936).

7. In the hope of avoiding misunderstanding, the writer wishes to state his preference for public investment projects of almost any kind, as against involuntary unemployment, whenever the choice actually narrows down to that; also his belief that housing, health, education, and conservation of natural resources are so important that the regular program of public investment should be expanded to any extent necessary to secure universally high standards in these fields. He would probably vote to include certain national development programs suggested by Hansen (e.g., rural electrification) on the regular public investment list, and to hold certain others (e.g., some of those related to reorganization and rationalization of transportation) in reverse for slack periods, although this is a tentative judgment, admittedly based on insufficient study of the fields in question.

It is sometimes suggested that expansion of public investment is required because of functional and geographic labor immobility—i.e., so that jobs may be provided in those places and on those types of work to which labor has been drawn in the past. This particular argument may be of some importance temporarily and in certain sections of the country.

8. Strictly speaking, consumer income will also depend on the level of business savings, i.e., undistributed profits.

9. In real terms, total consumption would be greater and saving less than if the gap were closed by expanding investment; i.e., the whole schedule or curve representing the "propensity" to consume would lie at a higher level, and the whole schedule or curve representing the "propensity" to save would lie at a lower level. But this need not interfere with anyone's personal thriftiness or right to save. Individuals would have more cash and their dollar savings would actually increase somewhat at the same time as their spending increased. This would not necessarily involve anything more than a shift along a given hypothetical schedule or curve relating dollars of consumer savings to dollars of consumer disposable income. (See below, especially section 7 and Table 28.1.)

10. The "mature economy" thesis is liable to overstatement, as pointed out by Kuznets. (Simon Kuznets, review of Alvin H. Hansen's *Fiscal Policy and Business Cycles*, in *Rev. of Econ. Stat.*, Vol. XXIV, No. 1[Feb., 1942], pp. 34–35.) Moreover, if the conditions of the problem can be changed by making effective demand correspond more closely to needs, intensive investment will obviously have greater scope than hitherto; this seems to be the one element of value in Moulton's comments on the subject. (See Harold G. Moulton, *The New Philosophy of Public Debt,* Washington, Brookings Inst., 1943, pp. 21–29, and other writings.) Generally speaking, however, after making all due allowances for the probable discovery of important new natural resources within existing frontiers, for a possible rise in the rate of invention, etc., one would hardly expect one factor (technological progress) to be able to provide as much opportunity for private investment in the future as was formerly provided by three factors combined (technological progress, rapid population growth, and territorial expansion). This is particularly the case in view of the power of monopolistic concerns to hold back the introduction of new processes, and the further fact that many new processes are likely to be capital-saving rather than capital-expanding. Private investment *may* flourish again as in the past, but no disparagement of American initiative need be involved in the suggestion that the chances are against it.

11. In the immediate demobilization period, a program to maintain consumption would aim at levels calculated to buy all the consumer goods that it will be possible for industry, under stress of reconversion, to produce; see section 12.

12. Keynes, *op. cit.,* p. 381; italics in original.

13. I.e., over-saving in relation to genuine investment opportunity; over-investment by the same criterion, or, in other words, in relation to the amount really needed.

14. This article will not discuss the ways in which public work projects and direct payments to consumers might be financed, but it will suggest that on the whole a full-employment program based on the underwriting of aggregate consumer spending might cost the government less than a full-employment program based on public investment. (See sections 7 and 15.) Presumably taxes that increase business costs or reduce consumer buying power would be ruled out as sources of revenue for such government expenditures, since they would operate to defeat the central purpose. On the other hand, savings that are not invested would provide a source from which funds might be secured by borrowing or taxation without detriment to production and with the positive advantage that policies along this line would tend to obviate the need for monetary expansion except as required by increased productivity of the economy. A parenthetical word may be added here about the public debt. The most important consideration with regard to the post-war public debt appears to be that it should not be allowed to occupy the center of the stage in discussions of general economic policy. This can hardly be emphasized too strongly. Proponents of measures to maintain the level of production and employment sometimes permit themselves to be sidetracked on this issue and then placed in a position where they seem to be advocating public deficits and a rising public debt as ends in themselves. It would be more convincing if they would show (1) that full employment, even if it involves expansionist public spending, is cheaper for society than unemployment, (2) that the measures they advocate for support of full employment involve less public spending than alternative measures capable of realizing the same objective, (3) that public borrowing is necessary to finance the necessary spending in so far as taxation and the issuing of

paper money are not deemed suitable, and—then only—(4) that the resulting rise in the public debt will not have the injurious effects that many believe to be indicated. (1) and (2) are the crucial arguments, not (4).

15. The question of the margin to be allowed between minimum and maximum limits of aggregate consumer spending is considered in section 8.

16. Prevention of *excessive* consumer spending will be discussed in section 8.

17. Or to a spendings tax; cf. discussion in section 8.

18. I.e., under-spending in relation to the underwritten amount, which in turn was originally judged sufficient to be likely to secure full employment without resort to fill-in public investment; see previous discussion.

19. So-called transfer payments, such as payments from social security funds, are excluded.

20. No change is assumed in inventories of consumption commodities.

21. Under certain circumstances, a fill-in (which in the illustration will raise government expenditures for goods and services above 24 billion) will still be needed, as is fully explained elsewhere. This qualification does not affect the main contrasts between the underwriting approach and the public investment approach which it is important to establish at this point.

22. See section 15.

23. Congress might levy the taxes in question, but suspend their application subject to the finding by this agency that it was necessary to carry them into effect (at some rate not in excess of the rate designated by Congress) in order to prevent an excess of consumer spending.

24. Also any self-subsistence production not otherwise allowed for.

25. Hence, net increases in consumer credit outstanding are treated as consumer dis-saving. (Money paid by consumers to buy residences is regarded as an element of saving, the houses themselves being treated as capital goods.) It should be noted that within a certain range the government could adjust total consumer spending (as defined in practice) toward guaranteed levels by restricting or encouraging the extension of new consumer credit. A progressive expansion of consumer indebtedness on a large scale would, however, hardly be desirable.

26. Cf. discussion of a closely related point in section 13.

27. For example, factory workers who *keep* their jobs will take home 23 percent less money when hours of work are cut from 48 (with time-and-a-half for overtime) down to 40, assuming that hourly rates remain unchanged.

28. Cf. Table 28.1. Experience following the last war suggests that a decline in efficiency may be expected at this time, irrespective of the level of employment.

29. This might include certain back taxes deferred to servicemen during the war, while the net total might take into account a small offset for Victory tax refunds not previously claimed.

30. Savings in this period might be reduced by a net expansion of outstanding installment credit, furthered to some extent by "lay-away" plans undertaken during the war; back payments by ex-servicemen on installment purchases and life insurance would have the opposite effect.

31. Actually, if circumstances were normal, a smaller tax would be sufficient, because such a tax would increase the ratio of saving to spending. Furthermore, in view of the expansion of consumption output expected later in the first post-war year, it might not be considered necessary to reduce current spending enough to secure a mid-year balance.

32. The same kind of effect would be produced if, as is sometimes suggested, primary stress were laid on the reduction of business taxes in general. This would not alter the case with respect to underwriting, but it would substantially reduce business cost, and hence also the appropriate total of consumer spending. Assuming a full-employment national income valued at 140 billion dollars (say, in 1946; cf. Table 28.1), gross national product with lowered business taxes would be less than 170 billion, and the value of consumption output less than 124 billion. But the question of how much this would narrow the gap between unadjusted consumer spending and the value of consumption output would depend on how much additional business and individual saving would result from the tax reduction, since this would determine how much less unadjusted consumer spending would be forthcoming at the same (140 billion) level of national income. So far as the budget is concerned, the government would doubtless incur less expense on account of consumer subsidies needed to make good the guarantee, but, on the other hand, it would lose tax revenue.

33. See Table 28.1 in section 7 and accompanying discussion.

34. See section 11.

29

What Chance for Free Enterprise?

It is unthinkable that after this war a situation will again be allowed to exist in America in which men and women will be unable to find jobs. But is there in fact any possibility that we can prevent the return of unemployment without, in the process, digging the grave of free enterprise? This question may seem indecent to economic prudes, and funny to planners committed to rigid interpretations of planning. On the other hand, all over the country, and in the armed forces, wherever located, there are people who really would like to know the answer.

The answer offered here is in the affirmative. Full employment need not preclude free, competitive enterprise. But that is not to say that free, competitive enterprise will be saved by giving pep talks or invoking "the American way:" It won't. Nor will it be saved by merely reapplying, more vigorously than before, the economics of the 1930's. Many economists seem to feel that the political problems involved in securing a full-employment economy after the war present a large question mark, but that the economic problems have all been solved. Surely the latter part of this proposition is not well founded in fact. At least if encouragement to economic individualism is supposed to be part of the picture, the last word has not yet been said.

The question at issue, so far as domestic public policy is concerned, is the proper relation between public investment in the broadest sense, control over aggregate individual purchasing power—or, better, aggregate consumer spending—and antitrust action. The trouble with the usual public investment approach is that it does not show how all the needed jobs can be assured without creation of an environment hostile to traditional forms of enterprise, and does not accurately control purchasing power. Also, on the theoretical side, it needlessly assumes that, when total investment and total saving are out of line, investment is the one that must change. The trouble with much of the consumer-demand theory is that it overlooks or minimizes the power of unregulated

An article published in the April, 1943, issue of *Free World*, under the title, "What Chance for Free Enterprise After the War?"

monopolies to prevent production and employment from expanding in step with expanding demand for commodities and services. The trouble with almost all current formulations is that they pay too little attention to the possibility of applying the underwriting principle in economic affairs on a broad national basis. Or else, if they advocate this principle, they limit economic flexibility by underwriting individual markets one by one rather than the national market as a whole.

If these contentions are correct, then it is still worthwhile to spend some time on the fundamental or strategic factors in economics. Work must be done on the details of their application in the post-war world, and some of this work as it relates to the ideas contained in the following pages is now going on in Washington. But the present discussion only deals with general alignments among the fundamental elements.

No one will deny that before the war we had already moved far away from nineteenth-century approximation of laissez faire. It would be somewhat academic to try to measure the further distance we have traveled down that road since Pearl Harbor. As a result of priorities, allocation of men and materials, price controls, and so forth, many small businesses are going to the wall, monopoly threatens to increase, or actually does increase, and the rates of operation of our going production enterprises are being more and more regulated by government. This last is an evident necessity, but it narrows the scope of free enterprise, at least for the duration.

Now the advocates of planned production take the position that, even for peace, the competitive system has reached the end of its usefulness and must be superseded. For the sake of the argument, let us make some concessions to that point of view. At some future date it is conceivable that competition, as we have known it, may practically disappear. This is debatable. And in any case, even if it were not, the date could hardly be predicted. However, the advance of modern technology has tended to concentrate production in larger units, and these have very often acquired the characteristics of monopoly or partial monopoly and created a need for regulation in the public interest. The advantage of size—at least, in many cases—is greater efficiency. The penalty is the disappearance of competition as the laissez-faire economists conceived it. It is not a foregone conclusion that technology need always favor bigness, any more than that technology is always the explanation where bigness exists. Moreover, certain services and also certain commodities can never be produced on a large scale. Nevertheless, the possibility arises that at some future date mass-production methods will have driven individualistic competition from practically every corner of our economy. In that case, public regulation of production is likely to become so general that it clears the way for systematic, over-all production planning.

The only reason for tentatively sketching this distant perspective is that it helps by contrast to define the post-war foreground. If we finally do come to over-all production planning—in a country with so deeply ingrained traditions of individual enterprise and competition—the explanation will most likely be technological. This can be ventured because public opinion hardly ever runs ahead of the facts; a lag is more to be expected. On the other hand, the explanation for the current trend toward administrative controls is altogether different. Obviously the war is responsible, not technological change. If this is so, then it reinforces the usual presumption (and the findings of certain public opinion polls) that most or, at any rate, very many Americans will want to go back to a free, competitive economy when the war is over. Barring the possibility of an extremely long war, or an outcome destructive of all the conditions that permit choices to be made, economic individualism will again make a powerful appeal.

How much economic individualism can post-war America stand?

No quantitative guess will be ventured here. Presumably the maximum possibility is somewhat smaller than the maximum possibility was before the war, because of technological progress in the meantime. But the real issue is whether any approximation of the maximum possibility can be made actual, and if so how. The indispensable condition for stability, democracy, and freedom after the war is sustained full employment. Is there any ground for supposing that we can have full employment in post-war America without accepting a far larger measure of governmental administrative control over our production system than is required by strictly technological considerations?

In certain quarters the tendency is to give up on this question without a struggle. A case in point is supplied in a newsletter put out by a leading firm of management engineers. The authors correctly diagnose our central post-war problem: "Our fundamental problem is how to create an industrial system that will insure a continuous production and exchange of goods and services that people need, so that all who want to work may have the opportunity to do so and the money with which they can buy all the things produced by other workers." But they then propose as a solution a system of planned production, with details unspecified but with the following general characteristics. "Its keystones would be: planning and budgeting industry operation, coordinating it nationally, creating and maintaining cooperation between individual companies and between labor, management, and stockholders, and having necessary governmental support." In other words, what they are suggesting is a further departure from individualistic methods of determining individual business rates of operation. This is probably also the view of many other Americans who are pessimistic about the possibility of getting full employment any other way. The view in question assumes that we cannot hope to secure coordinated control of the over-all volume of production and employment unless we establish some form of coordinated control of individual production quotas.

Without minimizing the difficulty of the problem or saying that competition can revive where the basic conditions for it have gone and cannot be restored, it may be pointed out that we have never had a program capable of combining assured full employment with a technologically given maximum of free competition. The two fundamentals of such a program would be a monetary-fiscal policy able to keep up the effective demand for commodities and services, and a monopoly and competition policy oriented to technological realities.

Both are essential. Neither one is sufficient without the other. Were we to try to sustain full employment through monetary-fiscal instruments alone, the attempt would fail. In a regime of pure competition we could probably control the over-all volume of production and employment rather accurately by controlling the size of the total demand for products, first taking into account any expected changes in costs. But, obviously, this could not be the case if monopolies were able to neutralize an increase in demand by raising their selling prices. On the other side, were we to put our trust entirely in a system of governmental regulation of individual rates of operation, and were we willing to push such a system of administrative controls to its logical conclusion, we could secure full employment, but only by sacrificing free production for market.

A monopoly and competition policy oriented to technological realities would have the following characteristics.

It would make proper distinctions between areas in which monopolistic situations are "natural" (inevitable for technical reasons) and areas in which monopolistic situations are "artificial" (based on unnecessary unfair restraints of trade).

Then, it would deal adequately with both types of situation. It would support and enforce competition in lines of production where competition has a real chance. For instance, it would help little business to borrow money on fair terms, make the patent system encourage innovation rather than buttress intrenched positions, and vigorously suppress restrictive and collusive practices in general. And at the same time, it would regulate the inevitably monopolistic lines of production as far as regulation was necessary. That does not mean that perfect efficiency in terms of low-cost production would result or be considered attainable or important. Rather it means that the new public utility rules (as they might be called) would be designed to prevent such raising of prices and limitation of output as might defeat the full-employment objective or interfere seriously with a balanced use of the nation's resources.

All this presupposes that it is or might be possible to distinguish areas that are inevitably monopolistic from areas of workable competition. Presumably that can be done with a reasonable degree of success if the available data are assembled and studied, in the light of modern economic theory, with the objective clearly in view. The sources for data include, for example, the case studies made by the Antitrust Division and Federal Trade Commission and the findings of the T.N.E.C. Monopoly Investigation. Out of such materials a practical set of criteria can probably be constructed for identifying workable competition on the one hand and monopoly (monopoly in the public sense rather than the narrow or pure sense) on the other. Our knowledge of the contents of these two major subdivisions of the American economy will then amount to more than a mere enumeration as of a particular date. Our knowledge will include, in addition, an understanding of the main distinguishing characteristics, with the obvious advantage that this will facilitate reclassification whenever reclassification becomes necessary.

A given industry may for a while possess the characteristics of competition and be subject to the rules of the game applying to competition, but later on, as a result of technological progress, that industry may have to come under the different rules applying to monopoly. The criteria will help show when this transition is required. Thus they will facilitate an orderly progression of our economy, based on technological realities. A slight variation of this procedure also might be worth considering. There will doubtless be borderline cases in which the technological picture is not clear. In these cases it might be best to leave the choice between operating under rules of competition and under rules of monopoly to the industry itself. Even in certain intrinsically less puzzling cases the choice might be left to the industry.

For example, an industry might be asked to choose between restricting the activities of its trade association to the point where exemption from scale-of-operations regulations could legitimately be granted and, on the other hand, permitting its trade association to suppress competition and in that case subjecting itself to the regulations in question. Any resulting losses from the standpoint of not securing the technologically possible maximum of free competition might be more than compensated by the gains from the standpoint of retaining more free choice. This could, however, be true only where a choice thus registered represented a fair consensus of the business men affected, and not a vote dictated by a powerful minority in the industry. And of course, it also presupposes, to begin with, a set of monopoly regulations capable of accomplishing what it is necessary to have them accomplish.

It is now time to turn to the other essential element, a monetary-fiscal policy able to keep up the effective demand for commodities and services. For only through such a monetary-fiscal policy can government give competitive enterprise its maximum support.

The dominant school of thought on this subject is preoccupied with the problem of investment—ordinarily interpreted to mean production of capital goods, including consumers' capital goods such as houses. Much has been said in recent years about the need to make up for deficiencies in private investment by expansion of public investment—which, again, may in part take the form of facilities to provide free services direct to the consuming public. In some quarters it is estimated that we must be prepared to have a public investment program after the war ranging in cost anywhere from zero up to twenty billion dollars a year, or else give up the idea of full employment.

On the whole, this is not, in the opinion of leading spokesmen of the investment school today, a matter of "priming the pump" to get things started. It is a matter of filling up gaps as they occur. Naturally the gaps do not always have to be connected with *investment* activity, or filled with public *investment*. While that is ordinarily supposed to be the case, other possibilities are also taken into account. More broadly, what is advocated is the filling of any gaps in private *employment* by means of expansion in public *employment*. More broadly still, what is suggested is that government assume *responsibility* for specific employment-giving production activities to the extent that private initiative falls short. It is of course true that public construction expenditures frequently represent payments for work supplied by private concerns on a contract basis, in which case government is not the actual employer. But in any case the essential idea is that government closes up the gaps.

The arguments advanced for this type of policy have rendered two great services. In the first place, they have stressed the fact that governmentally initiated production activity must be used as the final balancing item to maintain full employment. It is hard to see how anyone who supports the objective of full employment can quarrel with that. It is clear that the indicated principle must apply during the stresses and shifts of the immediate demobilization period. Moreover, it must apply at other times as well. For example, some fluctuation would be bound to occur in the level of private employment even if the final markets for the products of private enterprise were stabilized. Because of changes in the rate of introduction of new inventions, fluctuations in the rate of replacement of fixed equipment, and certain other factors, the capital goods industries in particular would tend to be busier at some times than at others even if the sale of consumer commodities and services were proceeding at an uninterrupted and steady pace. The further merit of the gap-filling approach to monetary-fiscal problems in that its advocates, looking around for large chunks of activity with which to fill large gaps, find themselves supporting (more strongly than ever) an extension of public enterprise or responsibility into certain fields in which it is indeed overdue.

There are fields into which government has not yet gone and should in future go, or into which it should go to a greater extent than it has hitherto, simply because certain badly wanted services will otherwise not be supplied. This ought not to startle anybody.

Roads and education, to mention two important historical examples, were once considered to belong in the province of private enterprise. Times change. Looking ahead to the kind of peace we want, it hardly seems open to question that government should lay out very substantial amounts to help clear our slums and bring decent housing to the people, provide some approximation of adequate medical care for everyone, move ahead toward universal educational opportunity, and conserve and develop the natural resources of the land we live in. Moreover, mention of these particularly obvious fields for public activity as well as expenditure is not intended to deny the existence of others, if the need can be fairly shown.

But precisely here is the weakness of the gap-filling approach, which tends to blur the line between need for products and need to create jobs. Normal or non-emergency public activities should in most cases go forward unconditionally. It is not a question of looking to see if there are employment gaps that require filling. It is enough that the end products of these particular public activities are considered by most people to be desirable for their own sake. On the other hand, emergency public works or work projects stand on a different footing. Of course, such work as serves no useful purpose should be barred in any event, and the authorized projects should be carefully selected so that the end products are as valuable as possible. But that does not alter the fact that in these cases employment provides the real justification, not our need for the end products.

Unfortunately, the gap-filling approach, pure and simple, invites confusion of this distinction. Its adherents are tempted to overplay the intrinsic usefulness (usefulness of the end products) of this or that public activity which can, to be sure, fill gaps, but would perhaps not gain general acceptance on that basis. Their argument rings slightly hollow. Under analysis it is found to imply the existence, year after year, of a tremendously broad zone of indifference, a zone millions of jobs and billions of dollars broad, with regard to which it is supposed to be practically impossible to say whether public activity is preferable to private enterprise or vice versa. This may conceivably be so, but, considering the magnitudes involved, it taxes the average man's credulity. Thus in one way it may even hurt a cause for which in other respects the same persons have fought with skill as well as devotion—the cause of the public services that are genuinely needed.

The difficulty arises because the gap-filling school has not devoted enough attention to keeping the gap from opening up in the first place or has not found the right means for the purpose. Many adherents of this school wish to encourage private initiative and make various suggestions as to how it should be done. However, their main concern is to show that gap-filling public investment is itself an encouraging rather than a discouraging factor. To this end they point out that the investment is to be limited to creating products not sold in competition with the products of private enterprise. With varying degrees of emphasis, depending on the extent to which they retain a faith in the pump-priming theory, they add that such public activities stimulate private enterprise indirectly as a result of their demand for raw materials and equipment. Finally, they lay particular stress on the so-called multiplier effect—the consideration that investment (in this case public investment) puts out purchasing power by way of its payrolls, which in turn helps enterprise as a whole find markets for its products.

Much of this, so far as it goes, is perfectly sound. If the pump-priming results anticipated by the more optimistic members of the school could be counted on, it would even mean that public investment could be permitted to taper off after a while because private enterprise would expand as a result of the stimulus received from the original increase in public investment. But that possibility—no stronger word is justified by the record—does not meet the ultimate objection. For it would still be true that, *during* all fill-in periods, the free competitive sector is narrower than it would be if the economic environment supported competitive individual enterprise up to the technologically given maximum. This is the issue that is never met by any program of filling gaps.

Clearly the country needs a policy of positive support for competitive enterprise as a whole, and lip service to that idea is not enough. Furthermore, the policy should be of a fundamental and practical nature. Most of the measures suggested, whether by the public investment school or by the opponents of government intervention, are either good but in themselves inadequate (for example, removal of taxes that deter enterprise) or else of highly doubtful effectiveness and in any case socially undesirable (for example, wage cuts).

By contrast, a fundamental and practical policy would include, with other encouraging measures, a direct and unequivocal support of aggregate consumer demand. It would peg this demand at levels sufficient to provide a market for the output of commodities and services private enterprise can bring to market when it is operating on a scale that leaves no employment gap to be filled. Consumer demand would not in the last analysis be supported indirectly by way of the purchasing power put out by a gap-filling public investment program; the objection to that has just been noted. Rather it would be supported and controlled directly, by having government give and stand back of a guarantee of aggregate consumer spending.

To begin with, government would estimate, on the basis of wage rates and other factors, the amount of consumer spending needed to take next year's full employment output off the market, and would peg the size of the consumer market as a whole by underwriting the total estimated in that way. This would amount to opening up the draft to keep the fires of enterprise burning. Without favoring one enterprise more than another, it would create the environment in which business initiative as a whole would have the opportunity to show what it can do. To describe this still differently, it would provide a full-size framework for private enterprise.

A radio manufacturer, for instance, would not have his own market underwritten, but, since he would know for certain that consumer demand as a whole would not shrink, he would benefit in proportion to his competitive ability to attract customers. An industry like the steel industry, in turn, while it would necessarily still face the competition of aluminum and magnesium, could count on a steadier flow of orders than is possible as long as nothing secures the aggregate sales of consumer goods embodying or produced with the help of steel, aluminum, magnesium, and all other materials.

Whenever full employment was not achieved as a result of the inducement given by this guarantee, government would expand its flexible program of public work projects. Thus it would indeed fill any remaining gaps—but with the distinction that the gap-filling program would here be the final line of defense against unemployment, not the front line. Finally, government would see to it that, by adjustment of the full-employment volume of payments to income thus brought about, a total of consumer spending emerged that was neither in excess of nor less than the amount guaranteed.

This it would do by subsidizing or taxing (or lending to or borrowing from) consumption directly, if and as necessary.

Such a policy would not correspond to the view that total saving must always govern total investment. Those who insist on the need for public investment hold that total investment can be allowed to decline when we achieve a more equal distribution of income, since that will weaken the tendency to save, which is of course strongest in the upper income brackets. In the meantime, however, they submit that we have no reasonable choice but to make investment outlays equal to the total of the voluntary savings accumulating at a full-employment level of income. But it is hard to see why that must necessarily be so. We might equally well cut down total saving, inasmuch as that can be done without interfering with the individual's right to save. Suppose, for example, that a tendency toward oversaving required government to subsidize individual consumption, under the consumption-pegging policy, in spite of the existence of full employment and a full-employment volume of money income. In that case, the funds for the subsidies could in whole or in part be borrowed by "tap issues" directed at the savers who had found no investment outlets for their surplus incomes.

So far as expense is concerned, such a program would *raise* the costs of government to the extent that an oversaving problem as such made consumption subsidies necessary for fulfillment of the guarantee. On the other hand, it would *lower* the costs of government, as against what a full-employment program by the straight gap-filling method would involve, to the extent that the incentive provided by the guarantee cut down the size of the employment gaps to be filled. The *net* effect upon costs might well be favorable, provided the program were linked up with advances on other critical fronts in our economy. The monopoly and competition policy already suggested would help translate the inducement of the guarantee into actual private production and employment, and would thus limit the expenditure for public works. A progressive system of taxes and a wise strengthening of our social insurance system to meet the needs of the aged, the sick, and persons handicapped in various ways—the common man's charter to which, as also to adequate labor standards, America already stands morally committed—would favor the spending of individual income and therefore minimize the oversaving tendency.

If the above analysis is correct, then what is needed next on the monetary-fiscal side is a working out in detail of the problems of mechanics involved in the direct adjustment of total consumer spending to guaranteed levels. There are two halves to this. A satisfactory way must be found to support consumer spending when, full employment notwithstanding, it tends to fall short. To date there has not been enough discussion of the problem to indicate the relative merits of tax reductions, tax rebates, special "national income security payments," and other techniques (including timed bond redemptions in the early post-war years) that might be used for this purpose. Further exploration should likewise suggest the most acceptable way of keeping consumer spending from exceeding the guarantee. Whenever that tendency is uppermost rather than the other, the suggested policy requires that the excessive demand be removed from consumer markets. That will avoid a price inflation danger such as we face today.

It will be seen that a monetary-fiscal policy along the indicated lines rests on the following argument. In general, the volume of public investment, including public services to the consumer, should be decided by judging the end products of the various government enterprises on their merits. To be sure, some public investment is needed for another reason—as a final balancing item to offset temporary declines in private investment. Ordinarily a rather small amount should be sufficient under the latter heading, although at times when an abnormally rapid physical transformation of the economy is under way, as will be the case in the demobilization period after the war, the amount may be fairly large.

The volume of private investment over a period of years should be allowed to work itself out as a result of the progress of invention, the rate of interest established, and the demand "derived back" from the demand for consumer commodities and services. Aggregate savings should be cut down to the level of aggregate investment as thus determined by its private and public components. The rest of our potential production energy, up to the level of full employment, should be thrown into producing commodities and services to be bought by individual consumers in the proportions they think best. To make this possible, government should underwrite aggregate consumer spending at appropriate levels, which can be done right away without waiting for income to be distributed differently.

After this war the first condition for justice, and even for peace itself, is that we make full employment the cornerstone of the American economy. Returning to the opening question—full employment will not necessarily permit us to follow along the trend line of maximum opportunity for free, competitive enterprise. But neither will it make that impossible. We ought to be able to combine full employment with a maximum of free enterprise, if we want to. The requirement appears to be a technologically valid policy for monopoly and competition linked up with a monetary-fiscal program centered on a pegged total of consumer expenditure.

30

Elements of an Economic Policy

A plan for winning the peace would help to win the war, for it would foster morale. A nation's fighting power depends on its faith in the future.

Without much doubt the peace aim of most Americans, if it could be articulated, would be to establish guaranteed full employment in the United States, while at the same time strengthening democracy and promoting effective, nonwasteful use of manpower and other resources. How can this aim be realized?

Consideration is asked for the following suggestions. The compressed form in which they are set down here is prompted not by dogmatism but rather by a desire to save the reader's time. (Economic analysis on which these suggestions are based was presented by the author in *Full Employment,* Yale University Press, 1941.) The reader in turn is asked, as he proceeds, to bear two things in mind. These proposals are intended as related parts of an over-all economic policy—for piecemeal adjustment here and there is not what the postwar situation will require. Secondly, the proposals assume that the people's elected representatives should lay down the guiding rules, and should change them from time to time to meet changing conditions, but then abstain from constantly usurping administrative functions.

It should be the policy of the United States Government to establish guaranteed full employment—a state of affairs in which all men and women willing and able to work will always have the opportunity to do so, at prevailing rates of pay and under prevailing hourly specifications and working conditions generally.

Stop there for a moment. What is full employment?

Full employment as referred to herein means employment of all except (a) unemployables and (b) a normal quota temporarily idle because of shifts in demand, technological progress, or any other forms of frictional (i.e., transitional) unemployment. Unemployability should be determined objectively, by medical test, in a manner

Published in the Summer, 1942, issue of *The Antioch Review*, under the title, "An Economic Policy to Insure Permanent Full Employment."

subject to popular control. This is not to suggest that unemployables, so defined, should not have a perfect right to find work if they can, but rather merely to delimit one of the fields where special assistance is needed and to indicate when involuntary idleness should not affect the unemployment figures. The amount of unemployment designated as the normal quota of frictional unemployment (which may vary seasonally) should be decided democratically; expert opinion should be taken and the final decision should be reached in a manner giving an adequate voice to labor and to all other sections of the population.

These observations in turn point to the need for two further preliminary comments. In the first place, the definition of unemployability herein advocated may create a situation in which the work of some employables is not worth, in terms of value added to product, no manner where they may be employed, as much as minimum wage laws of the United States require that they be paid; in that case, the difference between what they are deemed to be worth when most effectively employed and the minimum legal rates should be a charge on the general economy, to be met out of taxation. In the second place, to assure that prevailing rates of pay, hours, and working conditions shall be decided democratically, collective bargaining and the right to strike should be fully supported by the government.

So much by way of defining full employment. But there are other main objectives as well. The measures taken to support full employment should be such as require the least sacrifice of other desired ends. Not only must democracy be preserved and strengthened, but in addition full employment should not conflict with effective use of resources.

To secure a truly effective use of manpower and other resources, as judged by the success with which these factors are applied to satisfying the wants and needs of the people, planned public enterprise (i.e., production of a socially planned quota of the specified goods and services, whether for sale or for free distribution) is required in some cases. In other cases production is best left to private enterprise producing to order or to meet an anticipated market demand. In still other instances a compromise solution may be most serviceable; for example, joint councils representing management and labor in a given industry may practice some aspects of production planning with approval and collaboration of government, government representatives may sit on boards of directors, and so forth.

In order to promote private enterprise and limit government intervention in economic matters to the necessary minimum, it should in general be the policy of the government to secure full employment by the method of *underwriting the aggregate amount of consumer expenditure and preventing monopoly price exactions* (as hereinafter noted), thus encouraging private employment.

In each specific case where socially planned and organized production may be urged as a substitute for private enterprise, the burden of proof should be on the proponents of public planned production to demonstrate that that procedure would be superior to free or regulated private enterprise.

However, where competition cannot function and regulation of private monopoly or of associated private producers has proved to be unsatisfactory, other methods are obviously required. Wherever the superiority of public planned production—measured against existing practice and against what might be brought about by constructive technical innovations—appears at any time to be established beyond a reasonable doubt, public planned production should be instituted.

In addition, as a second and final line of defense against unemployment (the first line being the guarantee applied to total consumer demand, together with control of monopolies), a planned program of federal, state, and local emergency public projects should be maintained as a regular part of the nation's economic apparatus, and employment thereon should be expanded and contracted as may be required to keep the total number of jobs adjusted to the labor supply.

Insofar as private construction continues to be peculiarly subject to fluctuation in spite of stability in the market for ordinary consumer goods, construction projects (i.e., durable public works) will tend to preponderate in this emergency program. Conservation offers another great field for expansible public employment. However, a sufficiently wide range of projects of all types should be planned in advance so that a selection can always be made that will fit the kinds or skills of labor currently available, whatever they may be and wherever located.

Compensation to labor on emergency public projects should be at rates prevailing in private and nonemergency public work.

Come back now to private enterprise. Contrary to the view formerly held by most economists, prices are not flexible enough to keep the volume of production and employment in the field of private enterprise from contracting when anything happens to check the circulation of money around the production-consumption circuit. Moreover the circulation of money does not maintain itself automatically. It is therefore fundamental to a full-employment program that government take steps to maintain the monetary circulation.

It should be the purpose of government, by guaranteeing or underwriting total consumer expenditure (thus so to speak organizing a system of national income insurance, to operate as hereinafter indicated), not only actually to maintain an adequate flow of purchasing power, but, by assuring this flow of purchasing power in advance, to let the prospective demand exert its full stimulating force upon all enterprises producing goods or services for market. This suggestion is meant literally: the government should give an unconditional guarantee of aggregate consumer expenditure.

Insofar as the inducement thus offered to private enterprises stimulates economic activity, it will also swell the flow of consumer income and spending by way of the normal channels of income. It is to be expected that a governmental guarantee of total consumer spending will have some *tendency* to secure full employment without the need for emergency public employment, and that regular and emergency employment together will have some *tendency* to fulfill the consumer spending guarantee without the need for special subsidies to consumption by the government. But the consumer spending guarantee given by the government must in any case be accurately fulfilled, whether this requires additions to consumer purchasing power from the Treasury, or whether it requires subtractions from consumer purchasing power to prevent overfulfillment of the guarantee, with consequent possibility of price inflation.

How large a volume of consumer spending shall be stipulated for any given year or other period of time should be determined by experts after due consideration of the factors relevant to the problem, such as prevailing money wage rates, price-level policy (taken in relation to total productivity), the expected extent of the additional market provided by government orders, foreign investment, and consumer credit.

The spending guarantee should within limits of feasibility be presented for a number of years in advance. The purpose of this is to establish a confidently expected trend in total consumer demand, which not only will remove some of the general over-all risk from current investment activity (capital formation), but also, by making price trends more predictable, will lessen the fluctuations in investment activity that arise out of speculative anticipations of price changes.

To bring consumer spending up to the stipulated level when it tends to fall short, orderly and just means must be provided for putting additional purchasing power into the hands of consumers. Congress should therefore determine in advance how the additional income money is to be distributed if and when such distribution proves necessary—whether through established channels of the social insurance system in the form of extra benefits, or by payments to all family units and individuals in the nation, or in some other manner. In deciding upon the formula for distribution of additional income money, so far as that is required, Congress should take into account the desirability of reducing existing income inequalities.

The point need scarcely be labored, today, that it is as essential to prevent an excess of consumer spending as to prevent a deficiency. Monetary measures undertaken without full recognition of this fact carry with them the grave danger of inflation. Congress should therefore legislate in advance the form of taxation or other means whereby consumer spending is to be brought down to the stipulated level in case it tends to exceed that level.

The sources of funds for subsidies to consumption, when needed, are in general the same as the sources of funds for public works or for any other purpose of government. Governments may levy taxes, or borrow, or issue their own noninterest-bearing notes.

In accordance with its objective of a full volume of production and employment, the government should levy any taxes designed to pay for subsidies to consumption or for public works in such a manner that they do not burden production or reduce mass purchasing power, but fall rather on large wealth and large incomes, on inheritances, or on the idle bank balances of individuals and corporations.

The government should also borrow such idle balances as it may require for these purposes, compulsorily if necessary; for clearly it is antisocial to hoard money, refusing either to spend or invest it, and correction of this abuse in no way voids the rights of private *enterprise*, properly construed.

Generally speaking, it is better in maintaining the monetary circulation to tap existing idle pools of money than to create additional money to substitute for what is lying idle. However, if for any reason the program of taxing or borrowing existing money proves inadequate to accomplish the named objectives, the government should be free to issue its own non-interest-bearing notes.

Monetary and fiscal questions are intimately connected with the rate of interest. The government through its central monetary and banking authorities should control the net rates of interest paid on money borrowed at long and short term.

A low basic rate should at first be established, in order to encourage housing and the further development of the nation's physical plant generally, and in order to keep down the cost of any government borrowing incidental to fulfillment of the full-employment policy. Moreover, the future trend of the rate of interest should so far as feasible be determined and announced in advance, both to minimize uncertainties and wastes connected with the construction of houses and other durable equipment and to prevent fluctuations in hoarding such as arise from speculation regarding the future course of the rate of interest.

Ultimately the decision as to what constitutes an adequate rate of return on loaned money should belong with the people; first, because it has an obvious bearing on income distribution, second, because it plays an important part in determining how large a proportion of current economic activity is to be devoted to social saving, or in other words to the production of capital goods rather than goods for immediate consumption. Hence steps should be taken to make the rate of interest a political issue as soon as intelligent debate on the subject is possible, and to settle this issue in a democratic manner.

This in a sense is a digression. The next point, however, is absolutely central.

The government should take the monopoly problem in hand—construing that term broadly so as to include not merely cases in which there is a single seller but also related situations (duopoly, oligopoly, etc.). The concept of control over the volume of production activity exercised by way of control over the volume of consumer spending presupposes the kind of response to buyers' demand associated with (a) competitive producers, or (b) monopolies that, as the result of regulation or for some other reason, act not to maximize their profits but rather to approximate or at least parallel the results given by competition.

Conceivably the beneficial effect of a guarantee of an amount of consumer spending sufficient to assure a normal competitive profit throughout industry as a whole, with industry operating at levels yielding full employment, might be entirely destroyed by the price-raising and output restricting policies of monopolies. Dominating the production and distribution of the necessaries of life, they might levy an increasingly large toll of profit for themselves, without permitting either themselves or others to give the normal competitive response (expansion of production and employment) in the exceptionally profitable lines in question. Meanwhile not enough market demand would be left over for the products of competitive producers in other lines (who incidentally would also have to pay exorbitant prices for any products bought from the monopolies) to justify expansion on their part. Hence total employment would fall short of what could be expected to result from the same total consumer demand in a system of universal competition. These unfavorable tendencies are very much in evidence today, being greatly strengthened by technological progress where patent control is used to increase the dominance of corporations already powerful in their field, and by financial tie-ups, and so on.

In addition to restricting output directly, monopolies by their excessive profits accentuate income inequality, which is undesirable in itself and furthermore tends to depress total consumer spending and increase the volume of hoarded money. Also monopolies can be a grave threat to political democracy.

From all of these considerations it follows that private monopolies must be subject to adequate restraint or regulation to safeguard the general welfare, and consequently it should be the business of the government to see that adequate restraints and regulations are imposed. These may take the form of publicity, price regulation, vigorous action under the antitrust laws, encouragement of cooperatives to enter into competition with monopolies, measures to give small companies access to the loan markets on terms more nearly equal to those enjoyed by the big corporations, public yardstick plants, revision of the patent laws, obligatory output rules based on criteria other than maximum profit—or such other forms as may be held advisable. While so-called monopolistic competition is not necessarily undesirable, and indeed may often be the only kind of competition possible, and while even private monopoly as such is not to be condemned automatically, the crux of the matter is that the restrictive practices of profit-seeking private monopoly cannot be tolerated. The government should therefore prevent these restrictive practices; or, if that is not feasible, then federal, state, or local government should own and operate the economic facilities in question.

Turn finally to the problems of our economic relations with the rest of the world.

Foreign trade and investment must be viewed from the standpoint of the general interest. From that standpoint it is seen that they are desirable insofar as they serve to promote an *effective use of resources* by securing a balance of trade based on regional (international) specialization in accordance with comparative efficiencies, but undesirable where they are used in an attempt to expand the *volume* of domestic production by securing foreign markets not offset by home markets opened to foreign producers, or to exploit foreign labor or foreign natural resources or achieve political domination abroad. The effort to avoid or eliminate domestic unemployment by finding convenient foreign outlets for goods, money, or population leads down the road of economic imperialism to war. In view of the injustice and suffering ultimately involved, it can now be supported only by those who do not understand that a nation like the United States can establish permanent full employment without resorting to external economic expansion or aggression.

What is needed is not an isolationist approach. On the contrary.

While sources for many previously imported strategic materials can be developed at home, the superior foreign sources should still be kept open if it does not take war to keep them open. Existing export trade should be an object of consideration, so as to avoid, where it can be avoided, the dislocation of the particular industries and kinds of farming that rely upon it. When requests are received for funds for development of backward areas, loans should if possible be granted, provided repayment seems assured and the terms are generous and fair, i.e., not such as may drain the wealth, restrict the economic independence or infringe the political sovereignty of the borrowing countries. Every effort should be made to get rid of tariffs and other trade restrictions (on a bilateral or multilateral basis so far as that can be arranged) and thus to move toward a condition of free trade, qualified as required by defense and by considerations of long-run evolution; for in that kind of free-trade world, producing a surplus of those things at which we are most efficient to exchange abroad for those things at which we are least efficient, we can have a higher national standard of living than if we are obliged to be our own jack-of-all-trades. Indeed it is obvious that the more international cooperation in all spheres of peaceful action, the better.

What is essential, however, as the foundation for any kind of sound foreign policy, is recognition that the problem of *quantity* of production and employment—the problem of securing prosperity in the sense of full employment—must be solved by *domestic* economic measures. Only on this foundation can be built a structure of durable peace in which the good will that Americans feel toward other peoples can find adequate practical expression.

While taking steps to avoid needless exchange fluctuations, which discourage trade, and while renouncing the use of currency devaluation as a weapon of economic aggression, the government should vary the exchange value of its currency if and when that proves necessary to correct a deeply rooted tendency for the foreign demand for dollars to fall short of or exceed the domestic demand for foreign currencies at the existing valuation.

If necessary the government should also place limitations on speculative short-term capital movements, and on any other international economic activities, including long-term investment, that may be found to be sacrificing the general welfare to the private advantage of the few.

31

The National Income Insurance Idea

National income insurance means a guarantee ahead of time by the Federal Government of the total number of dollars to be spent in consumer markets in any given year. The purpose of such a guarantee would be to bring about full production and full employment in private industry through the assurance to private industry that the final market as a whole would be of adequate size as specified. The amount guaranteed for any year would be based on the amount of consumer demand deemed to be sufficient to afford a normal rate of profit, on the average, on the total volume of goods to be marketed at the full employment level. An over-all guarantee such as this would, of course, not be designed to eliminate the risks of competition. However, the producer's risks would be held within more reasonable limits than they are at present. This consideration extends to the risks attaching to long-term investment in plant and equipment, which, since they spring from uncertainty about consumer demand in the more distant future, would be reduced by the establishment of national income insurance as a long-run, continuing policy.

The program would operate as follows: The amount spent by each person or family would still depend on the individual money incomes received in the usual ways—namely, on the wages, salaries, dividends, etc., of production, including public works, and on social security benefits, farm benefits, veterans' pensions, annuities, and so forth. The only difference would be that there would also be an adjustment by the Government to make the total amount spent in consumer markets agree with the guaranteed total. That is, extra money income would be paid out when necessary to keep the total from falling below the guarantee, and some money income would be held out of action when that was necessary to keep the total from rising above the guarantee and thereby inviting price inflation. Thus whenever it was a question of avoiding a consumer expenditure shortage, the needed extra income would be distributed on some fair and reasonable

A statement in the *Congressional Record*, February 4, 1942, included in the extension of remarks of Rep. Jerry Voorhis of California.

basis approved in advance by Congress—say as "national income security payments" payable to all heads of families throughout the country. The postman could deliver these Treasury checks. The finance could reasonably be provided by taxes or loans from the stream of surplus savings, or—to the extent of expansion required by expanding production—by creation of Government credit under authority of Congress. Similarly Congress would specify in advance the tax or borrowing methods to be applied in the opposite case, to prevent the occurrence of an amount of consumer expenditure exceeding the guarantee. The size of the guaranteed total, to which the actual total would thus at all times be kept adjusted, would grow as the armament program tapered off, so that a rising private demand would automatically cushion much of the post-war shock.

This plan would not conflict with any other sound measures to promote employment, such as public programs for conservation, slum clearance, and other useful projects outside the area of private enterprise; encouragement to private initiative, invention, and investment; regulation of monopoly prices; joint management-labor planning to combat shortages in key industries; a tax program laying the burden more on the stream of large savings and less on mass consumption; the raising of substandard wage rates; protection of farmers' incomes; a suitable ceiling on hours of work; and a broad social welfare program, including expanded old-age pensions, adequate public-health provisions, Federal aid to education, and so on. On the contrary, national income insurance would supplement and reinforce all such measures. The special contribution of national income insurance would be the resulting certainty of a large and stable total demand at all times in the nation's final markets for goods and services. This should stimulate business enterprise to produce on a scale securing full employment without the same heavy reliance on public works that might otherwise be needed. Since the individual competitive enterprise would not be burdened with interference but rather would be assured an adequate market for which to compete, the nation's jobs would be more in ordinary enterprise and less on emergency public projects.

Index